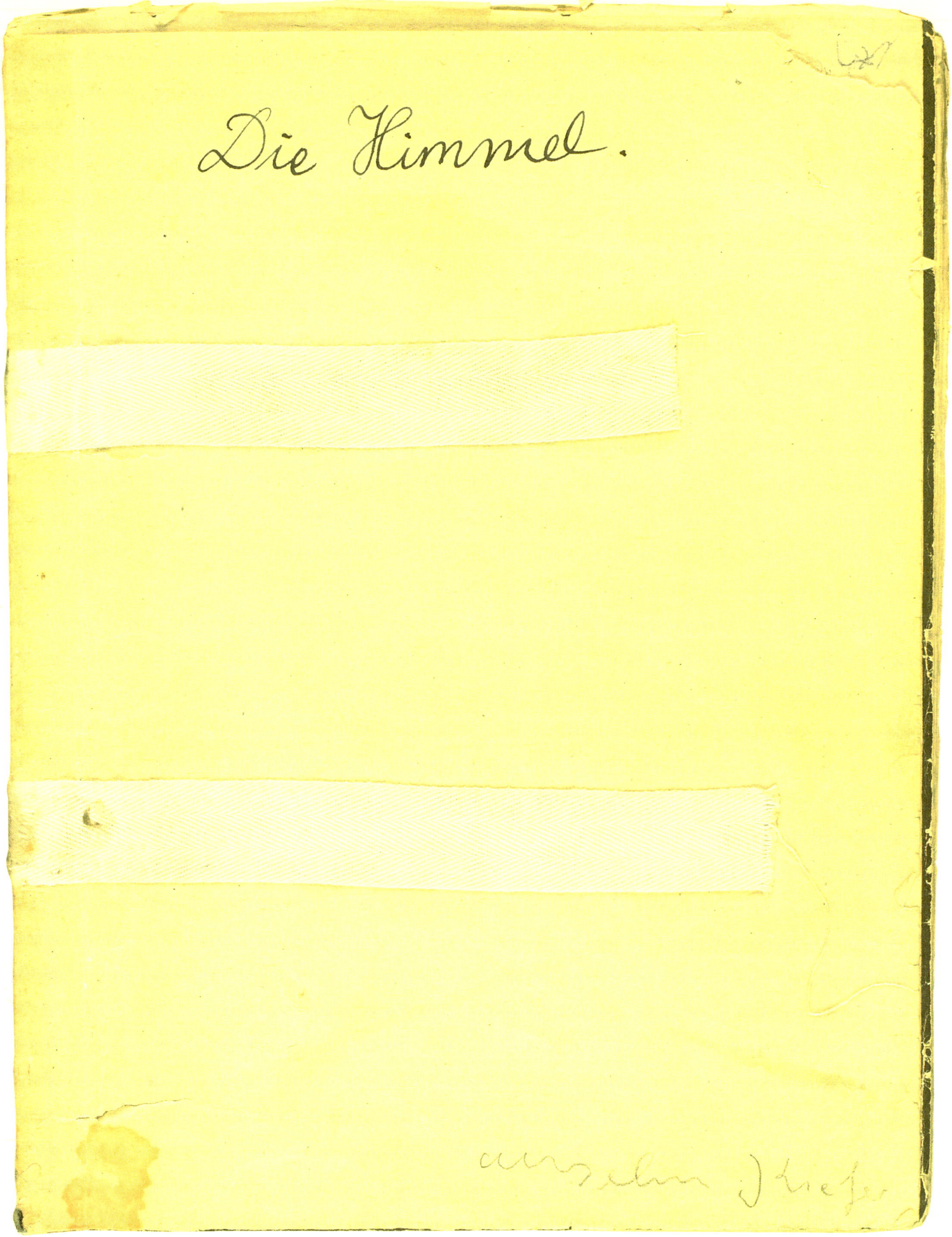
Die Himmel.
anselm Kiefer

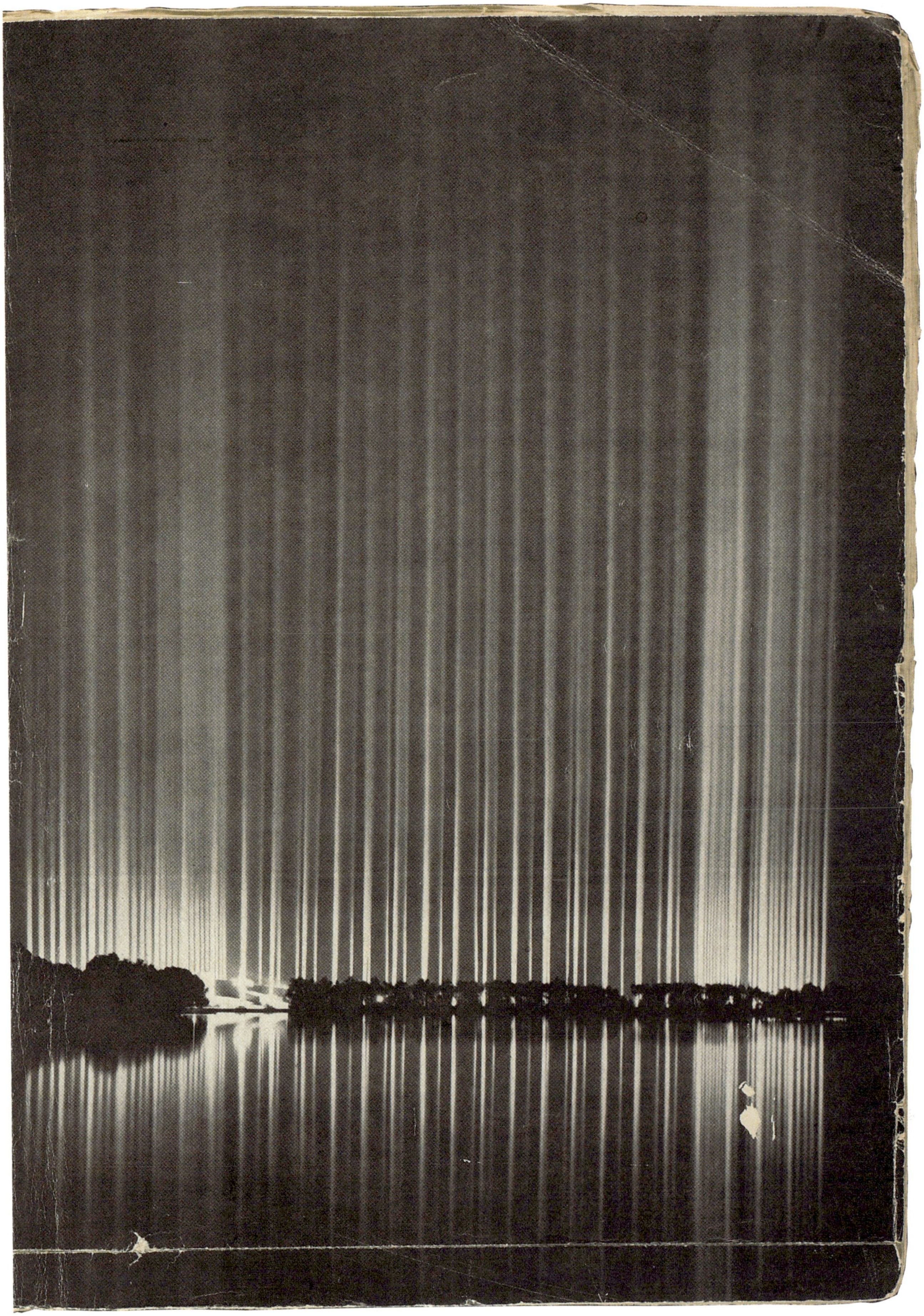

5|6

7|8

9|10

11|12

21 | 22

23 | 24

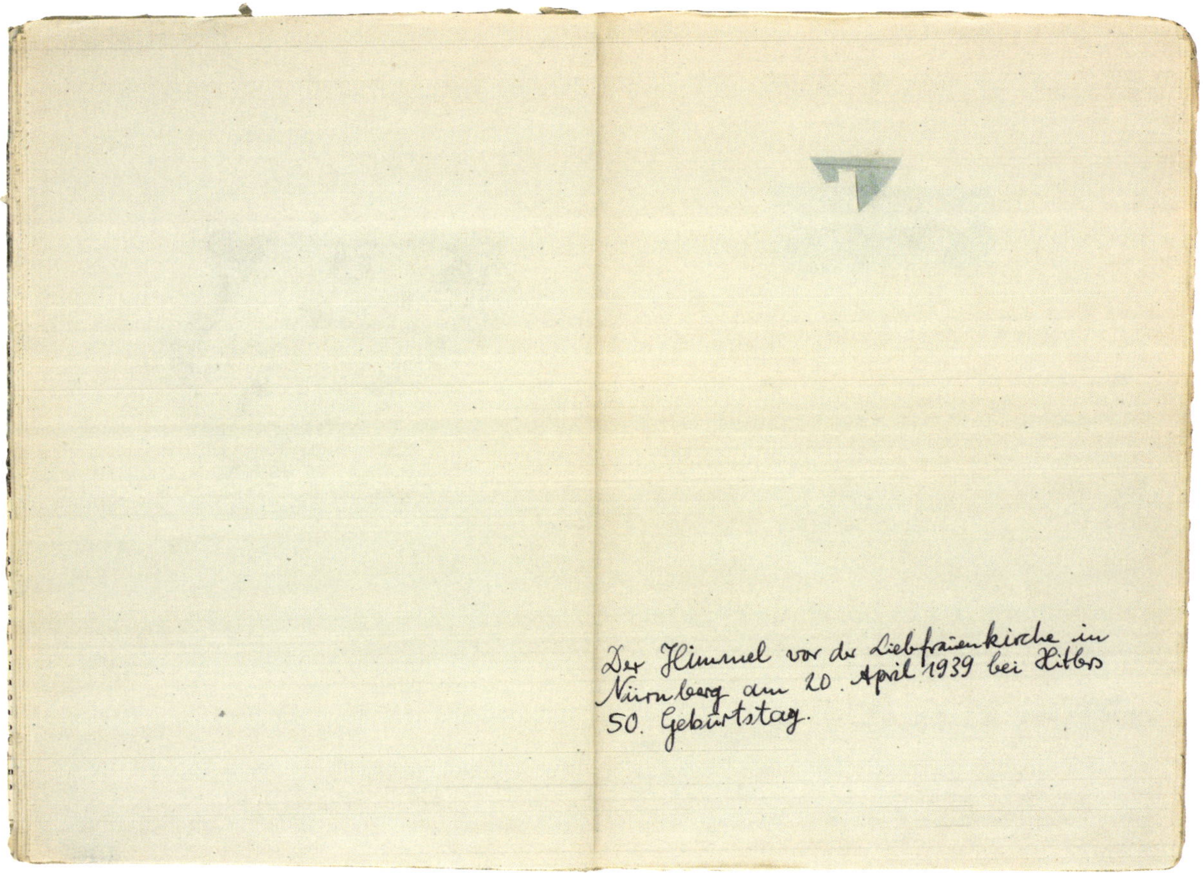
Der Himmel vor der Liebfrauenkirche in
Nürnberg am 20. April 1939 bei Hitlers
50. Geburtstag.

25 | 26

im August 1942 westlich von Stalin-
grad.

27 | 28

Der Himmel über einer brennenden deutschen Stadt von der Kanzel eines englischen Bombenflugzeuges aus,

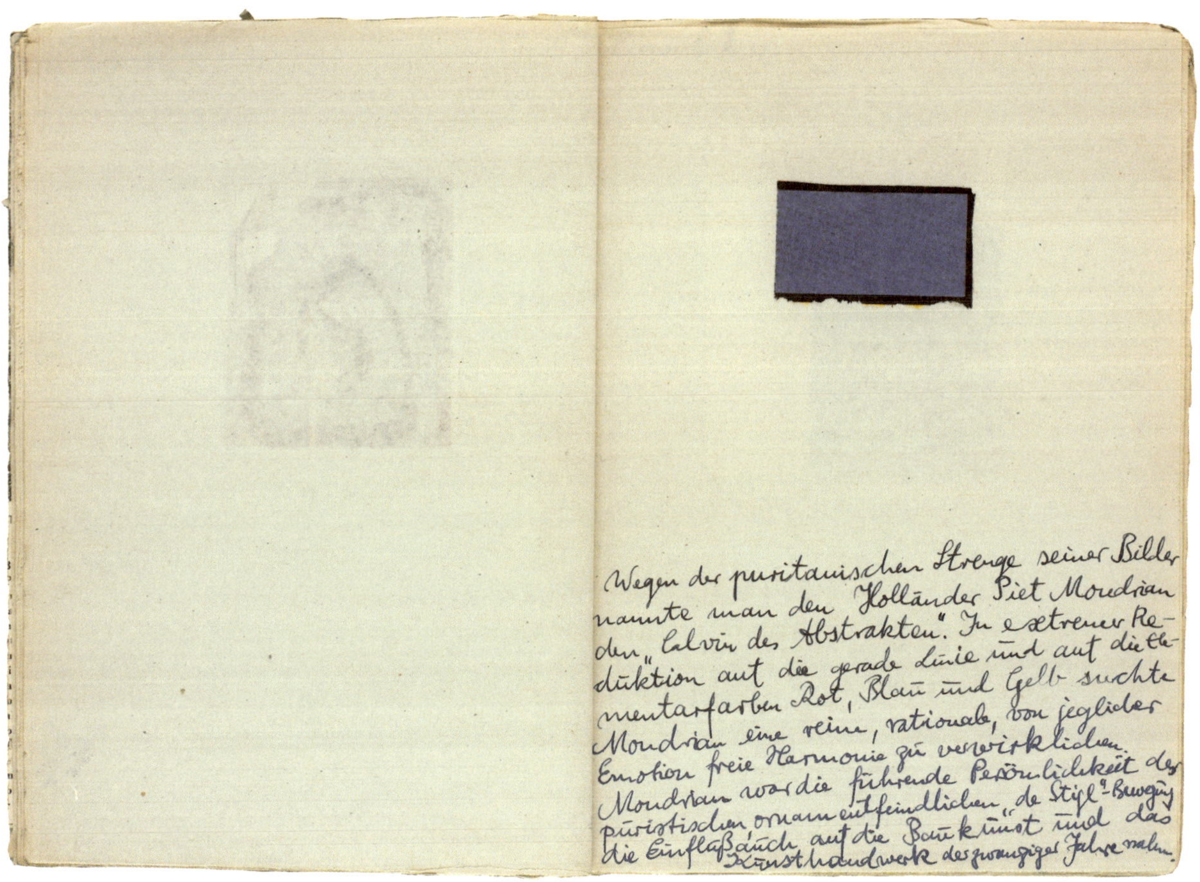
Wegen der puritanischen Strenge seiner Bilder
nannte man den „Holländer Piet Mondrian
den „Calvin des Abstrakten“. In extremer Re-
duktion auf die gerade Linie und auf die Ele-
mentarfarben Rot, Blau und Gelb suchte
Mondrian eine reine, rationale, von jeglicher
Emotion freie Harmonie zu verwirklichen.
Mondrian war die führende Persönlichkeit der
puristischen ornamentfeindlichen „de Stijl“-Bewegung
die Einfluß auch auf die Baukunst und das
Kunsthandwerk der zwanziger Jahre nahm.

33 | 34

Himmel-Ecke

35 | 36

37|38

39|40

41 | 42

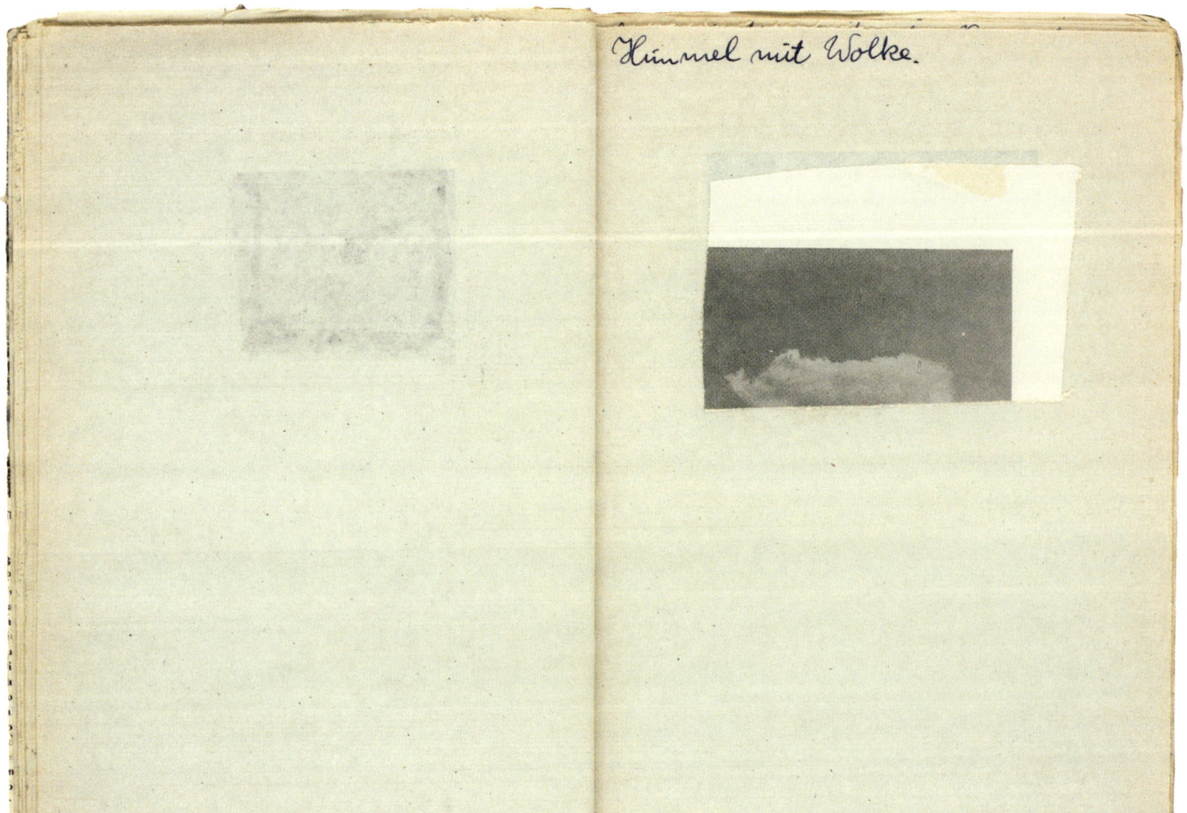

45 | 46

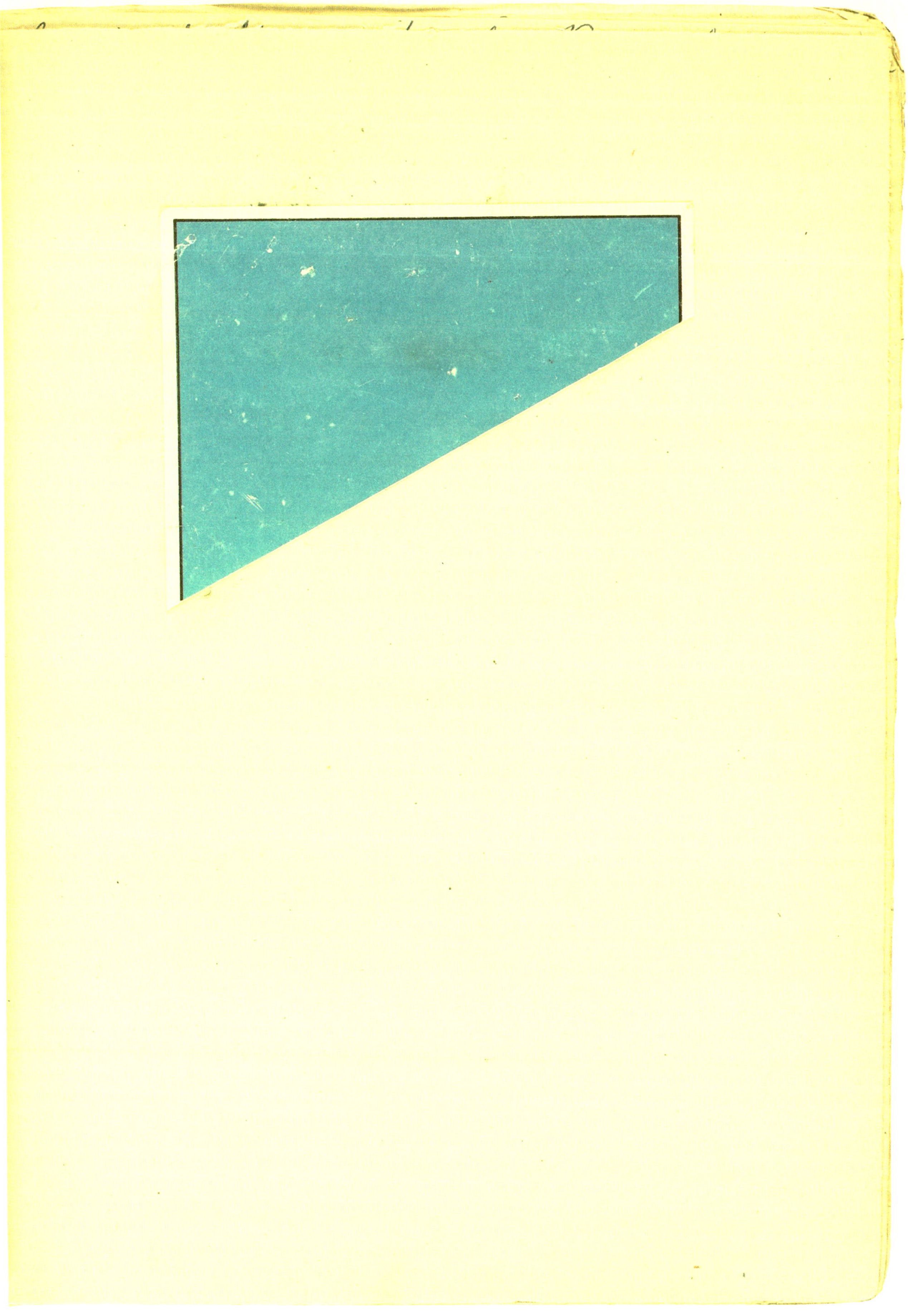

Landschaft, von der der Himmel genommen wurde.

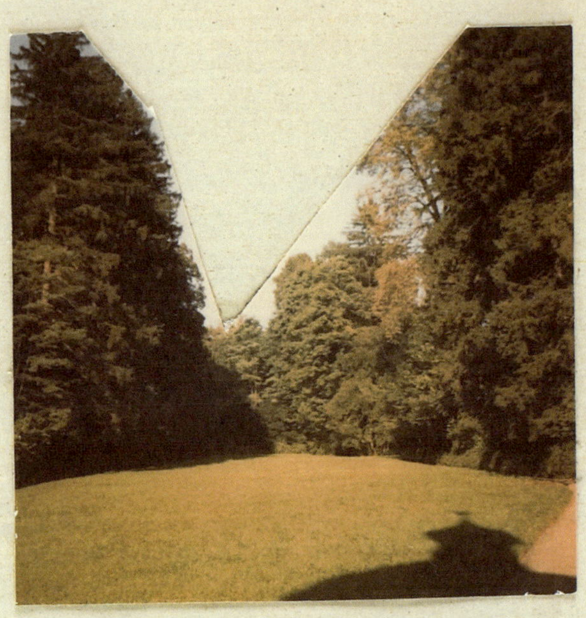

nach unten offener Himmel.

57 | 58

59 | 60

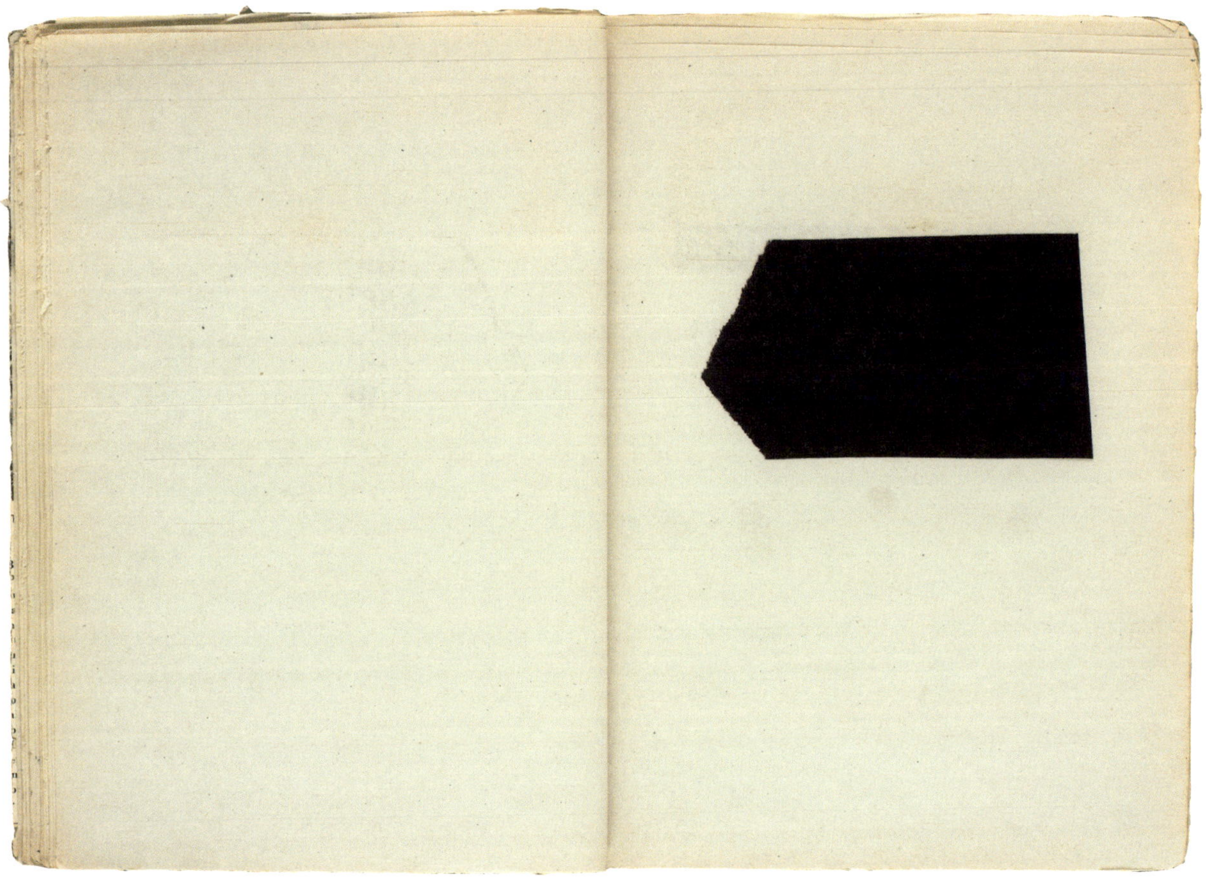

61 | 62

63 | 64

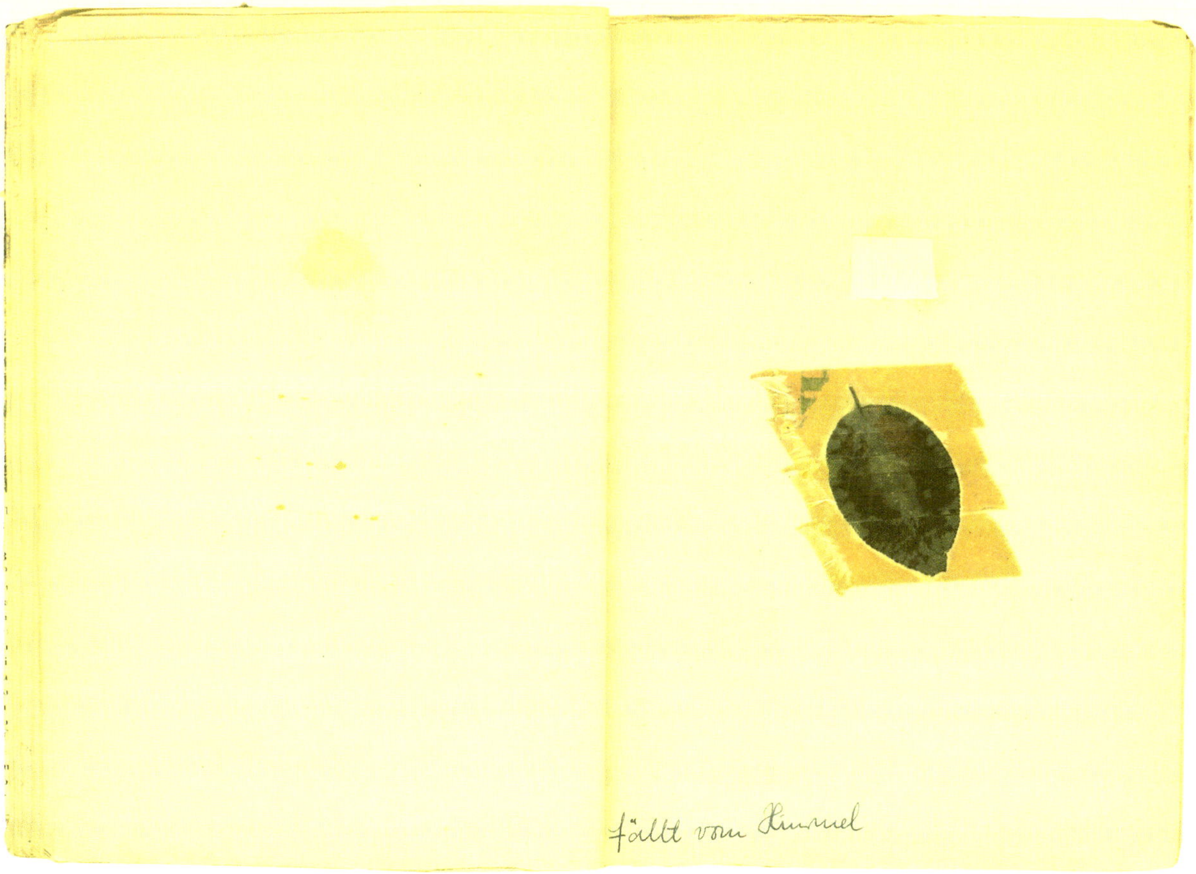

73 | 74

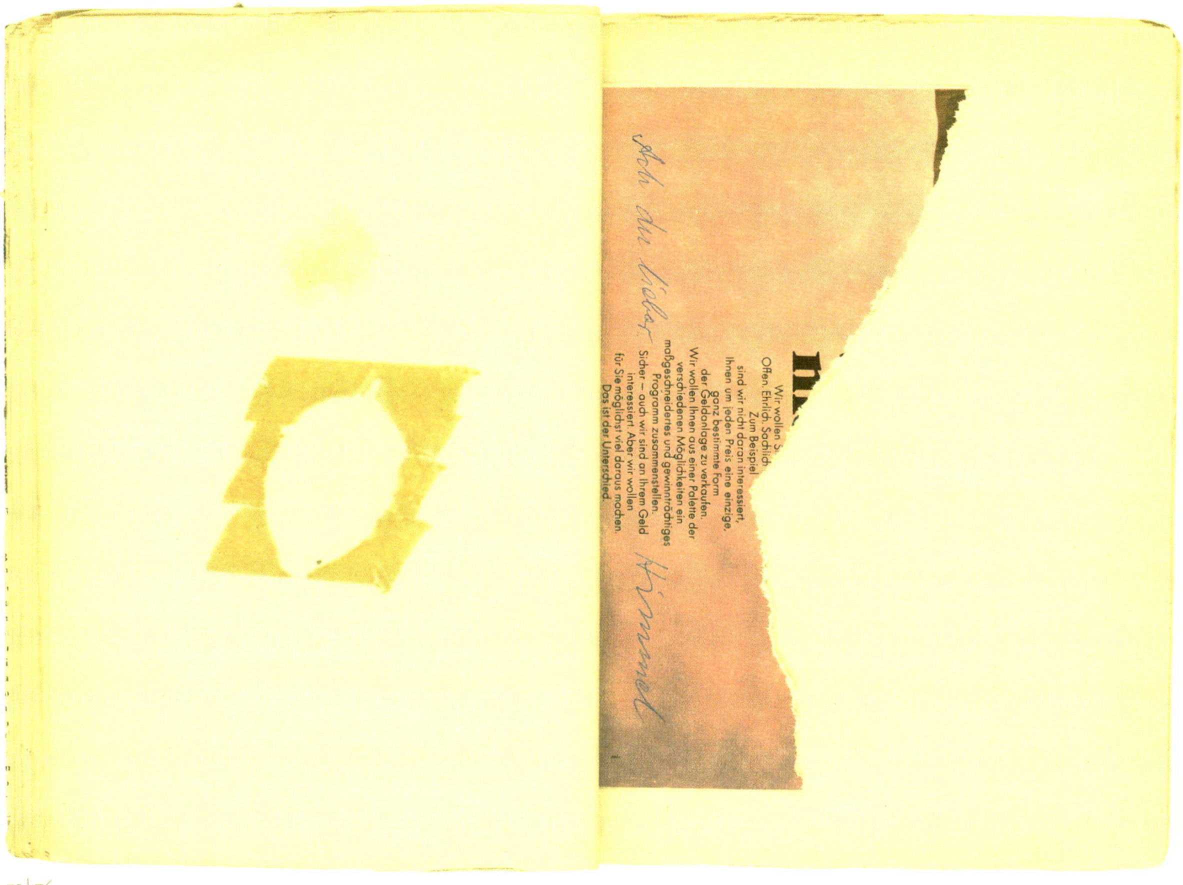

75 | 76

1000.-

Anselm Kiefer
Heaven and Earth

Organized by Michael Auping

MODERN ART MUSEUM OF FORT WORTH

in association with PRESTEL

Modern Art Museum of Fort Worth
September 25, 2005 – January 8, 2006

Musée d'art contemporain de Montréal
February 12 – April 30, 2006

Hirshhorn Museum and Sculpture Garden, Smithsonian Institution
June 18 – September 10, 2006

San Francisco Museum of Modern Art
October 15, 2006 – January 14, 2007

Contents

Lenders to the Exhibition

Albright-Knox Art Gallery, Buffalo, New York
Céline Bastian, Berlin
Buchhandlung Walther König, Köln
Carnegie Museum of Art, Pittsburgh
Dallas Museum of Art
Anthony d'Offay, London
Eric Fischl and April Gornik
Maxine and Stuart Frankel Foundation for Art
Hirshhorn Museum and Sculpture Garden,
Smithsonian Institution, Washington
The Jewish Museum, New York
Ludmer Collection, Montreal
Lester Marks, Houston
The Metropolitan Museum of Art, New York
Modern Art Museum of Fort Worth
Private Collection
Private Collection, Berlin
Private Collection, Courtesy of Gagosian Gallery
Private Collection, London
Private Collection Sanders, Amsterdam
Private Collection, San Francisco
San Francisco Museum of Modern Art
Jerry and Emily Spiegel
Walker Art Center, Minneapolis
Dr. and Mrs. Konrad M. Weis, Pittsburgh

Foreword

Like many of the ancient stories to which Anselm Kiefer's works refer, his paintings, sculptures, books, and works on paper present mysterious and deeply effective images. Kiefer's subject matter, both cathartic and dramatic, captures a basic human instinct that reaches for transcendence. It is undoubtedly for this reason that Kiefer's impact has been international in scope. The importance of the artist's work has been recognized throughout the world through major museum exhibitions in Germany, Switzerland, France, Spain, Mexico, Holland, Italy, Korea, and Japan.

In North America, it has been almost two decades since Kiefer's work was introduced through a large survey exhibition that toured the United States in 1986 and 1987. We can no longer lay claim to introducing Kiefer to an American audience. Here we present a more focused viewpoint, exploring a theme that has run throughout the artist's career: a symbolic dialogue between heaven and earth.

I would like to thank our chief curator, Michael Auping, for conceiving this presentation and bringing to it his usual energy and insight. His work over the past four years has resulted in a thought-provoking exhibition and book.

The exhibition travels to the Musée d'art contemporain de Montréal; the Hirshhorn Museum and Sculpture Garden, Smithsonian Institution; and the San Francisco Museum of Modern Art. Our thanks go to the directors of those institutions, Marc Mayer, Ned Rifkin, and Neal Benezra, for hosting this presentation in their cities.

Traveling an exhibition of this size, complexity, and fragility requires a financial commitment that we and our tour partners cannot bear alone. We are therefore extremely grateful to the Dedalus Foundation, New York, for their generous support of this exhibition.

Finally, we are indebted to Anselm Kiefer for his patience and assistance over the past few years. It is an honor to present this exhibition and to have the artist significantly represented in our collection.

Marla Price
Director

Preface and Acknowledgments

The influences and counter-influences between American and German art following World War II have created a particularly strong dialogue. In the late 1950s, American avant-garde art was exported to Germany with considerable force. The Museum of Modern Art's international blockbuster *The New American Painting* offered Europeans a grand introduction to the ambitiously personal visions of the New York School, or what has come to be known as Abstract Expressionism. Berlin, along with London and Paris, was one of a few well-chosen art centers to receive the exhibition. As it did in America, the New York School left its mark on German art for the next three decades. In the 1980s, the Germans returned the favor, sending America what might be thought of as the New German School. It did not come so neatly packaged in a single exhibition, or even in a single generation, but the wave of images emanating from Joseph Beuys, Georg Baselitz, Anselm Kiefer, Sigmar Polke, and Gerhard Richter, among others, has been nothing less than profound in its international impact, particularly its impact on America.

Although the works of these artists are now represented in American museums in substantial numbers, we would be less than honest if we proclaimed a full understanding of the meaning and intentions that lie behind their imagery. As Michael Werner, the influential German art dealer who engaged many of these artists early in their careers, said recently, "German art of this generation has too many layers and deep, painful splinters to be nursed into order by our generation. This will take a long time, but it must be important because these artists make us fight among ourselves."

The work of Anselm Kiefer has been particularly polemical and subject to intense debate. Not only does Kiefer remind us of aspects of recent German history that many people would prefer to forget, but he does so in a manner that is as Gordian and stimulating as it is mournful. A first impression of Kiefer's art is often one of daunting symbolic complexity in which multiple references to controversial philosophers, mystics, political figures, and events are juxtaposed to the sacral. Finding a pathway through this labyrinth of references is a matter of viewpoint, ranging from dense scholarly analysis to personal interpretation.

A number of important museum exhibitions in Europe and America over the past three decades have set out the artist's wide-ranging imagery and subject matter through large surveys. In this presentation and book, we follow a more focused path, tracking Kiefer's lifelong interest in a visual exploration of a dialogue between heaven and earth. This is not an exhibition about religion, although aspects of many different religions and mystical beliefs are referred to in Kiefer's imagery. For more than three decades, Kiefer has explored the dauntingly large question of why concepts such as transcendence and the idea of a supreme being exist throughout history.

In order to track the artist's interest in this subject, we have brought a number of rare early works from his personal collection together with works from various museum and private collections. Each of these works contributes in a different way to Kiefer's discursive approach to this grand theme. On behalf of the artist and the Museum, I would like to thank the lenders to this exhibition for their generosity in parting with their works for an extended period.

Accompanying the exhibition is this book, which contains three parts. At the core is an interview with the artist, in which he discusses his early conception of his imagery and his thinking regarding the concept of heaven. Preceding the interview is an introductory essay, which amplifies some of the circumstances and issues brought up in the interview, and discusses a number of the artist's projects whose size and magnitude prevent their inclusion in a traveling exhibition. Finally, a group of Notes on the Works, presented alongside the color plates, touch on the symbolic context that informs a number of works in the exhibition that are not discussed specifically in the essay.

I want to thank Anselm Kiefer for agreeing to discuss this slippery and difficult topic. Although the artist's reputation is that of an exceptionally private individual, I have found him to be particularly open and generous over the years this exhibition has evolved.

Of course, a major publication and an exhibition are more than a two-person dialogue. Within the Museum, I have had many partners, each of whom makes me appear more professional than I deserve. Marla Price, the director of the Modern Art Museum of Fort Worth, is always the first to encourage a new project, even when it is complicated and potentially controversial. I am grateful for her support, not just for this exhibition, but over the past decade.

I have come to rely on my administrative assistant, Susan Colegrove, to an embarrassing degree. My thanks go to her for keeping track of the many miscellaneous details that are the glue of an exhibition. I would also like to thank our research assistant, Laura Phipps, for her contributions.

Our editor, Pam Hatley, is one of the most forgiving and resourceful people I have ever met. To my mind, these are the key qualities of a successful editor. We have both worked closely with our designer, Peter Willberg in London. In collaboration with the artist, Peter has made this book beautiful. This is my eighth book with Peter, and I hope there will be at least eight more. At Prestel, I would especially like to thank Thomas Zuhr, Jürgen Tesch, and Victoria Salley for their support and for their dedication to this project.

Anselm Kiefer's works are complex, sometimes fragile, and highly valuable constructions. Bringing them to Fort Worth and touring them around North America requires a very special team. Rick Floyd, registrar, has borne the brunt of this task, and I am exceedingly grateful for his patience and attention to detail. Tony Wright, head of installation and design, has had the difficult task of supervising the movement of Kiefer's works within the museums.

I would also like to extend my appreciation to our tour partners, specifically Neal Benezra, Director, Ruth Berson, Deputy Director for Programs and Collections, and Gary Garrels, former Chief Curator, San Francisco Museum of Modern Art; Marcel Brisebois, former Director, Marc Mayer, Director, and Paulette Gagnon, Chief Curator, Musée d'art contemporain de Montréal; and Jim Demetrion, former Director, Ned Rifkin, Director, and Kerry Brougher, Director of Art and Programs and Chief Curator, Hirshhorn Museum and Sculpture Garden, Washington, D.C.

This project has also benefited from the knowledge and expertise of many individuals outside the Museum. Chief among them are Heiner Bastian, James Cohan, Anthony d'Offay, Larry Gagosian, Marian Goodman, Marie-Louise Laband, Jack Lane, Lorcan O'Neill, Sylvie Pages, Mark Rosenthal, Nan Rosenthal, Robin Vousden, Wim Wenders, and Ealan Wingate.

Finally, I thank Anselm Kiefer and his partner Renate Graf for their patience and hospitality over many years of visits. Atelier Kiefer is a very special place, which I hope this exhibition and book reflect.

M. A.

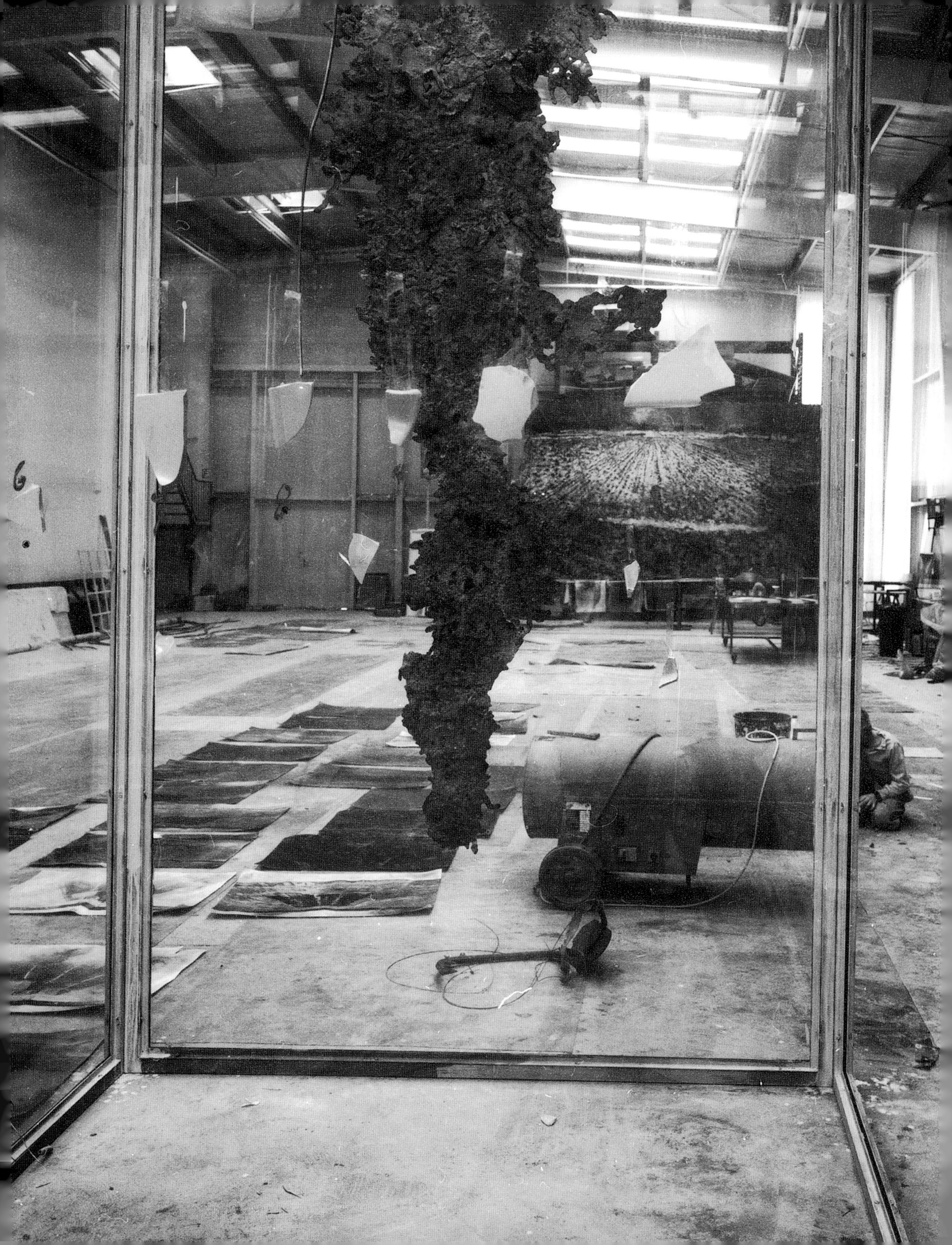

Introduction

Innumerable aphorisms and folktales speak to our inherent need to seek a heaven. At the same time, they caution against stargazing. Stare into the heavens and you ignore the earth and your fellow man; ignore the possibility of a heaven and you put a limit on the imagination. Balancing these needs of "church and state" has always been one of the fundamental challenges of all nations, but in certain eras, heaven would appear to be a distant memory, if not altogether absent. Wim Wenders's description of his poignantly titled 1987 film *Wings of Desire* pans back to such a purgatorial moment: "When God, endlessly disappointed, finally prepared to turn his back on the world for ever, it happened that some of his angels disagreed with him and took the side of man, saying he deserved to be given another chance. Angry at being crossed, God banished them to what was then the most terrible place on earth: Berlin. And then He turned away. All this happened at the time that we today call: 'The end of the Second World War.'"[1]

In the wake of Adolf Hitler's National Socialism, the political and religious fabric of Germany was in as ruinous a state as its landscape. It would seem that even art could not offer much hope. Theodor Adorno's now famous statement—"After Auschwitz, to write a poem is barbaric"—threw up an imposing challenge to all postwar artists who would pursue "false utopias" in lieu of remembering a dark recent past.[2] Few artists of this postwar generation have navigated the difficult terrain between the possibility of transcendence and the necessity of remembrance as dramatically and provocatively as Anselm Kiefer. Kiefer has pointedly stated that, for his generation, "There is always hope, but that must be combined with irony and, more important, skepticism."[3]

Born in Germany in 1945, only months before the end of the war, Kiefer's vision of transcendence is invariably laced with pathos. For Kiefer, the idea of heaven can elevate us only if it can carry the weight of history. Perhaps for this reason irony, skepticism, and hope—in no particular order of importance—run through his more than thirty years of artmaking like major arteries. The trails Kiefer would follow in exploring his identity, not only as a German but as an artist, would eventually come together in a broad synthesis of law; literature, including complex esoteric texts; and art. All of his works are informed by some configuration of this synthesis.

In 1965, before deciding to pursue artmaking, Kiefer began to study law. He did so as

The artist's studio near Buchen

a means of focusing questions on the interrelation between history, philosophy, and religion. Art, which had always been of interest to him, was at that moment hovering in the background of larger questions regarding his country's recent history, his Catholic upbringing, and the challenge of defining lofty, if not utopian, goals for the future of a postwar German artist. As a student of law, Kiefer's interest in the controversial German theological and legal intellectual Carl Schmitt reflected his understanding of the complexities and contradictions involved in integrating the goals of church and state. A devout Catholic, Schmitt's philosophy explored the most fundamental challenge of law and government: to reconcile the inherent tension between the concepts of free will, authoritarianism, and spirituality. Based on a worldview that mankind is essentially self-interested, Schmitt's philosophy fell on the side of authoritarianism for the sake of progress and what he envisioned as a greater idealism. In such texts as *Political Theology* (1922) and *The Spiritual–Historical Situation of Today's Parliament* (1923), Schmitt evolved an argument that man's inherent inhumanity toward man necessitates a social contract with a powerful governmental or religious leadership structure.

In 1938 Schmitt published an analysis of the seventeenth-century British philosopher Thomas Hobbes's use of the ancient symbol of the Leviathan, a formidable sea creature, to describe the magnitude of authority that must be invested in government, religion, and God in order for a society to operate effectively and efficiently. Schmitt joined the Nazi party in 1933, and for a time was a leading intellectual figure within the government. Yet because of his ardent but complicated views, in which he discussed esoteric traditions and secret societies, including Gnosticism, the Jewish kabbala, Rosicrucianism, and Freemasonry, he soon fell out of favor. Neither judge nor apologist for Schmitt, Kiefer was interested in the dilemmas posed by his ideas. "I was interested in people like Schmitt," the artist has said, "because they got caught between the power of government and the power of God." Kiefer would not shy away from the inherent historical friction between the political and the spiritual imagination. Indeed, it would become the leitmotif of his life's work.

Schmitt's broad-ranging texts introduced Kiefer to various forms of esoteric theology. "I was interested," Kiefer remembers, "in the possibility of going back, not just through German law and history, but through the history of the concept of spirituality." Kiefer also acknowledges that when he was investigating law and religion in the 1960s, the political landscape was fractured by strident viewpoints from the right and the left. While a war in Vietnam gathered attention and fierce debate and a German

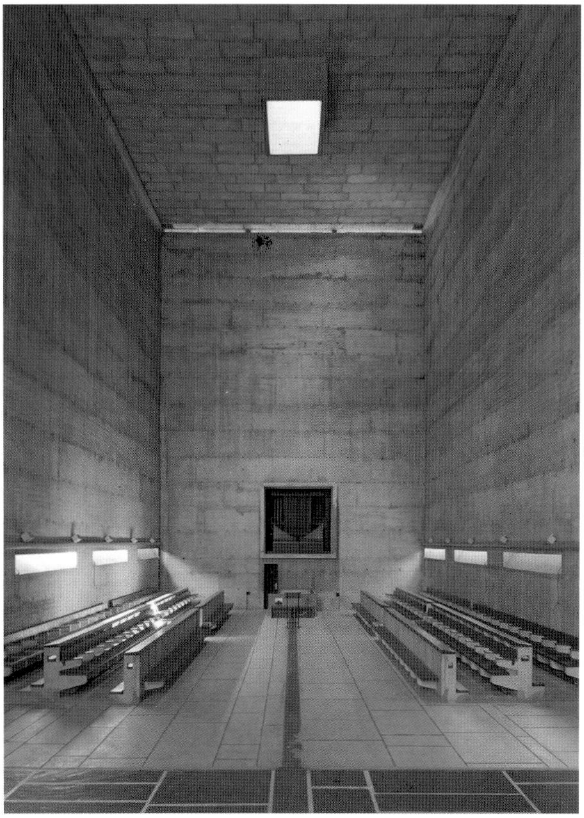

Le Corbusier, Couvent Sainte Marie de La Tourette

protest movement got underway, religion was confronted by death-of-God theology. As Kiefer puts it, "You couldn't depend on factions. You had to find your own way."

Kiefer would become increasingly solitary, a quality he would maintain throughout his career, as evidenced by the remote locations of his studios over the years. In 1966, he visited the Dominican monastery of La Tourette, designed by the acclaimed modernist architect Le Corbusier between 1955 and 1960. Kiefer spent three weeks living in a cell as a guest of the monks, as the artist remembers it, "just thinking quietly—about the larger questions." His interest in the Dominicans, and their culture of spirituality and scholarship, merged with his natural curiosity about the importance of modern art in society. The son of an art educator, his early interest in the paintings of Vincent van Gogh, the sculptures of Auguste Rodin, and the poetry of Rainer Maria Rilke, and later the work of Marcel Duchamp and Andy Warhol, would evolve into a more critical reflection on the intellectual and spiritual value of the modern image.

Toward this end, Kiefer placed himself in an unusually potent environment at Le Corbusier's monastery. La Tourette and the widely known Chapel of Notre Dame du

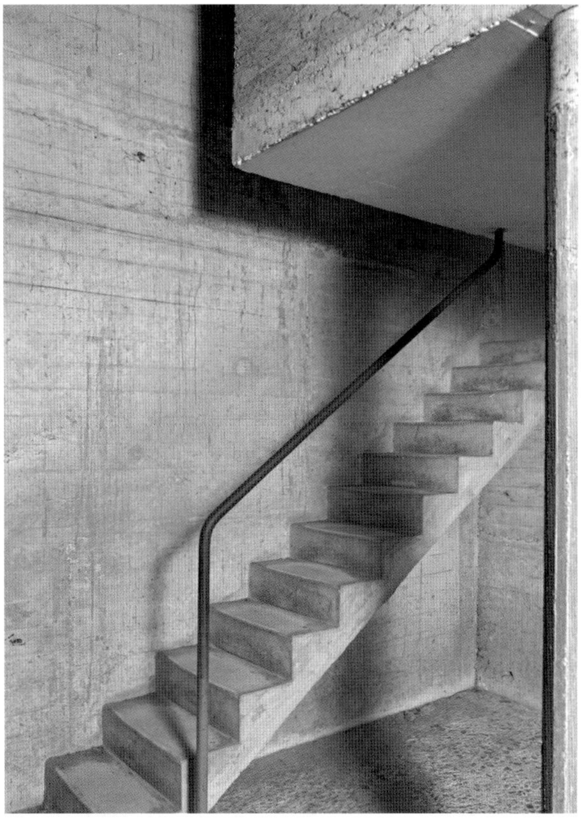

Le Corbusier, Couvent Sainte Marie de La Tourette

Haut, Ronchamp, are considered by some to be the pinnacle of Le Corbusier's career. The influential architect (born Charles-Edouard Jeanneret) had come to believe that the sleek, white villas he had built while he was in his forties were not the deepest reflection of his spirit. La Tourette, a stark concrete structure built in a forest clearing above the vineyards of Beaujolais, has been described as "one of the most haunting, numinous buildings of the twentieth century,"[4] incorporating Le Corbusier's love of medieval monasteries with a powerful modern vocabulary.

There is a twisted historical irony involved in pairing Le Corbusier with the Dominicans. When Christianity became an "official church," it was transformed from persecuted to persecutor. Swiss by birth, Le Corbusier was a descendant of medieval Cathars (the Pure Ones), Gnostics whom Pope Innocent III declared to be heretical, and who were almost completely annihilated by the Dominicans and the French soldiers who carried out the Pope's crusade. It would not be lost on Kiefer that the architect of this great building would have been burned at the stake by his client seven centuries earlier.

La Tourette is a powerful, sculptural container—theatrical in the best sense of the term—and an inspired staging area for exploring twentieth-century materials, forms, and symbols and their relationship to the spiritual. Kiefer's art would eventually engage an ambitious and somber theatricality of its own. His visit to La Tourette marked a turning point. Not long thereafter, he turned his energies to art. Abandoning his studies in law and romance languages, Kiefer entered the university in Freiburg, where he studied with the painter Peter Dreher. Dreher introduced the young artist to art as a field of investigation "without boundaries."

Kiefer's subsequent meetings with Joseph Beuys reinforced many of his ideas about the possibility of a content that engaged a larger context for art. Beuys's appointment to the Düsseldorf Academy and his openness to students, even those who, like Kiefer, did not attend the school officially, was significant. Beuys's work incorporated a wide range of materials and images which challenged the American-styled European abstraction that dominated art academies in Germany in the decades following the war. Beuys is also acknowledged as the first German artist to directly address the Holocaust in his imagery.[5] For Beuys, who had participated in the war from the German side, Germany and in fact the world was in a state of acute trauma, not only from the effects of the war itself, but from the ironies and contradictions that led to it. Speaking of the town in Germany where he was raised, Beuys painted an inglorious, if perhaps exaggerated, image of an unquestioning Germany: "Everyone went to church, and everyone went to the Hitler Youth."[6] Kiefer appreciated Beuys's broad-ranging viewpoint, in which history, mythology, religion, and art formed a matrix. Beuys proposed art as a utopian synthesis of various inter-questioning disciplines that was capable of creating an enlightened worldview. While Kiefer was inspired by Beuys's openness and his grasp of a wide range of esoteric knowledge, including alchemy, his viewpoint was less utopian. Beuys became a public figure, while Kiefer would remain far more private and hermetic, with a darker, more skeptical vision. If Beuys was the shaman, Kiefer would be the Gnostic, the questioner of all received knowledge.

In many of his earliest works, Kiefer began to ask fundamental questions regarding the nature of religion and its relationship to intellectual and political life. He would begin by contemplating the concept of paradise. In Kiefer's earliest surviving work of art, created three years after his visit to La Tourette, he tackles nothing less than the Kingdom of God in a book entitled simply *The Heavens* (1969, pages 1–16). Measuring less than 8 × 10 inches, *The Heavens* has the look of a child's scrapbook, with small, simple images of skies and clouds cut from magazines and pasted onto otherwise empty white pages. In addressing the grand subject of his title, the young artist's approach combined insightful modesty with dark ironies, indicating that the road to paradise is invariably warped. His use of image fragments reflects a belief that heaven cannot be summarized into a single image or place, but is better symbolized by a series of glimpses, each convincing and unconvincing from different viewpoints.

In Kiefer's visionary polemic, even light has its dark side. One of the first pages of *The Heavens* contains a photograph of an architectural light installation by Albert Speer. Like Schmitt, Speer was a controversial German figure whose ambitions toward exalted schemes combining the political and the spiritual found unholy results. Known as "Hitler's architect," he produced the most grand and imposing structures associated with the Nazi party. In *The Heavens*, Kiefer reproduces Speer's installation of Klieg lights pointed to the sky, creating a cathedral of light. The luminous energy that shines down in churches and paintings to indicate God's divine presence can be directed skyward to help expose and shoot down enemy aircraft. Kiefer's awareness of the delusions that go with warring "heavenly governments" points in many directions. On another page, a small rectangle of red sky is accompanied by text reading "The heavens above a burning German city seen from the cockpit of an English bomber." *The Heavens* initiates the artist's penchant for exposing the shadowy wrinkles of any utopian fabric. As Kiefer puts it, "Religion can pretend to be pure. History cannot."

The Heavens echoed a 1968 installation of the same title, in which the artist placed collage elements representing different views of heaven on the walls of a small room. It was his first installation work, in which he consciously used architecture to create a symbolic space.[7] In the installation, Kiefer was creating his own "Dome of Heaven," a concept that would lend its name to the title of a small watercolor he created two years later. Here Kiefer draws from one of the most fundamental artistic expressions of many world religions—the vision of heaven depicted in painting or mosaic on domes and related vaulted forms.

In the watercolor *Everyone Stands Under His Own Dome of Heaven* (1970, page 54), the dome of a church or the cockpit of a German bomber is transformed into a child's snow globe, which covers a tiny figure whose straight right arm is raised as if saluting the sky. Kiefer has cited Hitler's use of religion as a propaganda tool, but he also points out that it is human nature to use heaven selectively. "From the time we are children, we create ourselves by imagining a heaven. We each have a different one. It's like color. No one sees the same blue. Some may see black."

This early period in the development of Kiefer's art has to some extent become obscured behind the controversy that accompanied the artist's *Occupations* series of the early 1970s. In 1975, Kiefer published a series of photographs in the German magazine *Interfunktionen* in which the artist gives the *Sieg Heil* salute at various locations in southern Europe, often in front of historical monuments such as the Colosseum. These photographs have been variously interpreted as ironic, humorous, and neofascist.[8] For Kiefer, the title *Occupations* carries a potential double meaning, simultaneously referring to the Nazis' ambition to control all of European culture and later the world, and the fact that the misguided vision and atrocities of the Nazi party would occupy the conscience of generations of postwar Germans. Kiefer comments, "The Nazi occupations had consequences for all of us for many years. Some people will always remain occupied by it."

The *Occupations* operate on a thin line between farce and catharsis. Benjamin H. D. Buchloh, the editor who commissioned Kiefer's *Interfunktionen* contribution, recalled it as "a real working through of German history. You have to inhabit it to overcome it."[9] A similar transference took place in the United States in the early 1970s with the so-called "Klan" paintings of Philip Guston, which depict hooded figures. Guston, who had feared and loathed the Ku Klux Klan since his teenage years in California, felt a need to address the image of the group in his own mind. Indeed, he referred to these works as self-portraits: "My attempt was really not to illustrate, to do pictures of the KKK . . . The idea of evil fascinated me, and rather like Isaac Babel who had joined the Cossacks, lived with them and written stories about them, I almost tried to imagine that I was living with the Klan. What would it be like to be evil? To plan, to plot."[10]

In one of the *Occupations* photographs, Kiefer mimics Caspar David Friedrich's well-known painting *Monk by the Sea* (1809). The German Romantic painter's image of a solitary monk contemplating a vast ocean and the earth's horizon has been interpreted as a powerful yearning for unity between man, nature, and God. Kiefer's photographic rendition, replacing the monk with himself and his Third Reich salute, takes the *Occupations* to a comic, if not pathetic, level in which the German soldier suggests his eventual occupation of heaven and God.

With one eye on heaven, Kiefer invariably keeps the other on human imperfection and its reflection in history. This balance is not created from the moral high ground of a self-anointed innocent. In Kiefer's mind, the artist cannot point fingers, as his visions may also be his delusions. Kiefer's use of the artist's palette in different contexts underscores this point. As a symbol of the imagination, Kiefer's palettes trace a symbolic journey between the day-to-day realities of an artist's changing and often fragile role in history, and a transcendent heaven.

An early work entitled *The Starred Heaven* (1980, page 77) shows the artist as a scruffy, nightgown-clad angel with a palette for a heart. He stands on a snake beneath a starry sky. Written over the photograph are the words of the eighteenth-century German philosopher Immanuel Kant, whose writings explored the boundary between reason and metaphysics: *The starred heaven above me, the moral law within me.*[11] Kant held that human knowledge is the result of the mind reasoning the conditions of its own experience. Because metaphysical propositions seek a truth beyond all experience, they cannot be established within the bounds of reason. In his half-mocking, half-serious portrait, Kiefer engages Kant's dilemma, proposing that the heart in the form of a palette, rather than the mind, may be the means of bridging the two realms.

Like many of Kiefer's symbols, however, the palette is placed on a thin edge between hope and despair. In Kiefer's various studios, a lead palette has often hung from the ceiling as a talisman representing the artist's challenge to seek a higher plane of vision. It also lies on the floor, covered in debris and unable to separate itself from the soiled studio wasteland, or is painted hovering above Hitler's "scorched earth" (page 71). In his desperate attempt to communicate beyond the halls of philosophy, church, and state, an artist invariably finds himself in a kind of purgatory. *Palette* (1981, pages 78/79) shows a traditional nineteenth-century palette precariously suspended by two strands of burning rope. *To the Unknown Painter* (1982, page 81) depicts a palette beaming rays through an imposing domed ceiling. The palette is dwarfed by the scale of the surrounding architecture, which bears a close resemblance to one of Albert Speer's ceremonial interiors. It has been impaled on the end of a long stick, implying the display of a defeated, beheaded enemy, perhaps a reminder of Hitler's war on "degenerate" art. In this context, Kiefer's palette might also remind us that before Hitler was a politician, he dreamed of becoming an artist. When Hitler's application to the Vienna Academy of Fine Arts was rejected, he was bitterly disappointed.[12] Had he been accepted, might Hitler's and Speer's imaginations have then created halls dedicated to the human spirit rather than political domination?

Speaking of *The Starred Heaven*, Kiefer comments, "I was using myself as the hero of an imagined myth or revolution. It is humorous, pathetic, but it is an important part of researching about who we are in this universe. We are capable of thinking very high and very low. Placing ourselves between heaven and earth is more difficult." In Kiefer's view, artists are vain if they think they are heroes, although he acknowledges that art may be the only space where an individual can be utterly free to question himself, as well as his relationship to his god. For Kiefer, this involves facing the limits of our knowledge and, perhaps even more important, the limits of our memory, particularly of our beginnings.

In the early painting *Man in the Forest* (1971, page 57), Kiefer depicts himself in a nightshirt in a tall forest. In his right hand he holds a burning branch, which lights his way. A German who for most of his life has lived and worked on the outskirts of cities and towns, Kiefer has said simply, "Our stories always begin in the forest." Posing as the mythical Gilgamesh in search of the meaning of life, Kiefer returns to the forest, a natural community whose history is that of man. Trees and plants play a significant role in many of Kiefer's images, as symbols of life cycles, medicinal magic, and fragility within a "civilized" setting. Indeed, as Kiefer's fire lights his way, it threatens to burn down the surrounding forest.

In *Resurrexit* (1973, page 61), Kiefer is replaced by a snake, which now occupies the forest floor. The artist has apparently escaped up a wooden staircase that has magically grown from the treetops. The stairs ascend, creating a triangular form that points beyond the trees into the sky. Conflating the terms *resurrection* and *exit*, Kiefer's title plays on the belief that the artist must find a way of looking beyond the circumstances of everyday life. These stairs, in fact, do not lead to heaven, but to Kiefer's studio at the time, the attic of a former schoolhouse. Located in Hornbach, a remote village in the Oden Forest, the wooden schoolhouse appealed to Kiefer as, in his words, "a place to teach myself history." Here the artist would enact a number of scenarios in which the heaven above and the moral law below would make contact.

In Kiefer's *Attic* series of the early 1970s, to which *Resurrexit* belongs, the artist choreographed various events, historical propositions, and philosophical dilemmas using his wooden studio as a stage upon which different symbols and personas play out the drama. Kiefer's attic space is analogous to his suspended palette in *Heaven – Earth* (1974, page 65), in which art must negotiate its own time and space.

In the stagelike painting *Quaternity* (1973, pages 62/63), also from the *Attic* series, a snake identified as *Satan* enters the room, joining three flames designated *Vater (Father)*, *Sohn (Son)*, and *hl. Geist (Holy Ghost)*. Reanimating a debate of the early Christian church regarding the existence and role of the devil, Kiefer presents evil, or Satan, as a fundamental element in his spiritual matrix. The artist has remarked, "History has shown us that there is always a darkness inside the light . . . Maybe we should be looking more carefully into the darkness." Acknowledging that Satan was once an angel, Kiefer reminds us of the mutable character of angels, which throughout history have taken many different forms, including that of a serpent. Like humans, then, angels are an impure form, a reflection of the human need to create a dialogue between heaven and earth. A number of Kiefer images could be described as angels—jet planes, meteorites, propellers, stars, nuclear power plants, palettes, books, buildings—images that reflect and attract the imagination but carry a mixed history.

The flames also play a paradoxical role in *Quaternity*'s drama, suggesting a spiritual presence at the same time they threaten to destroy the wooden room that contains them. For Kiefer, fire is a powerful symbol mediating between heaven and earth, originating in the skies (lightening and stars), as well as in the hand of man. A source of great destruction, it is also a symbol of creation and invention, from the so-called "creative spark" to the Big Bang theory. "Creation and destruction are one in the same," Kiefer has said. "I work with this process in the studio." Kiefer has, in fact, over many years used intense heat and fire in the making of various works, melting metals and applying flames to the surfaces of his paintings or heat to earthen surfaces, causing them to crack and break apart, equating physical transformation with creation.

The pages for Kiefer's books entitled *Cauterization of the Rural District of Buchen* (1975, pages 72/73) are made from sections of paintings the artist burned in a final, frustrated attempt to, in his words, "heal the imagery, to come to a raw stage, the *nigredo*." Here Kiefer refers to the most fundamental state in alchemical transformation, in which matter is burned down to a blackened base before being regenerated into later stages of white and gold. The putrid, blackened stage is central to this creative process.

Paradox fills every page of *Cauterization*. As if in response to Adorno's stand that it is barbaric to make art in the aftermath of Nazi atrocities, Kiefer creates a two-sided image. Because so many of the pages are simply black, he has in effect created a book of abstractions, images without form. The title and process of creating these books, however, creates a poignant if not barbaric poetry. Not only do these small, burnt remnants remind us of charred battlefields and the burning of books during the Nazi era, they also refer specifically to the rural district of Buchen, a city located near Kiefer's home and studio in the Oden Forest, where large quantities of chemicals remained stored at an underground military site. Fighting fire with fire, Kiefer performs a kind of ritualistic healing or "cauterization" of an infected landscape.

Kiefer's early interest in the poetry of Paul Celan cannot be overlooked in this regard. Celan's haunting meditations on the Holocaust could be regarded as the *nigredo* of German poetry, the dark edge of a lineage that stretches from Friedrich Hölderlin in the eighteenth century through Rainer Maria Rilke in the early part of the twentieth. Celan's *Death Fugue*, written in a concentration camp in 1945, is far more than a description of death camps. Employing stark and pungent language fragments, Celan cut deeply into a human psyche that can produce hope and destruction in equal doses. In Kiefer's imagery, as well as his own use of words in combination with images, he has absorbed some of Celan's sense of the tragic becoming surreal, where graves are dug in the sky and milk is black.[13]

Kiefer's response to the lyric weight of Celan's poems is felt throughout his art in powerfully material ways. His extensive use of lead is analogous to the cold and gray atmospheres evoked in many of Celan's poems, and also echoes Celan's interest in alchemy. Alchemists were traditionally identified as "artisans" who attempted to reconcile dualism, which divided matter from spirit, by seeking the spirit within matter through extreme heat and subsequent purification. Metal was central to alchemical experimentation, with individual metals representing various degrees of pollution or purity in stages on a continuum to the most spiritual metal, gold. Lead is the first and the oldest of the seven metals of alchemy. It is also considered the least pure and the most ambiguous.

The discovery of metal and its role in the spiritual development of culture through alchemical imagery was a crucial stage in world knowledge. Writing about the history of religions, Mircea Eliade underscores the historical importance of "the imaginary world *(universe imaginaire)* which came into being through the discovery of metals . . . Not only did the manipulation of metals contribute considerably to man's conquest of the material world; it also changed the world of meaning. The metals opened for him a new mythological and religious universe."[14] Creation myths, which form a subtext to many of Kiefer's fragmented allegories, and which the artist describes as being "about forgotten beginnings," often involve metals as a symbolic element.

As the base metal in the alchemical process of making gold, lead is the ground zero of transformation. For Kiefer, lead is the metallic equivalent of humankind, an impure and ambiguous matrix operating at a low level in the cosmos but capable of achieving a higher state: "I feel closest to lead because it is like us. It is in flux. It's changeable and has potential to achieve a higher state of gold. You can see this when it is heated. It sweats

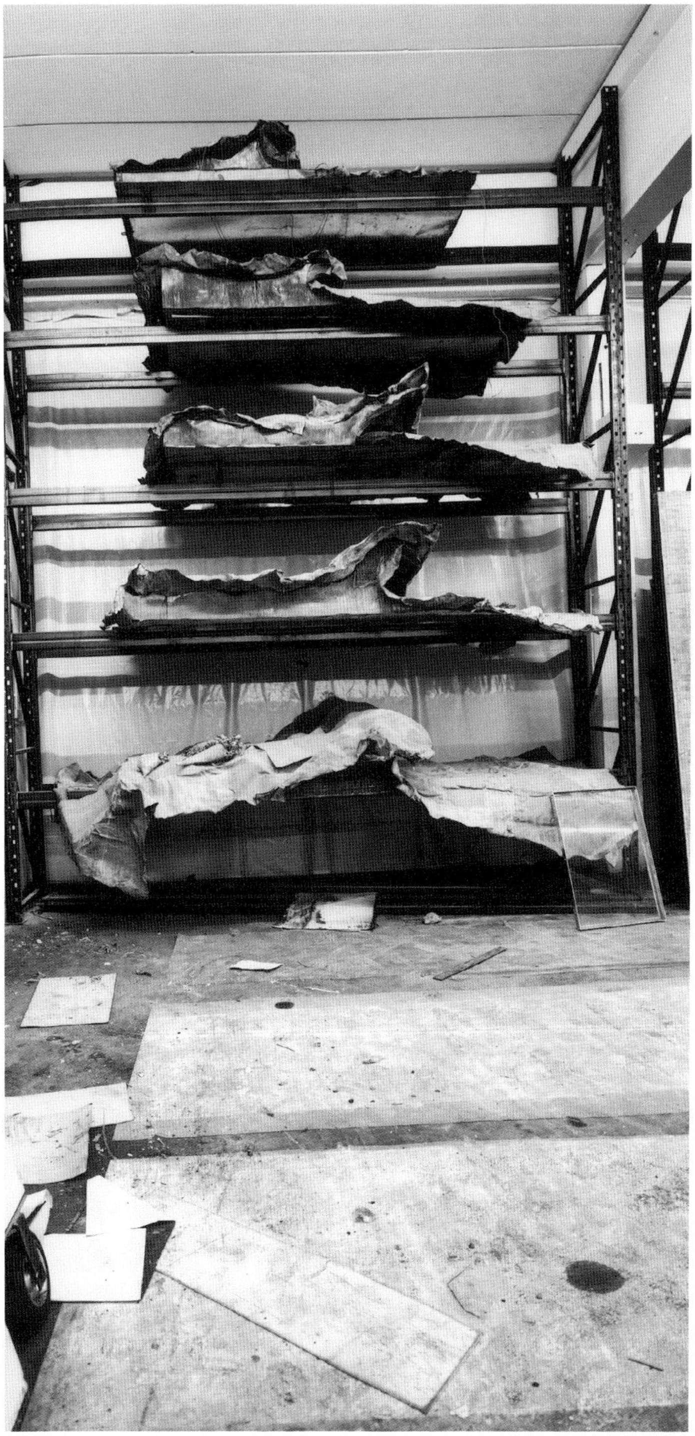

Lead in Kiefer's studio near Buchen

white and gold. But it is only a potential. The secrets are lost, as the secrets of our ability to achieve higher states seem lost or obscured." Alchemy at this level suggests a spiritual transcendence, and becomes an allegory of humankind's attempt to escape earthly boundaries. Alchemists employed the image of a white dove contained in lead to express the idea that matter can be transformed into spirit. Lead is also the symbol of creativity itself; since late antiquity, it has been associated with the planet Saturn, the "highest" of planets and the domain of artistic inspiration. The Saturnine temperament, however, is a melancholic one.

The presence of lead in and around Kiefer's work spaces is inescapable: when it is not scattered on the floors of his studios, it is nailed to a wall or hanging from the ceiling. Stacks of lead line the private road leading up to his current studio compound in Barjac, France. "For me," Kiefer has said, "lead is a very important material. It is, of course, a symbolic material, but also the color is very important. You cannot say that it is light or dark. It is a color or non-color that I identify with. I don't believe in absolutes. The truth is always gray."

A large cache of Kiefer's lead inventory comes from the roof of Cologne Cathedral, the tallest Gothic structure in Germany.[15] In the sculpture *20 Years of Solitude* (1971–91, pages 92/93), these lead sheets from Cologne act as the foundation for a series of small, white, semen-stained books. The title refers to the solitary nature of the artist's search for glimpses of transcendence. More pointedly, elevating his sperm above a cathedral roof reflects Kiefer's complex relationship with Catholicism. Raised Catholic, the artist has had to balance his appreciation of and curiosity about Catholic imagery with his innate skepticism of symbols of authority. A church building, no matter how grand, and a Bible, no matter how convincing, cannot, in Kiefer's words, "deliver us to heaven. It is my body that holds my spirit, as it is in nature." Conflating the microcosmic (the human body) and the macrocosmic (the heavens), as the early alchemists had done, Kiefer in essence writes his own bible using his sperm. What to some could seem like an act of defilement is for Kiefer another symbolic act of regeneration and self-determination, and perhaps a challenge to a religious authority that found itself in a controversial position, at the least, regarding its leaders' knowledge of the Holocaust and their delicate relations with the Nazi state. Echoing Barnett Newman's well-known statement about Abstract Expressionism—"We are making it out of ourselves"—Kiefer creates a personal heaven from his own seeds. Placed on the salvaged lead, the honey-yellow stains float like stars above the deconstructed cathedral roof.

Among the different mediums Kiefer has worked with over the years, including watercolor, painting, printmaking, sculpture, and architectural installations, bookmaking has been a consistent and central part of his art. The artist devotes an entire studio to this activity. Indeed, a large library and bookmaking studio are situated between his living space and his painting and sculpture studios.

Books have many connotations, particularly for Germans, whose history of printing (the Gutenberg Bible) and of burning books is part of a national psyche. For Kiefer, the book has immense symbolic power as a container and transmitter. From the Bible to ancient illustrated manuscripts and books of law, it projects the history of world knowledge. The codifying of laws and languages, the formulation and circulation of theories of creation, the rise of religions and the nation-state, and the scientific revolution have played out in books. Kiefer's books are often paradoxical in nature. Many of them are large, indicating their symbolic importance. At the same time, the artist applies elements of subversion: a lead book with blank pages that cannot be read and immense wings that cannot fly. One of the key aspects of all of Kiefer's books is that they are predominantly visual. While words or phrases may occasionally appear (for the most part, names, locations, and events from the distant past), they are used to contextualize a visual and material narrative. Kiefer describes his books in Jungian/archetypal terms. "You do not have to read my books," he has said. "You only need to scan. I am not picturing words. I am trying to recreate a memory. You cannot read memory through illustrating. It is more directly given through images and materials." Reminding us that the first books were clay tablets, many of Kiefer's pages are covered with earth. Such pages evoke biblical deserts and the caves at Lascaux, taking us back to the beginning of the imagination of the sacred. Flowers occasionally emerge from Kiefer's earth pages and eventually become stars, creating a wistful dialogue between earth and heaven. Ancient texts have in fact described the universe as an immense book.

For Kiefer, books and architecture operate in parallel worlds; both are powerful containers that record the history of human aspirations. Like books, buildings are images of authority which the artist reforms, literally eroding their iconic presence and placing them in a larger framework of time. Imposing buildings that suggest transcendence over the earth must ironically always return to it. The ruin represents the vanity of human aspirations for power and glory. While monuments attempt to fix meaning against the flow of time, Kiefer makes the overwhelming vastness of time the subject of many of his works. His images of ceremonial halls, ancient brick buildings,

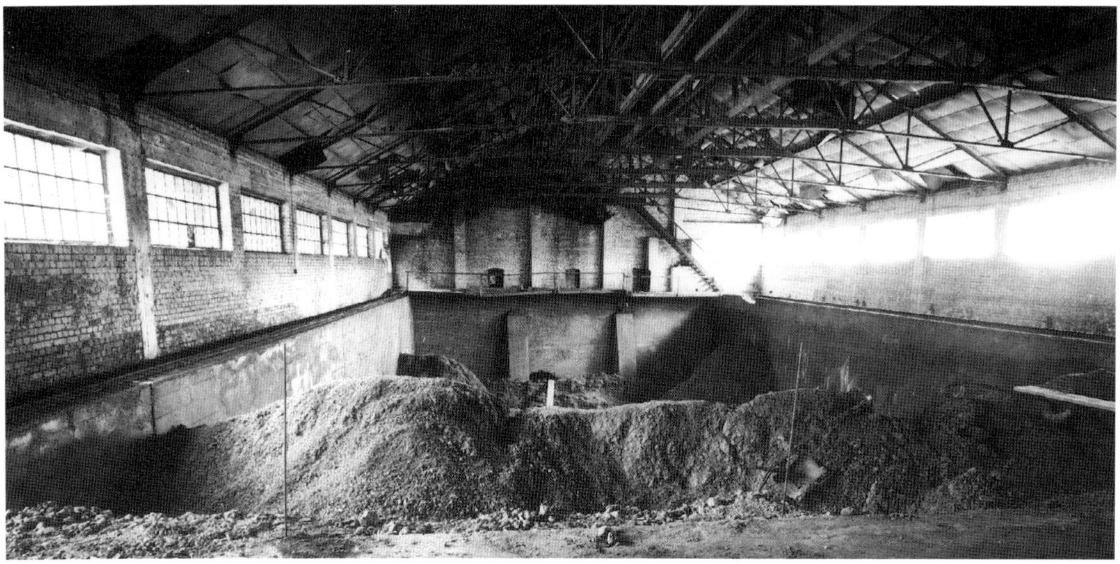

The Brick Factory, near Buchen

and pyramids are obscured by the sandy mist of time. Time is in fact an intrinsic part of the process of their making. Applying layer upon layer of sand, ash, earth, and emulsion, Kiefer literally builds his images over weeks and months using trowels and brooms as paintbrushes. He then leaves the works outside for equal, if not longer, periods. The results are weathered monuments that move in and out of focus. An Albert Speer interior covered by a thick layer of ash, an ancient Mexican pyramid stained with blood and gold, or a massive brick kiln all suggest human history riding a far more pervasive wave of time. "Each of these buildings," the artist contends, "has a history created by its own fiction and need to demonstrate its philosophy of existence. That fiction is part of the debris of history. My images connect with that debris. They attempt to connect with the beginning or the end, with a deep and lost memory between here and there."

Kiefer's recent interest in stars and astronomical charts is an elegy to a time when the night sky evoked the possibility of a mysterious heavenly realm that pushed at the edges of the human imagination. Planets were mysterious messengers that suggested the narratives of our beginnings. For Kiefer, those narratives are not only spiritual but material. He describes the earth as a kind of alchemical fragment, "a piece of metal that is still burning inside, still being forged from a great fire." In Kiefer's cosmology, the universe is an immense athanor, or alchemical oven, where spirit and matter are in a continual process of creation and destruction.

Kiefer has often described the artist's studio as a microcosm of this athanor, where images and materials are constantly under breakdown and reformation. Building on that image, in the 1980s Kiefer purchased an abandoned nineteenth-century brick factory in a town called Höpfingen, also near Buchen. What he initially described as simply a "studio expansion" soon evolved into a massive installation in which the building and Kiefer's art created a symbiotic dialogue verging on allegory. The building consisted of a long, dried-up mud pit with ovens or kilns at one end. The ovens soon became symbolic containers housing various metals, unfinished or abandoned paintings, and massive bunches of brittle dried flowers. Salvaged World War I and World War II tanks were positioned on the perimeter of the property. The Brick Factory embraced direct and cryptic references to war, death camps, alchemy, and the faint hope of some form of purification. A lead palette, hung from a high ceiling, hovered over the dried, cracking pit. Again, it is significant that the palette was made of lead—an alchemist's symbol of the possibility of transformation from base matter into spirit.

Brickmaking is humanity's equivalent to the creation of stars. Forged through heat and compression of matter, bricks and stars can be seen as the building blocks of earthly and celestial architectures. While bricks fall into ruin, we imagine stars burning infinitely. Kiefer, however, also presents a cosmos in continual ruin. In some of his recent images of a star-packed universe, the mythological heaven of the past is replaced by a scientific one, in which celestial bodies are measured and given numbers for their speed, color, and light. Kiefer identifies his stars with these numerical designations, which would appear to represent a fixed system of distances. But as Kiefer points out, this too is an illusion of sorts, as the planets that emit the light we are measuring have long since died.

Kiefer is less fascinated by the destination than the search. His natural, existential skepticism regarding a place called heaven is outweighed by his remarkable, even baffling ambition to explore the need for one. In the early 1990s, Kiefer settled in the south of France, where he works in a complex of nineteenth-century buildings originally designed as a silkworm nursery. This 200-acre complex in Barjac, which the artist has named La Ribaute, has become a total work of art. Along with areas for the making of ever more monumental paintings and sculpture, it houses a vast network of above- and underground installations. Kiefer's choice of studios has always had a metaphoric connection to his subject matter, sometimes conscious, sometimes coincidental. In the 1970s, when he was working in a former schoolhouse in the Oden Forest, the artist was admittedly in a period of intense "study," establishing the foundation for

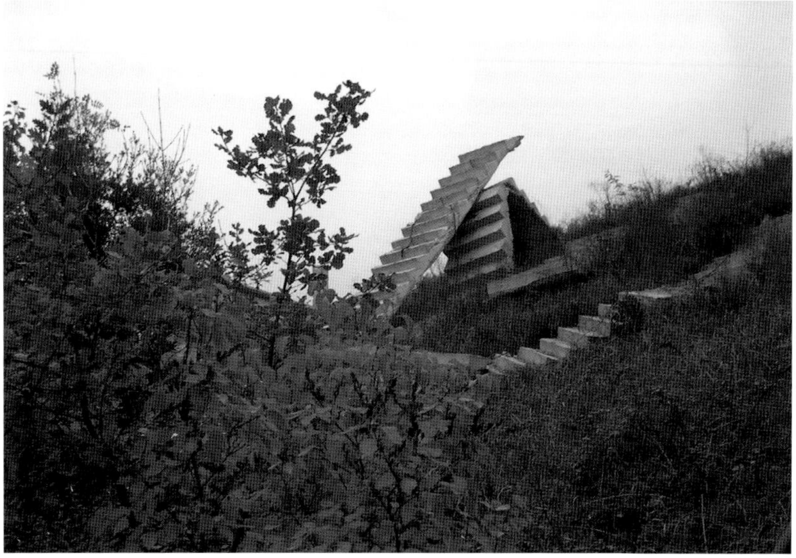

An installation on Kiefer's land, Barjac

what would be an ever-growing field of symbols. The abandoned brick factory near Buchen, where the artist created many of his earliest architectural installations in the 1980s, was significant for its wall of ovens, coinciding not only with his meditation on Germany's Nazi past, but his growing interest in alchemy and its concept of the athanor.

Kiefer's choice of an abandoned silkworm nursery may also be a part of his symbolism. The Zohar, or Book of Splendor—a thirteenth-century Spanish mystic's guide central to kabbalism from medieval times, from which the artist can quote—refers to personal enlightenment using the symbol of a silkworm that encloses "itself within, weaving itself a palace."[16] Kiefer's decision to move to a large and remote piece of land results from his ambition to create a work of far greater inclusiveness and complexity than any he has previously attempted—a *gesamtkunstwerk* that synthesizes painting, sculpture, and architecture. This is Kiefer's eccentric "Dome of Heaven." Since his arrival in Barjac, he has been an obsessive builder, developing acres of new stages and spaces that recapitulate and extend, physically and symbolically, many of his earliest images. It is a grand alchemical search envisioned to last a lifetime yet never be completed.

With the exception of a modest living area, all of the buildings on Kiefer's land, as well as the land itself, have become a monumental staging area for exploring the

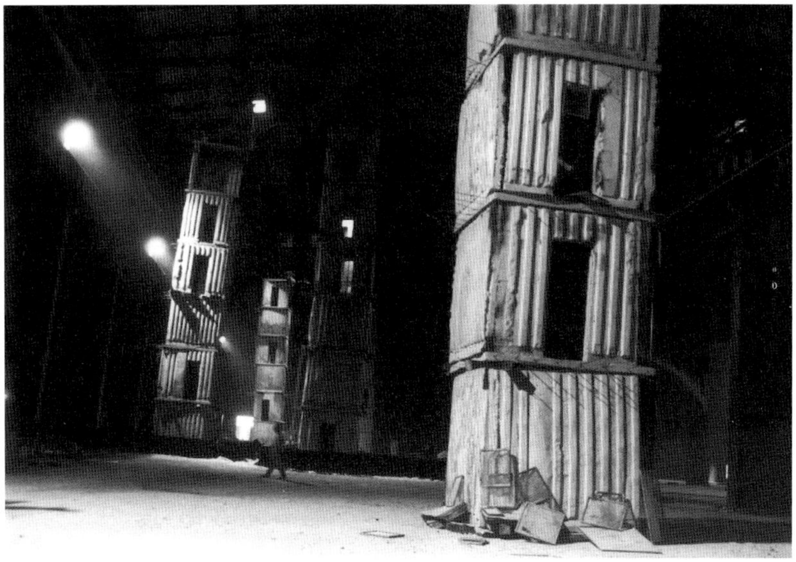

The Seven Heavenly Palaces, Hangar Bicocca, Milan

relationship between heaven and earth. Not only does Kiefer appropriate the architecture of the silkworm nursery buildings into his art, he has over the last decade constructed his own symbolic architecture in the form of towers that climb into the sky, underground spaces that tunnel below the surface of the land, and massive concrete stairs that rise out of the earth, punching their way through the horizon. He is, in essence, creating his own church, one quite different from Le Corbusier's La Tourette or Henri Matisse's famous Chapel at Vence, which is located nearby. While Matisse's space is filled with light and color, Kiefer's vast complex consecrates darkness and instability.

In his series of tower-like monuments, Kiefer returns to the concrete he so admired at La Tourette. The sleek, horizontal containment of Le Corbusier's monastery, however, has been transformed into deliberately crude architectural elegies to a once-secret explanation of the path to God and heaven—perverse extensions of the Merkaba tradition, with its divine chariot that carries mind and spirit through seven heavenly palaces described by kabbalistic mystics. In the fall of 2004, Kiefer constructed seven such towers in a dark and sprawling hangar in Milan.

If Kiefer's precariously balanced towers of concrete rooms seem to be unlikely steps to heaven, his tunnels, which wind underneath the property for thousands of yards, are even more perplexing. Referring to this underground activity in a typically paradoxical manner, Kiefer remarks, "There is no reason to assume that heaven is in the sky or that it is filled with light." The tunnels lead to variously sized rooms lined with lead or concrete, or left raw and cavelike. Containing symbolic objects—palettes, broken ceramics, piles of bricks, broken glass—they are dimly lit, often with only a single, bare light bulb, functioning like ancient or primitive chapels, which the artist has ritualistically reconfigured over months and years. These towers and chambers may represent an attempt to create a new poetics of spirituality, or the ruins of a failed one that ended when Judaic and Christian authority came to political loggerheads.

In this respect, Kiefer's interest in ancient Jewish culture should not be explained away simply as guilt for his country's persecution of Jews. He explains it as a matter of "reassembling." "It is all one thing," he contends. "I cannot imagine German culture without Judaism. Everything that makes German philosophy and poetry interesting to the world is a combination of Germany and Judaism. One thing is that Germans committed the immense crime of killing Jews. The other is that they amputated themselves.

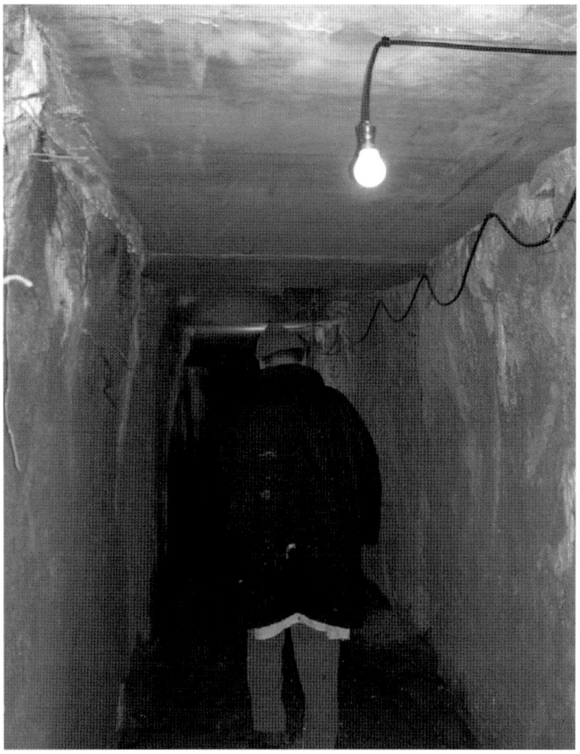

The artist in Barjac, 2003

They took half of German culture and killed it."[17] Kiefer's art can be seen not only as a form of mourning and working through the catastrophe of the Nazi era, but also as the artist's personal attempt to rebuild German culture into the more complex spiritual matrix that existed in a much earlier time. Kiefer's creation in 2000 of six monumental lead paintings for the arched niches of a chapel at La Salpêtrière Hospital in Paris was a clear attempt to reconstruct this type of complexity. The fact that the chapel is in a hospital, a place of healing, is not insignificant. For Kiefer, this was an opportunity to connect the break between Judaism and Roman Catholicism. The ensemble addressed the theme *Shevirat Ha-Kelim*, or "The Shattering of the Vessels."

According to kabbalistic wisdom, the existence of disharmony in the material world can be ascribed to two momentous events: the original constriction (*Tsim Tsum*) and the Shattering of the Vessels. God's constriction was necessary in order to make room for the world. This constriction, however, concealed the divine essence, creating a profound division between God and humanity, which resulted in a dark, vacant space. For Kiefer, the imagination is the only means capable of traversing this vast space. Tsim Tsum could in fact be understood as a metaphor for the creative process, in which the artist withdraws into himself in order to render a new image of the condition of the world. Although Kiefer may sublimate some of his Catholic background in order to explore the mystical side of the history of religion, the power of the image—so much a part of Catholic teaching—remains dominant in his approach: "My understanding of a text is only complete when I can make an image of it. The process of spiritual knowledge is almost purely visual for me."

The Shattering of the Vessels is likewise a powerful visual image for Kiefer. In this later stage in creation, the divine light emanates, shattering ten vessels that were meant to contain it. The scholar Gershom Scholem writes, "The breaking of the vessels continues into all the further stages of emanation and Creation; everything is in some way broken, everything has a flaw, everything is unfinished."[18] This can be understood to represent the "fractured" state of our world, in which the kabbalist strives to restore balance and wholeness. The paintings for La Salpêtrière consist of lead panels that filled each arch in the chapel. Kiefer's signature material, mystically associated with the air and the earth, projects an ambiguous space between light and dark. From one of these spaces hang large ceramic pots, some of which are cracked or broken. Another panel includes long dried flowers that project from the gray field, some drooping downward and others reaching up, as if growing out of the murky, leaden space of the painting. In

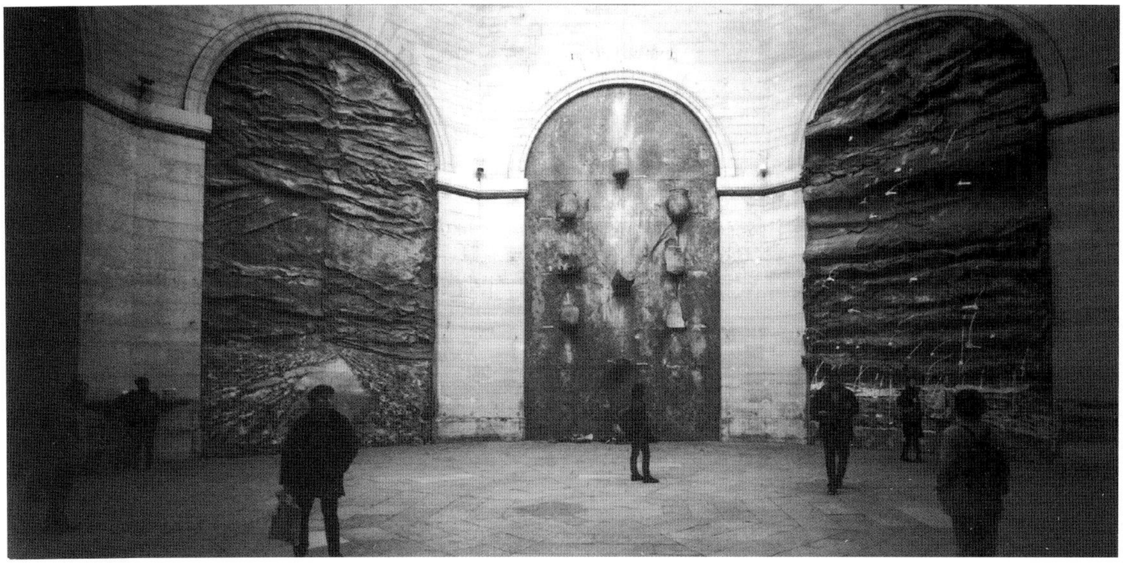

Shevirat Ha-Kelim, Chapelle de la Salpêtrière, Paris

another panel, an immense, craggy tongue of once-molten lead reaches down to the bottom of the painting. In the center of the chapel's floor, the artist placed stacks of lead sheets, like pages of a new book yet to be bound, covered with shattered glass.

While Tsim Tsum has been compared to scientific theories of the Big Bang, it might also describe the fractured metaphysics that challenge the possibility of world peace and order. The single thing that binds all cultures, regardless of politics or religion, is a need to engage the fundamental reason for human existence. Indeed, the immense darkness created by Tsim Tsum could be conceived as a universal wound that, given the world as it is now, cannot be healed. "Our tragedy is that we don't know our beginnings," Kiefer says. "This is not just a German problem." Neither priest, rabbi, nor evangelist, Kiefer's task is ultimately a personal one: to rejuvenate his own visualization of our precarious condition.

"The great epoch of the spiritual which is already beginning, or, in embryonic form, began already yesterday . . . provides and will provide the soil in which a kind of monumental work of art must come to fruition."[19] These words were written by Wassily Kandinsky, the great pioneer of abstract painting, almost one hundred years ago. Kiefer's project in Barjac can be considered an extension of this exploration. Twentieth-century art began with a discussion about the spiritual, and throughout his career Kiefer

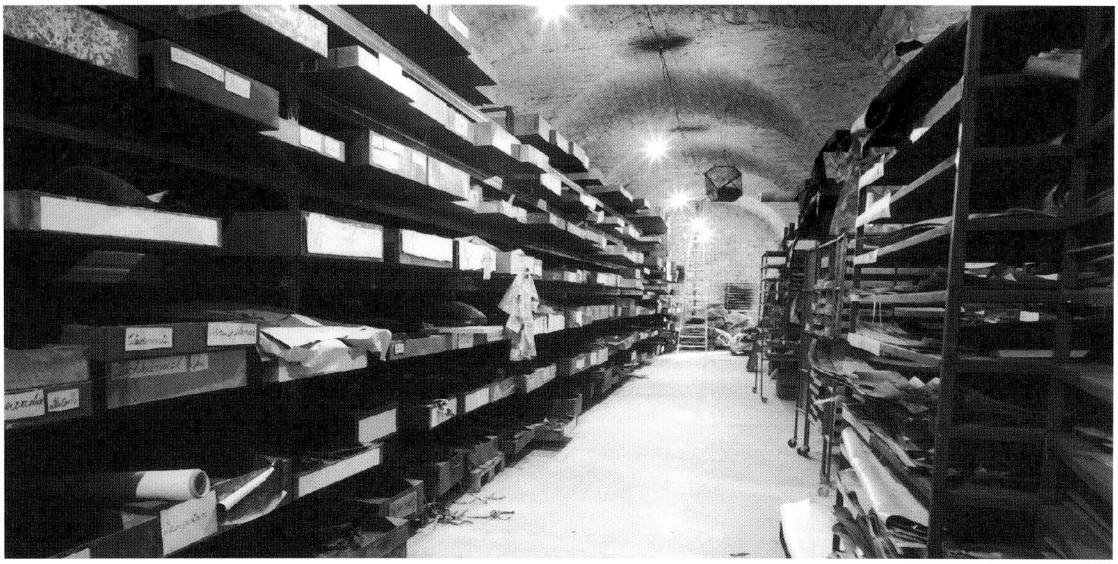

A storeroom in Kiefer's studio complex, Barjac

has endeavored to keep the discussion going. His is a romantic quest splintered with doubt. "I am not trying to illustrate religion," Kiefer has said. "I'm a storyteller with a broken story."

Kiefer engages the complex challenge of forming a poetic–spiritual image in our time, in relation not only to Adorno's warning, but also to that of the Old Testament. The Second Commandment—"You shall not make for yourself a graven image, or any likeness of anything that is in heaven above, or that is in the earth beneath, or that is in the water under the earth"—places the artist in an untenable position. Abstraction would appear to be the most logical solution, and indeed, it has been the central means of exploring the visual nature of spirituality in the twentieth century.[20] Following World War II, the powerful abstract fields created by the Abstract Expressionists acknowledge the Second Commandment at the same time they stir deep, perhaps ancient questions about the individual and the nature of existence. As it has developed over the decades, however, abstraction has tended to lose its potency, at times hardening into mannerist gesture by succeeding generations. When Kiefer calls out to *Aaron*, *c.* 1979—the brother of Moses who attempted to reengage the forbidden image—he does so from the ironic standpoint of a generation of Germans who see contemporary abstraction as a kind of silence or a negation of historical and spiritual memory.

Kiefer sees his challenge as one of elemental reconstruction. His imagery comes in dramatic and continually shifting panoramas reminiscent of Abstract Expressionism but filled with an archaeology of symbolic debris. His studio appears as a sprawling junkyard of eccentric materials and found objects he has collected over his almost four-decade career. They lie in piles over many acres or are stacked on immense steel shelves and stored in a vast underground library of boxes. Both conceptually and materially, Kiefer is a redeemer of lost or discarded images and forms, which, for the artist, resonate with mythic content that reflects our need to answer fundamental questions: Why do we exist? Are we from heaven? Are we meant to end up there, or does it exist at all? If so, how can we conceive of it?

From the late eighteenth century and the beginnings of what historians identify as a Romantic strain within the art of Western culture, the artist's gaze has often been directed toward heaven—a space where chaos becomes order. For the artist, it is an inward search for a preconscious image that speaks to our beginnings and a rationale for our creation. This is as true for Caspar David Friedrich as it is for the Abstract Expressionists, for whom Kiefer has often expressed admiration. The vast abstract fields of Clyfford Still, Mark Rothko, and Barnett Newman present a monumentally abstract approach to the concept of the sublime in which man stands in awe at the space between the individual and the cosmos. The titles of Newman's paintings, also inspired by kabbalistic and biblical texts, reflect an ambition to imagine the earliest moment of creation: *The Break*, *Genesis*, *The Beginning*, *Pagan Void*, *Zsim Zsum*. For Newman, it was a matter of scale: "One thing that I am involved in about painting," he told David Sylvester, "is that the painting should give man a sense of place: that he knows he's there, so he's aware of himself."[21] Sylvester remarked that Newman's and Still's paintings were not abstracted realities, but "the real space of the mind and its imperfect attempt to grasp the whole."[22]

Kiefer's art can be seen as a synthesis of this Romantic tradition, absorbing the abstract pathos and imposing size of Abstract Expressionist painting, yet reaching back to recover images and symbols that carry distant memory. Kiefer's art is based on the assumption that a deep field of lost images housed in the memory of the modern mind will resonate through intuitive structures made by the artist. Inscribed on a number of Kiefer's paintings and installations are the words *Am Anfang*: In the Beginning. Combining materials and images of his time with words that carry echoes from an ancient past, Kiefer attempts to take us back to the beginnings of religion, when the desire and means of transcendence were still a matter of debate, when the relationship between heaven and earth was still being constructed. In this belief, he creates his own phenomenology of religion, one that contains the impurities and ambiguities of the lead he continues to employ in his work. Kiefer envisions a leaden age rather than a golden one. As he remarks, "Looking for light is a tyranny we can't afford now."

Light has been a crucial symbol in European religious art, early on as an emblem of God's grace passing down to earth and later as a symbol of psychological awareness, connoting personal enlightenment. Kiefer's leaden light seems to bypass both of these traditions, creating an unsettling twilight in which the spiritual, psychological, and historical seem to collide without resolution. Even when he is not using lead, Kiefer's landscapes are always overcast, as if caught in an infinite winter, suggesting either the aftermath of a cataclysm or the prelude to one, creating a space that carries the weight of history within a reach for transcendence.

When Kiefer talks about "hope," he does so with a weary look. In one of his most recent paintings, *Heaven on Earth* (1998–2004, pages 146/147), a muddy road leads away from the viewer to a distant horizon. Clouds of barbed wire—an indelible symbol of concentration camps—block our path into the artist's illusionistic space. Kiefer's road to heaven, informed by an awareness of history, is paved with a skepticism that is turned as much against scientific certitude as it is against theological authority. He does not assume the existence of a paradise, only the ancient need to imagine one.

1 Wim Wenders, "An attempted description of an indescribable film: From the first treatment for *Wings of Desire*," 1986, reprinted in *The Logic of Images: Essays and Conversations*, trans. Michael Hofmann (London: Faber and Faber, 1991): 78.
2 Theodor Adorno, "Cultural Criticism in Society," in *Prisms*, Samuel and Sherry Weber, trans. (London: Neville Spearman, 1967): 34.
3 Unless otherwise noted, quotations from the artist in the Introduction and the Notes on the Works are from a conversation with the author, October 5, 2004.
4 Jonathan Glancey, "Divine Inspiration," *The Guardian* (January 14, 2002).
5 Thomas McEvilley, "Communion and Transcendence in Kiefer's New Work," in *Anselm Kiefer: I Hold All Indias in My Hand* (London: Anthony d'Offay Gallery, 1996): 1.
6 Caroline Tisdall, *Joseph Beuys: We Go This Way* (London: Violette Editions, 1998): 21.
7 The installation, first produced in the artist's studio, no longer exists.
8 See Christine Mehring, "Continental Schrift," *Artforum* (May 2004): 178–183.
9 Ibid.
10 "Philip Guston Talking," lecture at the University of Minnesota, 1978, transcribed by Renee McKee, in Nicholas Serota, ed., *Philip Guston: Paintings 1969–1980* (London: Whitechapel Art Gallery, 1982): 50.
11 The full quotation is translated, "Two things fill the mind with ever new and increasing wonder and awe, the more often and the more seriously reflection concentrates upon them: the starred heaven above me and the moral law within me." *Critique of Practical Reason* (1788; repr. London: Longmans, Green and Co., 1923): 260.
12 Adolf Hitler, *Mein Kampf*, 1925–26, trans. Ralph Manheim (Boston: Mariner Books, 1999): 19–21.
13 Paul Celan, "Death Fugue," in *Selected Poems and Prose of Paul Celan*, ed. John Felstiner (New York: W. W. Norton, 2001): 30.
14 Mircea Eliade, *The Forge and the Crucible: The Origins and Structures of Alchemy* 2nd ed. (Chicago: The University of Chicago Press, 1978): 181.
15 Damaged during World War II, the replacement of Cologne Cathedral's lead roof was part of a long restoration process.
16 Daniel C. Matt, *The Zohar: Pritzker Edition*, vol. I (Stanford: Stanford University Press, 2004): 110.
17 In Alan Riding, "Unseen as He Stares Down History," *The New York Times* (April 3, 2001).
18 Gershom Scholem, *On the Kabbalah and Its Symbolism*, trans. Ralph Manheim (New York: Schocken Books, 1996): 112–13.
19 In *The Spiritual in Art: Abstract Painting 1890–1985* (Los Angeles and New York: Los Angeles County Museum of Art in association with Abbeville Press, 1986): 11.
20 Ibid.
21 In David Sylvester, *Interviews with American Artists* (New Haven and London: Yale University Press, 2001): 39.
22 David Sylvester to the author in an unpublished interview, 1986.

Plates

Winterlandschaft (Winter Landscape), 1970

The early watercolor *Winter Landscape* typifies Kiefer's balancing of hope and skepticism. A disembodied head floats between the sky and a vast, barren field. Blood from the figure pours onto the snowy ground and stains the clouds as it moves through the sky. For Kiefer, barren earth is a powerful metaphor for historic memory, the ultimate page upon which history is recorded.

This work may also refer to Kiefer's early interest in Vincent van Gogh's paintings of fields, as well as the Dutch painter's tortured romanticism, which resulted in his cutting off part of his own ear. As if pulling Van Gogh through recent German history, Kiefer's romanticism is ambiguous. The severed head looks up to the dark and ominous sky. While the figure seems to search the heavens for an answer, the image may also be interpreted as a warning about burying our heads in the clouds. Human blood—which the poet Robert Duncan once referred to as "the ink of history"—connects earth and sky, suggesting that history is an ever-present force in shaping our image of heaven.

It is significant that Kiefer has painted a winter landscape. The motif of winter, twilight, or nightfall runs through much of his imagery. Typically, the four seasonal phases of the sun's orbit are seen as relating to the stages of human life. Kiefer would extend that relationship to a time in history that suggests the barren end of a cycle and the uncertainty of a new beginning.

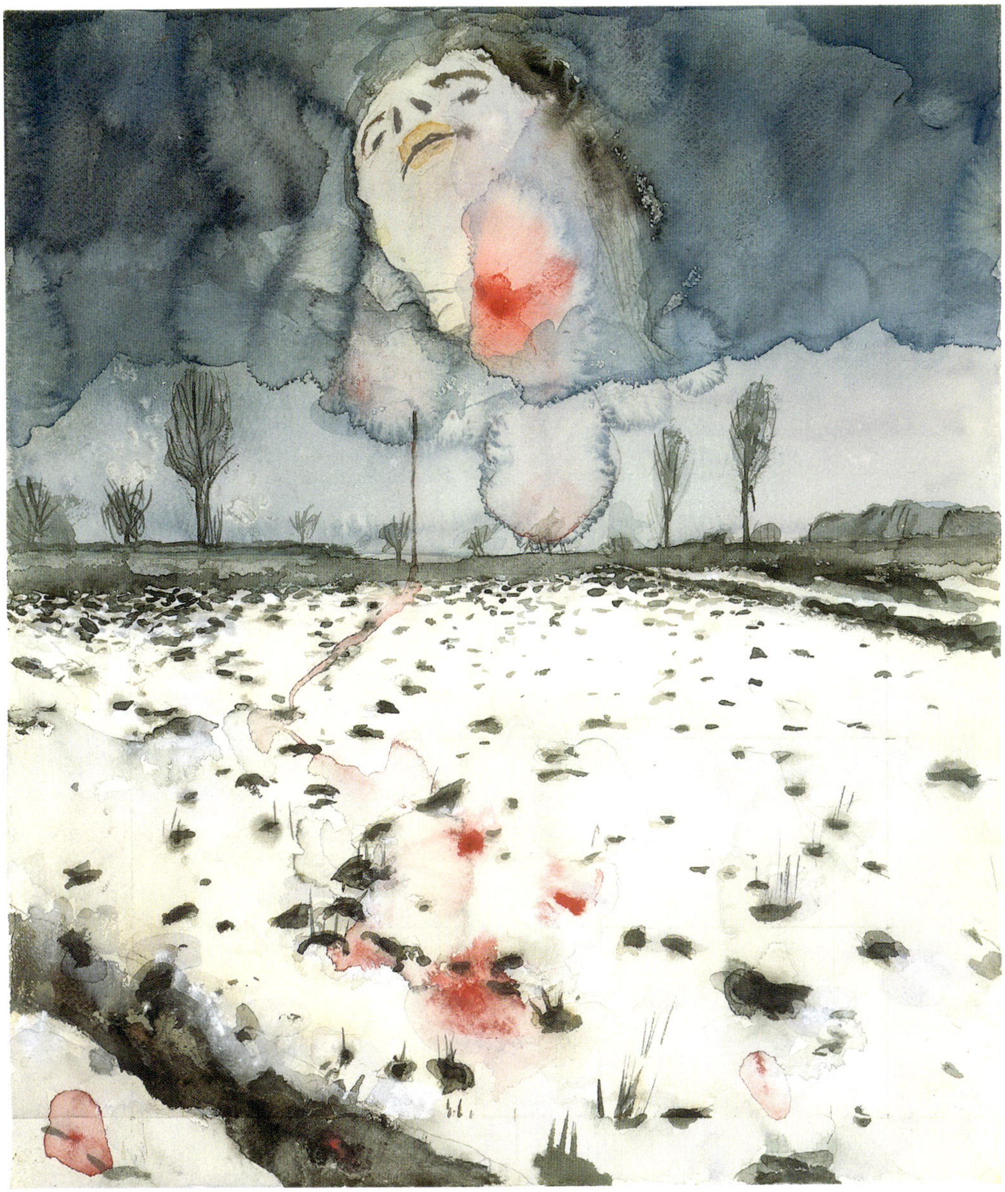

Winterlandschaft (Winter Landscape), 1970
Watercolor, gouache, and graphite pencil on paper
16 7/8 × 14 inches (42.9 × 35.6 cm)

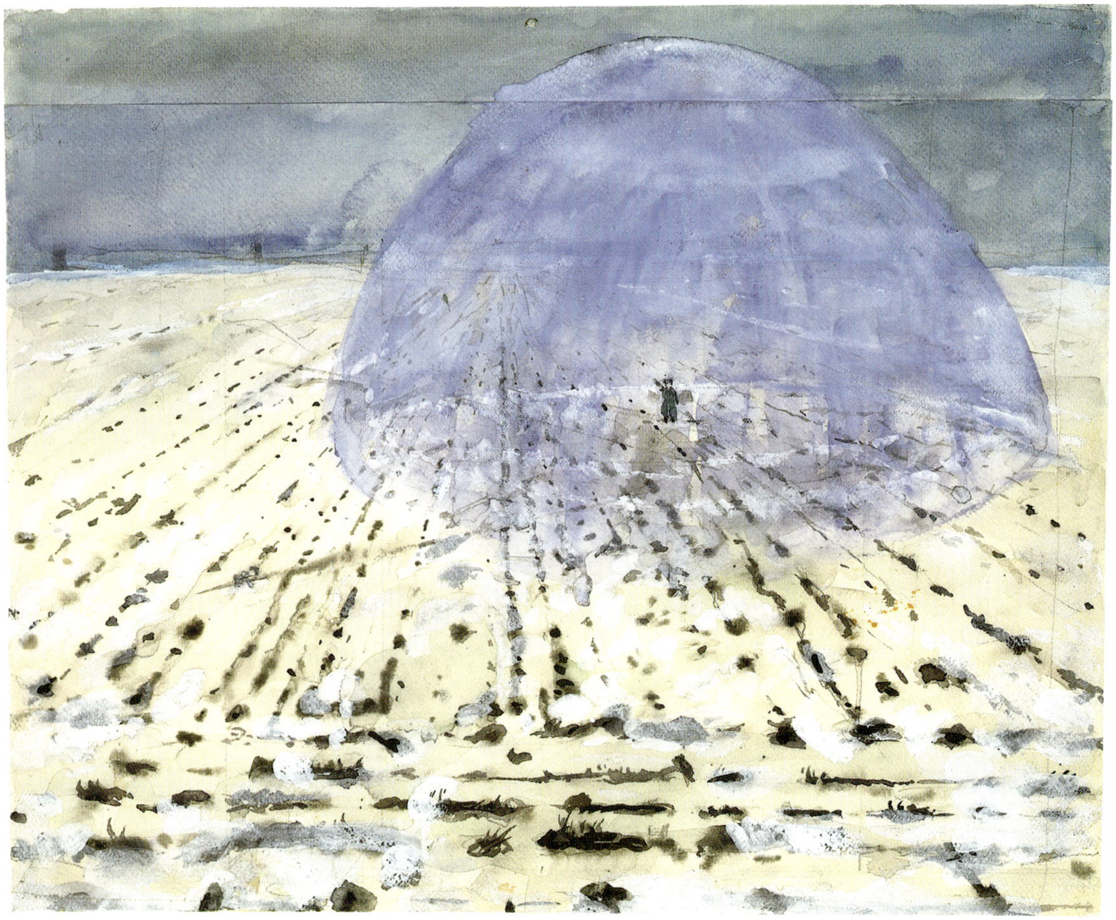

Jeder Mensch steht unter seiner Himmelskugel (Everyone Stands Under His Own Dome of Heaven), 1970
Watercolor, gouache, and graphite pencil on joined paper
15 ¾ × 18 ⅞ inches (40 × 47.9 cm)

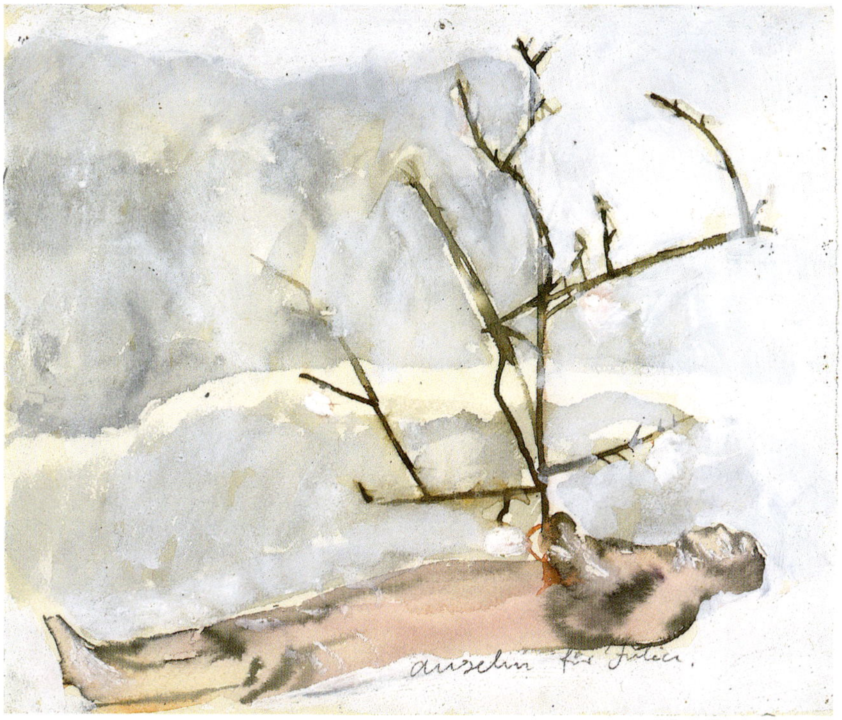

Liegender Mann mit Zweig (Man Lying with Branch), 1971
Watercolor, gouache, and graphite pencil on paper
9 ⅝ × 10 ¾ inches (23.8 × 27.3 cm)

Mann im Wald (Man in the Forest), 1971

Liegender Mann mit Zweig (Man Lying with Branch), 1971

Man in the Forest, one of Kiefer's earliest paintings, introduces a number of symbols on which he would elaborate in subsequent works. The painting depicts the artist wearing a nightshirt, holding a burning branch in a dense pine forest. Forests have played an important role in Kiefer's biography. The artist, whose surname means "pine tree" in German, was raised on the east bank of the Rhine, in the Black Forest region. He later chose to study in Freiburg, near the frontier border of France. In 1971, he established his first studio in the town of Hornbach in the Oden Forest in the Rhineland-Palatinate. "The forest is very important to Germans," Kiefer has said. "Our stories always begin in the forest." A key moment in German history is set against a dark forest, in which Arminius (Hermann) led the ancient Germanic people in victory over Roman invaders at the Battle of Teutoburg Forest in A.D. 9.

Kiefer's trees, while referring to a symbol of German nationalism, also evoke the ancient tradition of tree worship that includes the Norse legend of the Yggdrasil, in which the universe is envisioned as a sprawling evergreen; the Tree of Knowledge of Good and Evil in the biblical Garden of Eden; and the kabbalistic Tree of Life. In *Man in the Forest*, the trees extend from the ground to the top edge of the painting without tapering, suggesting their extension far into the sky, restating the mythic connection between earth and the imaginative realm of the heavens.

Kiefer is dwarfed by the presence of the trees, but he holds a fiery branch, demonstrating his inventiveness and potential power over nature. The fact that he wears a nightshirt, however, indicates that this is a dreamscape. Kiefer imagines himself as a Gilgamesh-like figure in the epic story that explores the nature of humanity, heroism, and the gods. As a young artist, then, Kiefer begins his own image/story with what is perhaps the oldest written story on earth. According to legend, Gilgamesh was superhuman, so powerful that the gods were forced to create counterforces to balance his desires and actions. Kiefer remarks, "As you can see, we have always been a problem for heaven."

The symbol of the branch is also prominent in *Man Lying with Branch* of the same year (page 55). Here Kiefer refers to historical images of a tree sprouting from a human form. By comparison, Kiefer's image shows not only envy of nature but also a desperation to reconnect with it. Unlike the historical images of this subject, Kiefer's version depicts the branch not growing from the body but stabbed into it, causing blood to squirt from the figure's side.

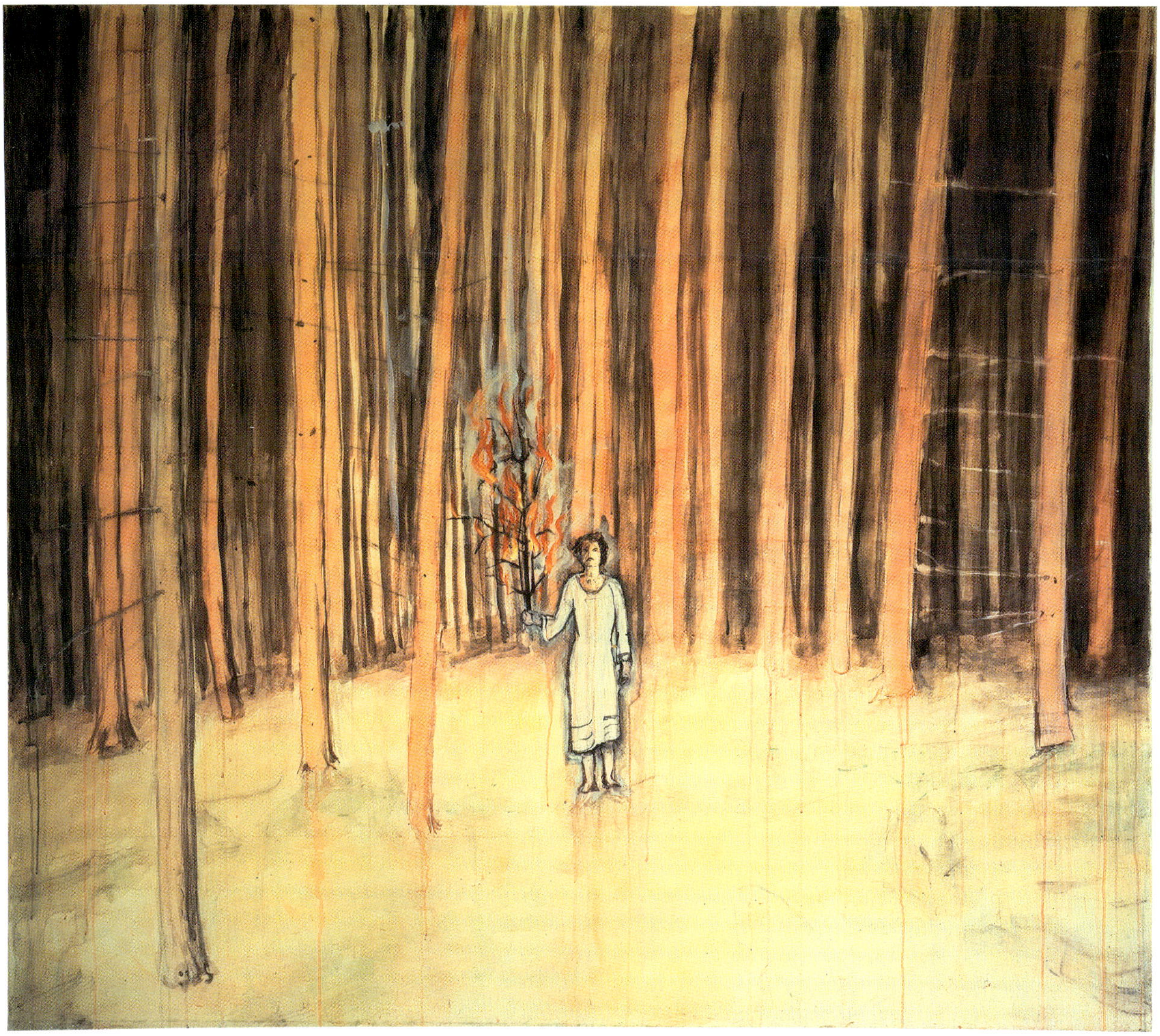

Mann im Wald (Man in the Forest), 1971
Oil on canvas
68 ½ × 74 ½ inches (174 × 189 cm)

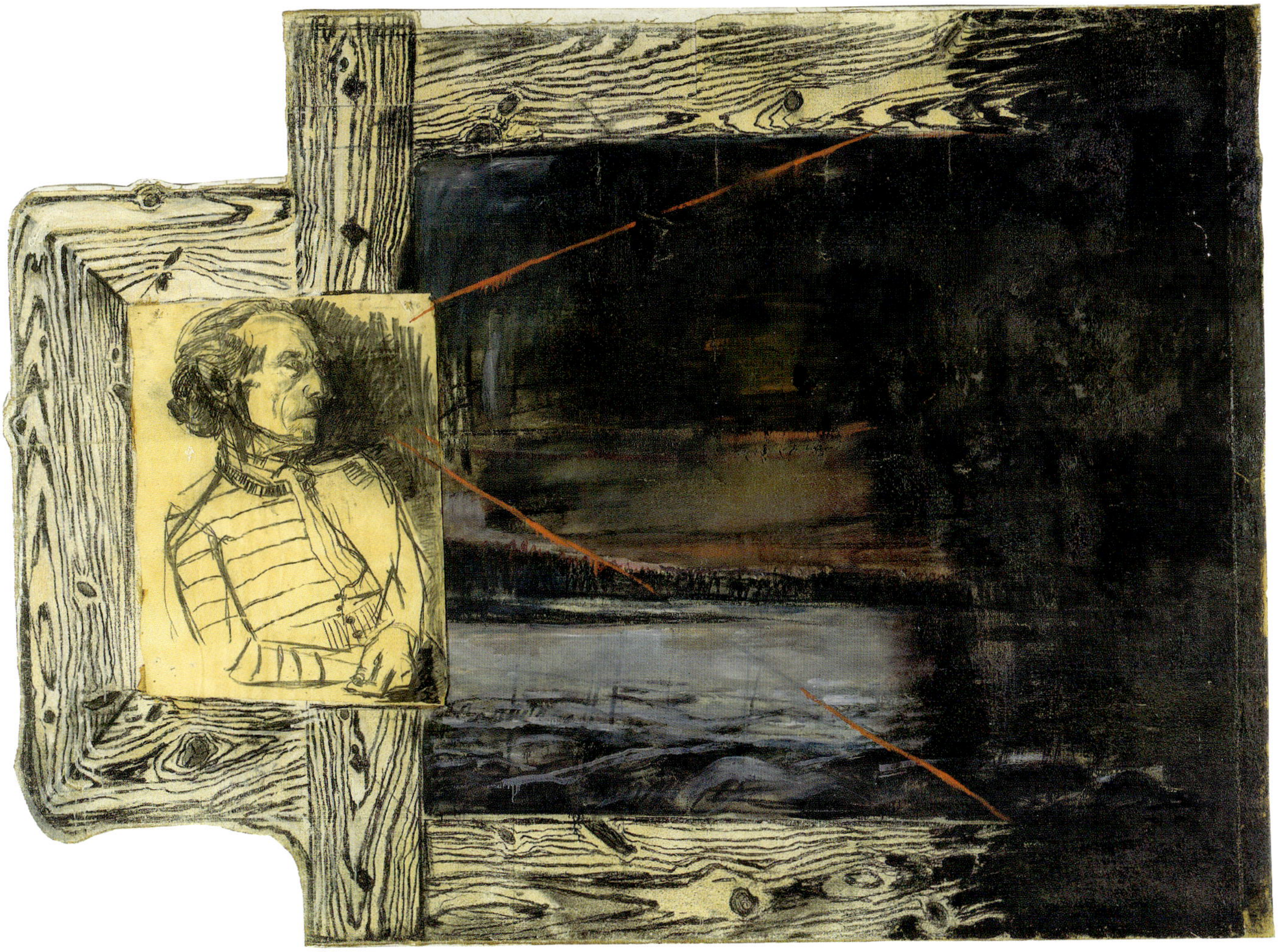

Landschaft mit Kopf (Landscape with Head), 1973
Oil, distemper, and charcoal on burlap, with charcoal on cardboard
82 11/16 × 94 1/2 inches (210 × 240 cm)

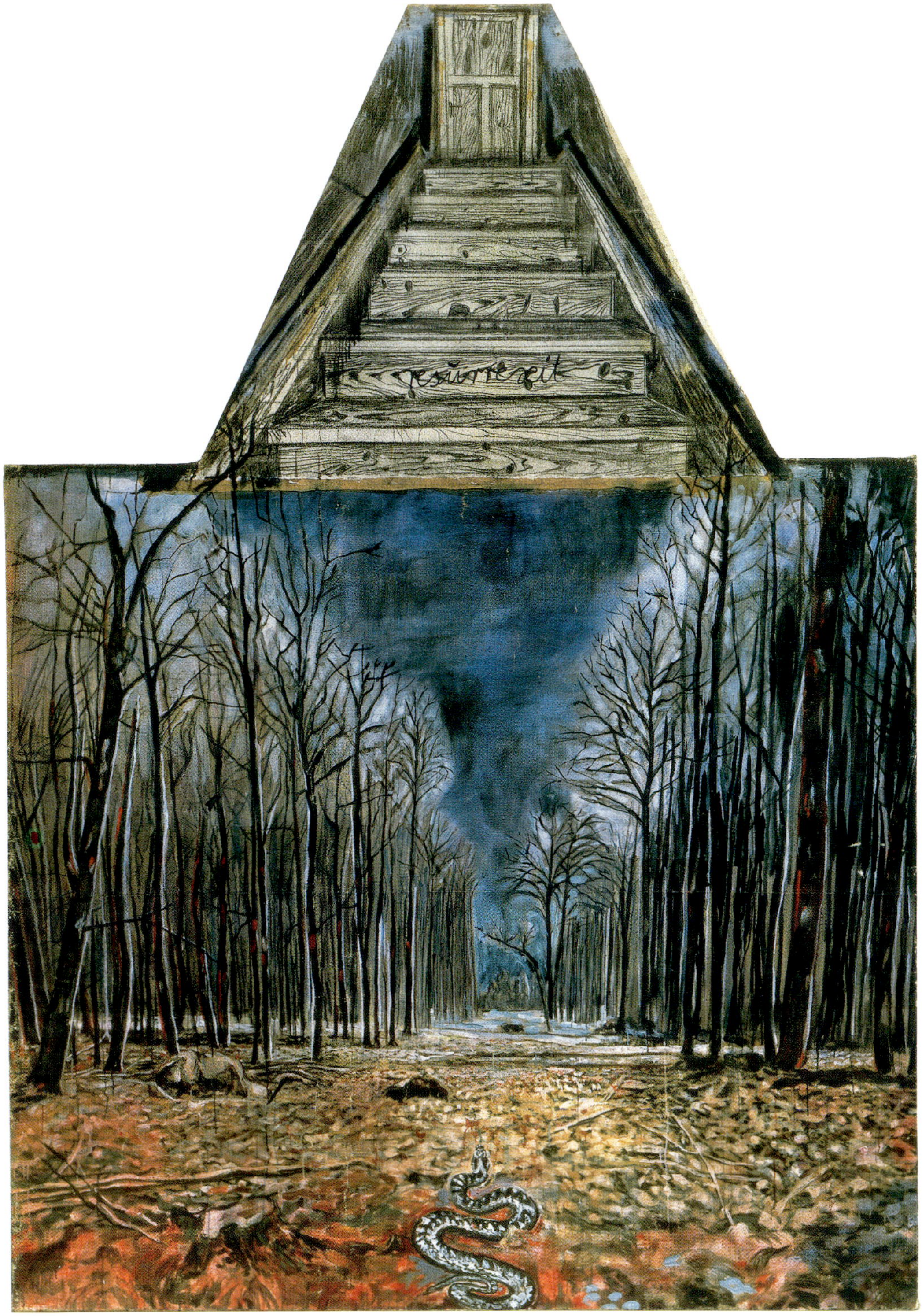

Resurrexit, 1973
Oil, acrylic, and charcoal on burlap
114 3/16 × 70 7/8 inches (290 × 180 cm)

Quaternität (Quaternity), 1973

In the monumental *Attic* paintings of the early 1970s, forest and fire again come together, but on the imaginary stage of the artist's studio. The *Attic* paintings were completed while Kiefer was living in a remote village in the Odenwald district, a region of wooded uplands between Frankfurt and Stuttgart. It is a landscape of legend, near the Black Forest and the Nibelungenstrasse, or road of the Nibelungs, the ancient mythological German peoples. Living in a large wooden building that was formerly a schoolhouse, Kiefer used the attic as his work space. The room's exposed wooden walls, ceiling, and floor became an architectonic forest in which mythological and historical events were recreated through the artist's eyes.

In *Quaternity*, the grain of the attic interior is rendered in a detailed drawing that covers the entire surface of this nearly fifteen-foot-wide canvas. Kiefer's dramatically tilted perspective beckons us onto his imagined stage. Literally employing the remnants of fire, Kiefer has executed the drawing in charcoal. He has said, "There is always the distant memory of an ancient fire that creates and destroys. Everything comes from and returns to fire. It is as powerful as time."

From the charcoal matrix of wood grain, three painted fires erupt, identified as *Vater (Father)*, *Sohn (Son)*, and *hl. Geist (Holy Ghost)*. Also invited into the attic is the image of a serpent—which he labels *Satan*—entering from a dark shadow on the right, establishing a dialogue with the flames. Like *Man in the Forest* (page 57), *Quaternity* is constructed on paradox. The flaming Trinity, which suggests an atmosphere of spiritual transcendence, also threatens to consume the building that houses it, much as the flaming branch in the earlier painting threatens the surrounding forest. The serpent is half in light, half in darkness. This symbiotic relationship between redemption and destruction, good and evil, would be a central theme in Kiefer's subsequent art.

As the number four has wide-ranging symbolic resonance, so the term *quaternity* appears in many contexts across time and disciplines, from the modern psychologist Carl Jung's writings on the concept of intuition to ancient alchemical treatises on "shadow-integration." In this case Kiefer alludes to a theological debate within the early Christian church. If the Trinity represents invincible, all-consuming purity and power, what, then, is the origin and role of the devil? How and why was the devil allowed to come about? The fourth-century debate concluded that the devil was not a part of God, but left the issue of the role of the devil in society largely unresolved. In *Quaternity*, Kiefer presents evil, or Satan, as a fundamental element in the spiritual matrix, joining the Father, Son, and Holy Ghost with connecting lines that represent an exchange of energy between them. Kiefer's symbols are seldom static in their meaning. While the serpent is generally associated with evil, in Kiefer's iconography it could represent the emergence of the Leviathan or the impure character of humankind. More pointedly, it may be a surrogate for the artist himself.

Like the forest, the attic is a symbolic space. We store our past in this dark and secret realm, which we visit infrequently and often with mixed feelings, if not trepidation. While some of Kiefer's attic scenes could suggest a political allegory of the rise of Nazi Germany, *Quaternity* evokes a broader Christian drama surrounding the relationship between good and evil.

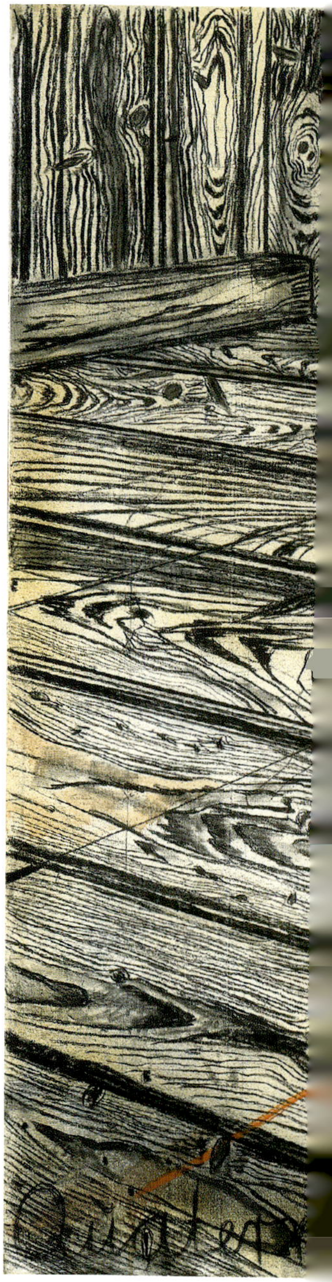

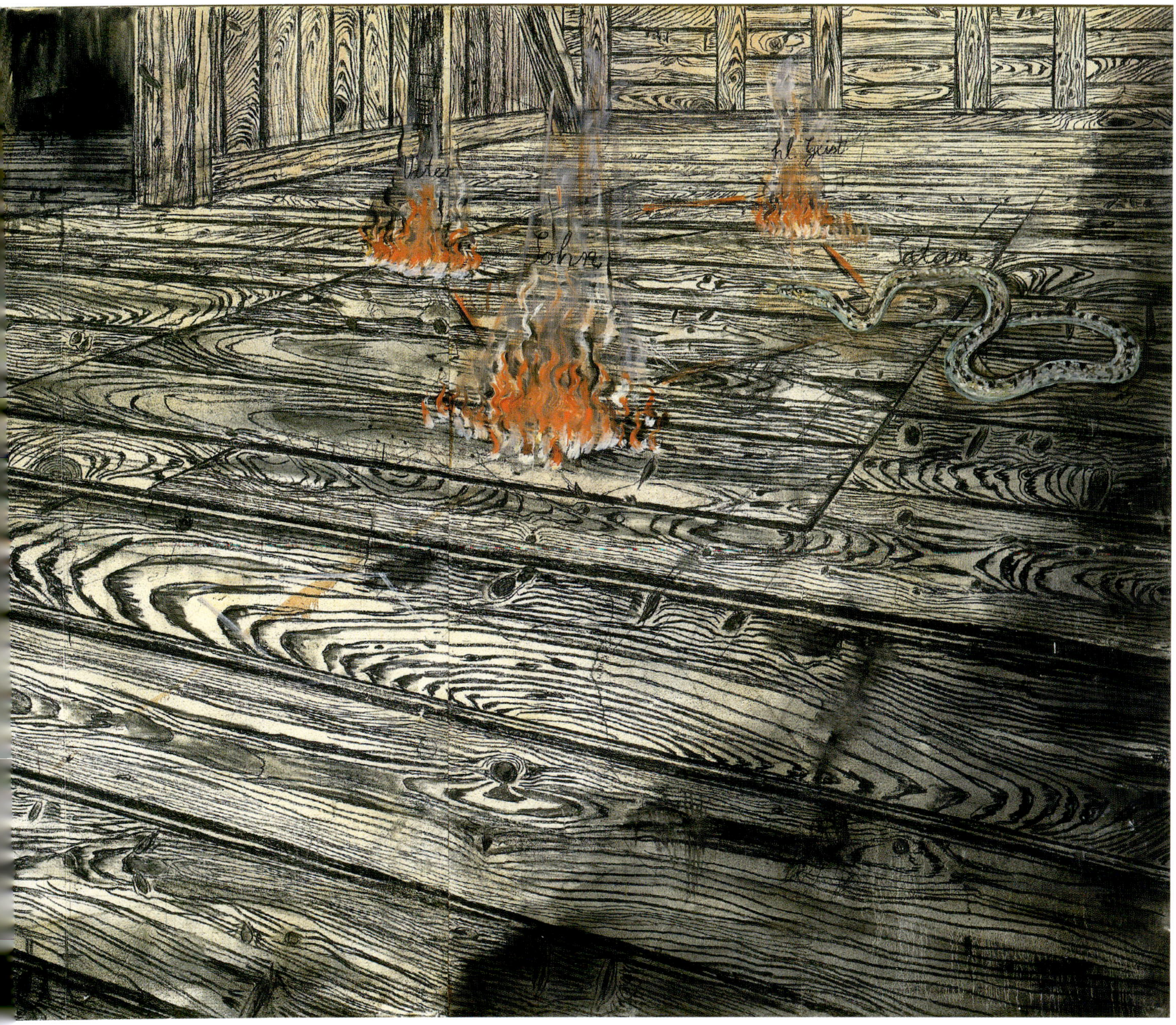

Quaternität (Quaternity), 1973
Oil and charcoal on burlap
117½ × 170¼ inches (298.4 × 432.4 cm)

Himmel – Erde (Heaven – Earth), 1974

Sende Deinen Geist aus (Send Forth Your Spirit), 1974

The artist's palette is a recurring image in Kiefer's work, variously symbolizing art, the artist, and more broadly, the powers of the imagination. In *Heaven – Earth*, Kiefer has painted the outline of a palette encompassing the heavens and the earth. A line connecting *Himmel (Heaven)* with *Erde (Earth)*, is inscribed *malen (to paint)*. *Send Forth Your Spirit* depicts a palette suspended between heaven and earth. From a dove in flight emanates the text *Sende Deinen Geist aus*, a phrase from the Catholic mass meaning "send forth your spirit." The text connects with the palette, which in turn connects with the landscape below. Behind the dove, a sun with a bluish-gray center radiates light in a dark sky. To the right of the palette, partially concealed, is another phrase from the mass, *[und] wird alles neu*, meaning "everything becomes new."

With its powers of flight, a dove is used in many cultural and religious traditions to symbolize the spirit. In Christianity the dove represents the mystical component of the Trinity, the Holy Ghost. Alchemists used the image of a dove encased in lead to express the idea that matter can be transformed into spirit. With these early images, Kiefer not only connects heaven with earth, he also freely combines symbols of Catholicism and older mystical traditions. The artist places the palette at the center of a transformational process whereby the highest expression of the spirit can be understood on earth.

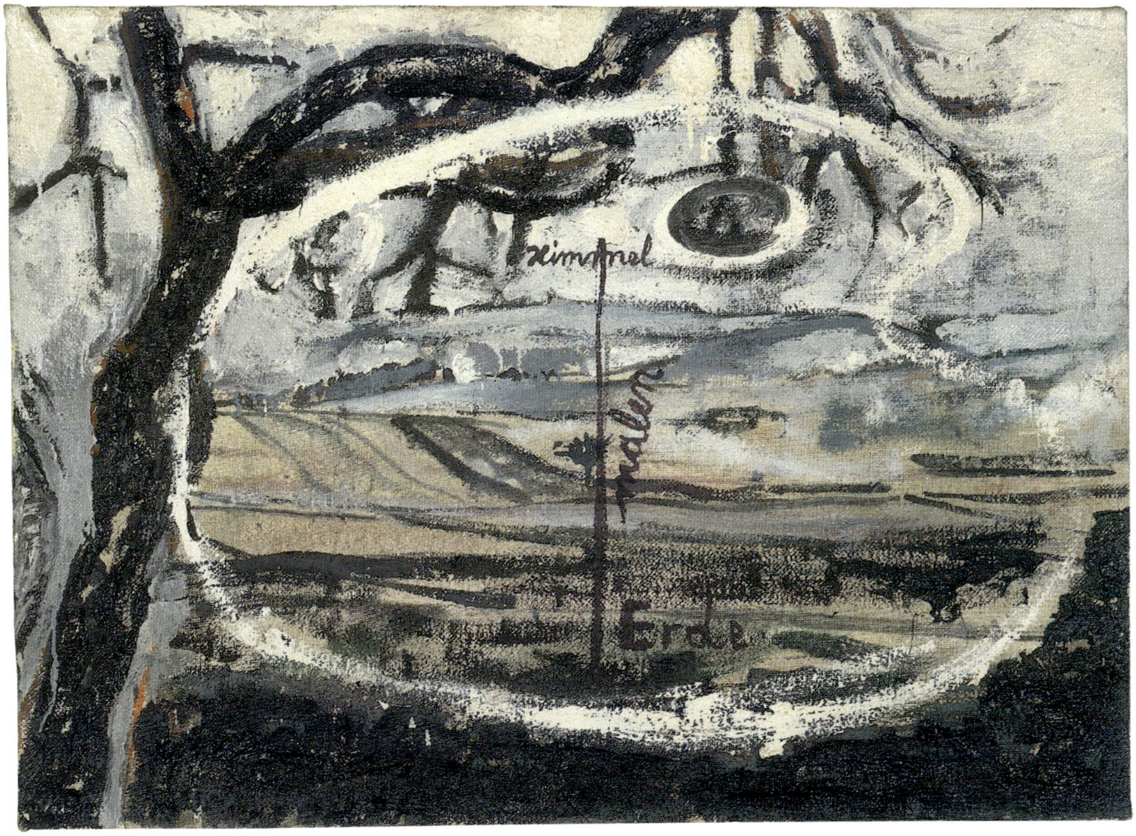

Himmel – Erde (Heaven – Earth), 1974
Oil on canvas
27 ½ × 37 ⅜ inches (70 × 95 cm)

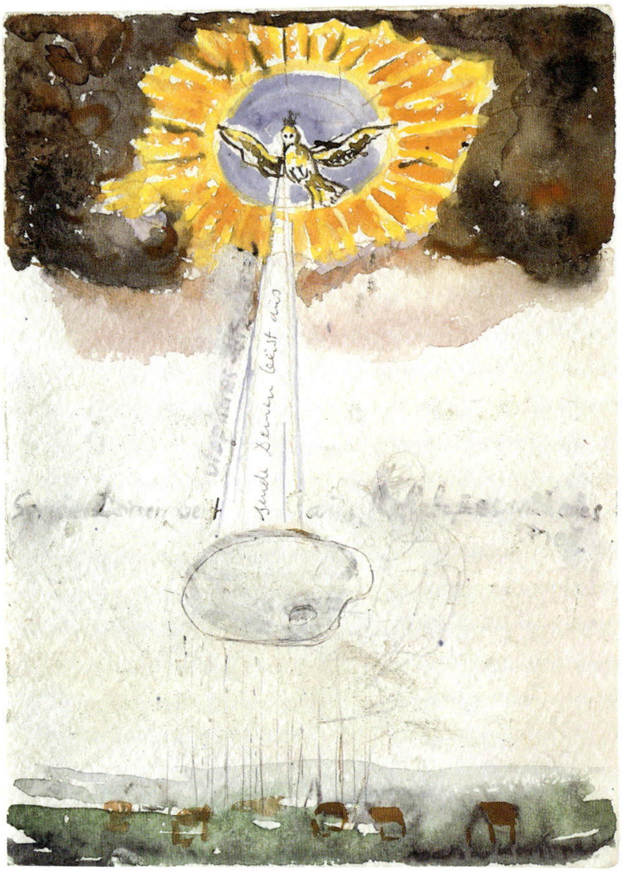

Sende Deinen Geist aus (Send Forth Your Spirit), 1974
Watercolor, gouache, pen and ink, ballpoint pen, and colored pencil on paper
13 3/8 × 9 1/2 inches (34 × 24.1 cm)

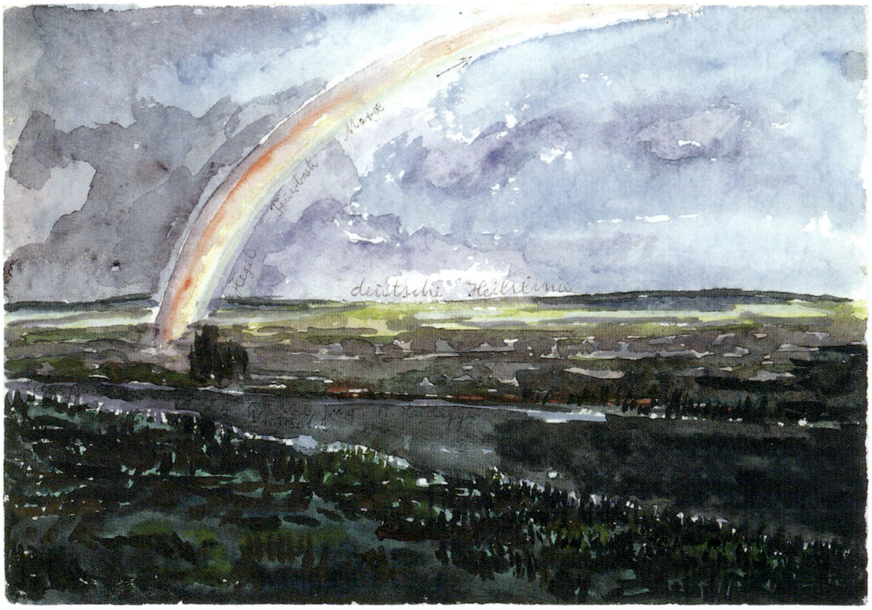

Deutsche Heilslinie (German Lineages of Salvation), 1975
Watercolor, gouache, and ballpoint pen on paper
9 ½ × 13 ⅜ inches (24.1 × 34 cm)

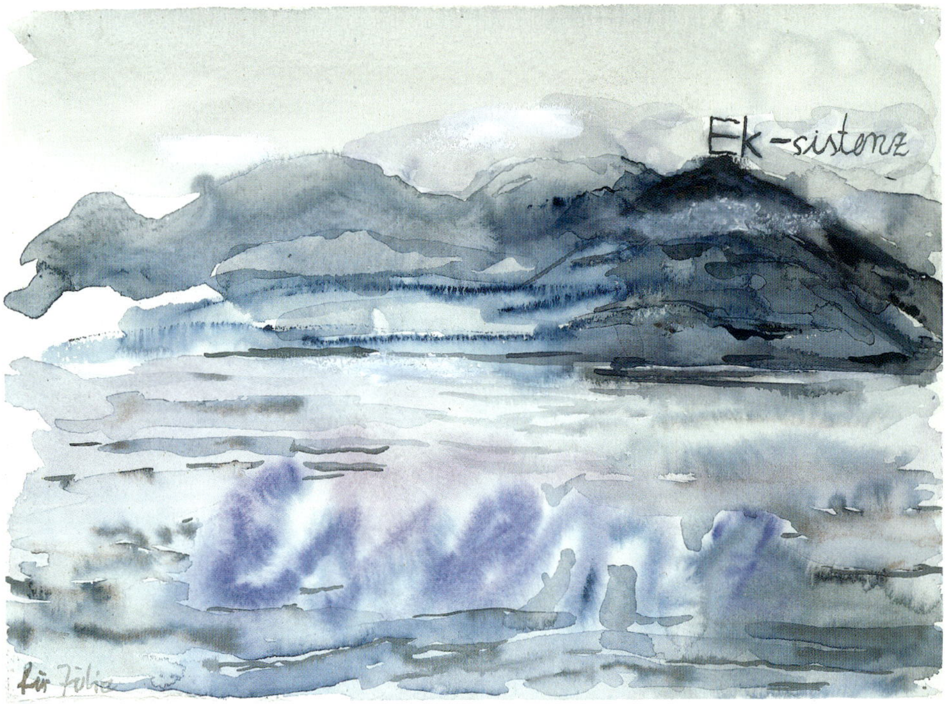

Essenz/Ek-sistenz (Essence/Ex-sistence), 1975
Watercolor and gouache on paper
11 ¾ × 15 ⅝ inches (29.8 × 39.7 cm)

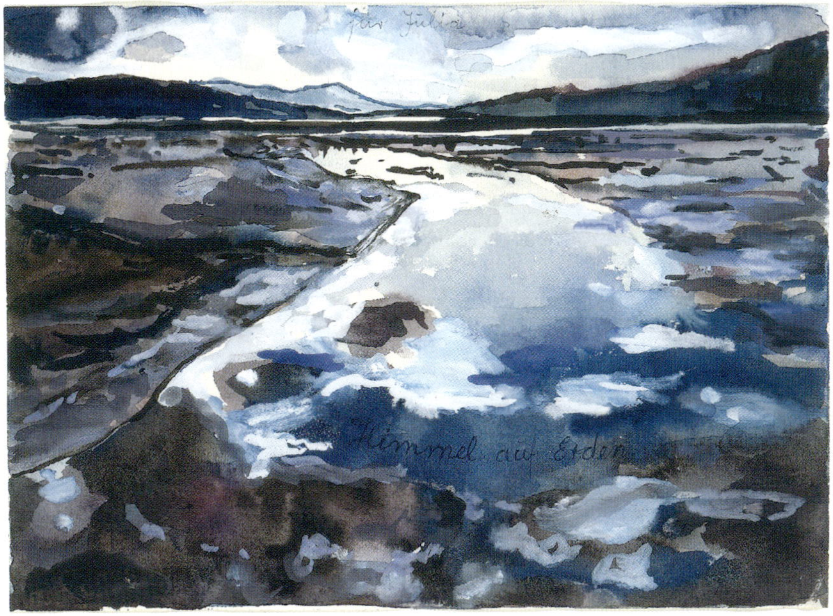

Himmel auf Erden (Heaven on Earth), 1974–75
Watercolor, gouache, and ballpoint pen on paper
9 ½ × 12 ⅝ inches (24.1 × 32.1 cm)

Malerei der verbrannten Erde (Painting of the Scorched Earth), 1974

Ausbrennen des Landkreises Buchen (Cauterization of the Rural District of Buchen), 1975

In the series of books titled *Cauterization of the Rural District of Buchen*, Kiefer engages the transformative and healing possibilities of fire, using his immediate surroundings as a stage set and his own works as *prima materia*. In the creation of these books, the artist burned a number of his paintings, then cut them down to form sooty pages. Other pages consist of staged photographs of explosions in rural landscapes. The fields in the photographs are from the titular rural district of Buchen, where Kiefer lived and worked at the time.

When Kiefer made these books, the region of Buchen was the site of a military installation where large quantities of benzene were stored, presenting a great danger to the area. In the staged photographs of an exploding Buchen, Kiefer realizes the collective nightmare of a region used as a storehouse for military fuel.

The carbonized books followed a series of paintings in which Kiefer portrayed charred landscapes, such as *Painting of the Scorched Earth*. These works bring to mind not only the scorched-earth policy used by the Nazis but also the cruelty and destructiveness of the Roman emperor Nero.

The word *cauterization (ausbrennen)* refers to a paradoxical medical process that heals by burning damaged tissue. In *Cauterization of the Rural District of Buchen*, Kiefer invokes these healing possibilities, seeming to fight fire with fire.

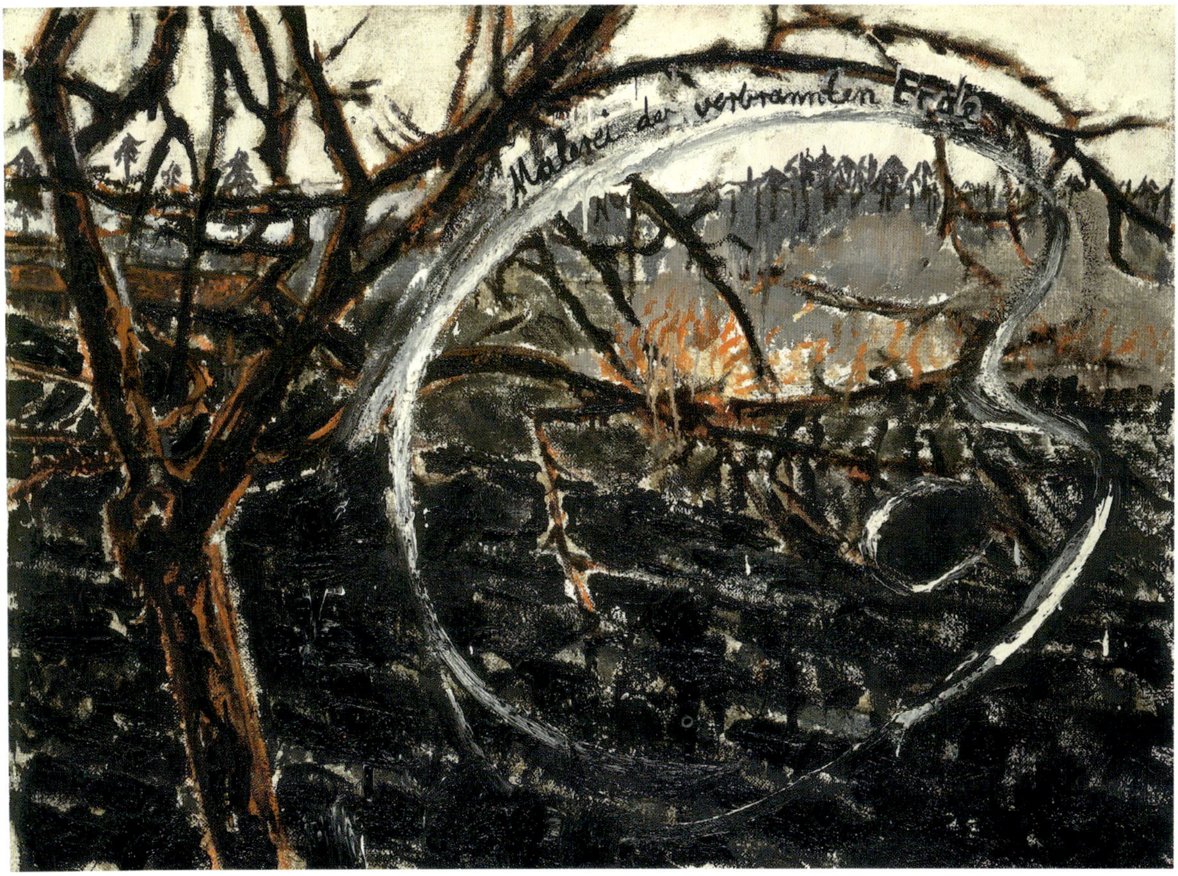

Malerei der verbrannten Erde (Painting of the Scorched Earth), 1974
Oil on burlap
37 ⅜ × 49¼ inches (95 × 125 cm)

4|5

6|7

10|11

56|57

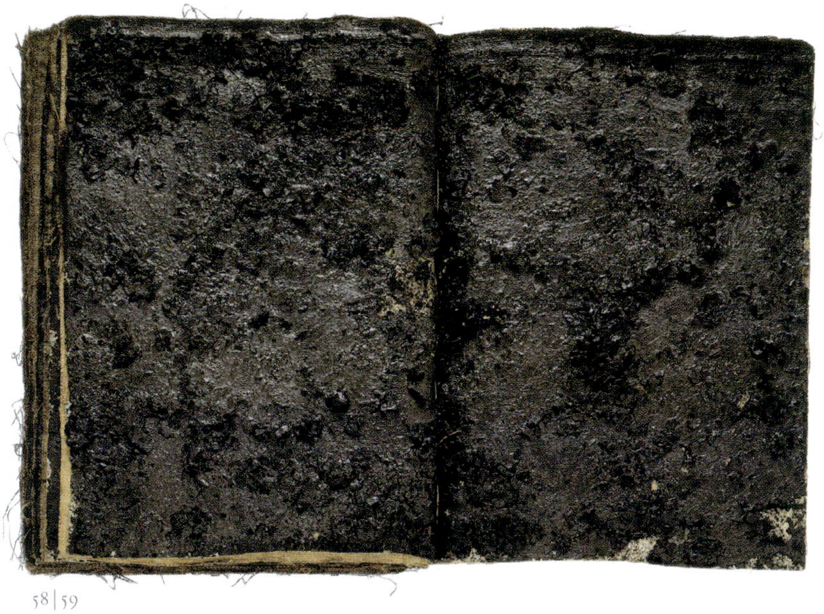

58|59

Ausbrennen des Landkreises Buchen (Cauterization of the Rural District of Buchen), 1975
Book, 60 pages. Oil, charcoal, and glue on twenty strips of burlap, bound
23 ⅝ × 16 ½ × 3 ⅛ inches (60 × 42 × 8 cm) (bound volume)

Aaron, c. 1979

In this painting, Kiefer refers to the biblical figure of Aaron, the older brother of Moses and the father of the Jewish priesthood, who helped lead the Jews out of Egypt. A complicated and charismatic figure, Aaron was said to be his brother's spokesman. He is the instrument of many of God's miracles; God caused his staff to turn to a serpent and also to blossom and bear almonds.

Aaron is not represented in this work by a figure, but by his name, which is followed by an exclamation point, suggesting a loud call. The large name is enclosed in a dense forest of vines or barbed wire. In the background, fires erupt in the treetops. Kiefer made several works at this time referring to the Iconoclastic Controversy of the Byzantine era, which surrounded the prohibition of the religious use of images. By using Aaron's name rather than a figure, Kiefer may be further exploring this moment in the history of art.

While Moses was on Mount Sinai receiving the written law, Aaron constructed the Golden Calf and encouraged the Jews to worship it. For disobeying the Second Commandment—"You shall not make for yourself a graven image, or any likeness of anything that is in heaven above, or that is in the earth beneath, or that is in the water under the earth; you shall not bow down to them or serve them; for I The Lord your God am a jealous God."—Aaron was prevented from entering the Promised Land. Kiefer suggests his identification with Aaron as the artist or image-maker whose role is to seek the grandest of visions. Yet these visions can only grasp a part of the whole, and are invariably subject to "higher judgments." Kiefer may also be pointing out a more contemporary historical allegory in which his generation has been effectively banned from giving image to Germany's recent past and its suppression of the Jewish faith.

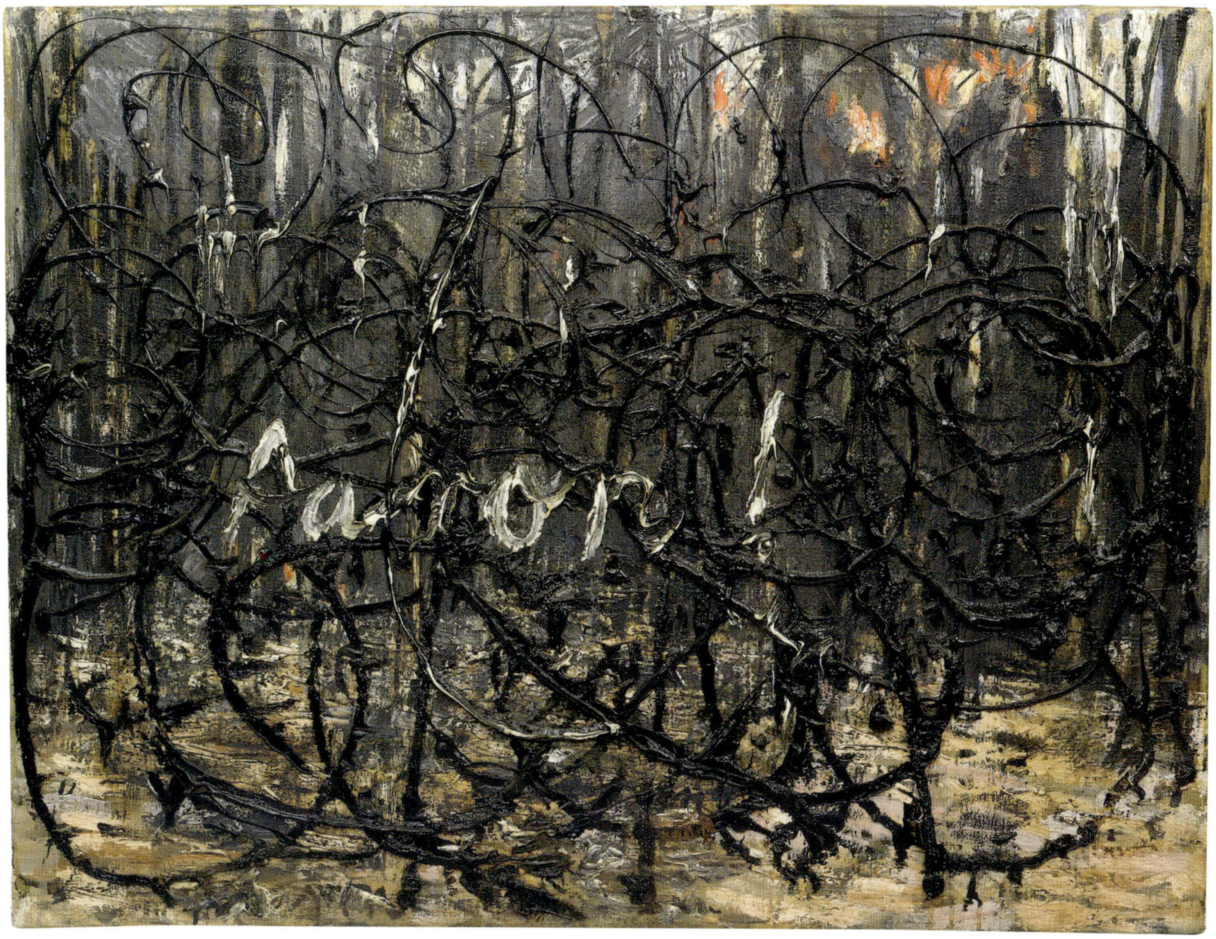

Aaron, c. 1979
Oil on canvas
28 × 35⅞ inches (71 × 91 cm)

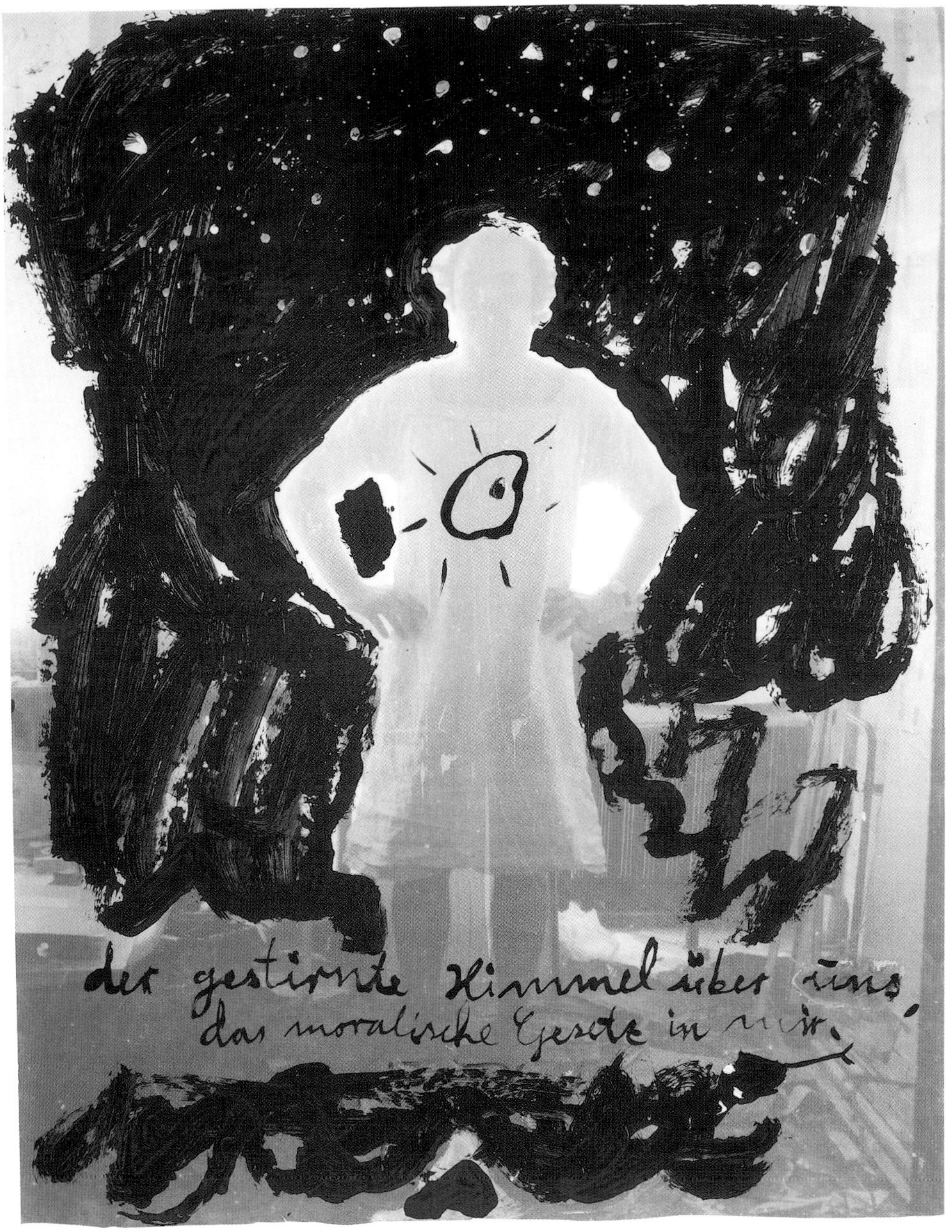

Der gestirnte Himmel (The Starred Heaven), 1980
Photograph (1969), with acrylic and emulsion
32 ⅞ × 23 inches (83.5 × 58.5 cm)

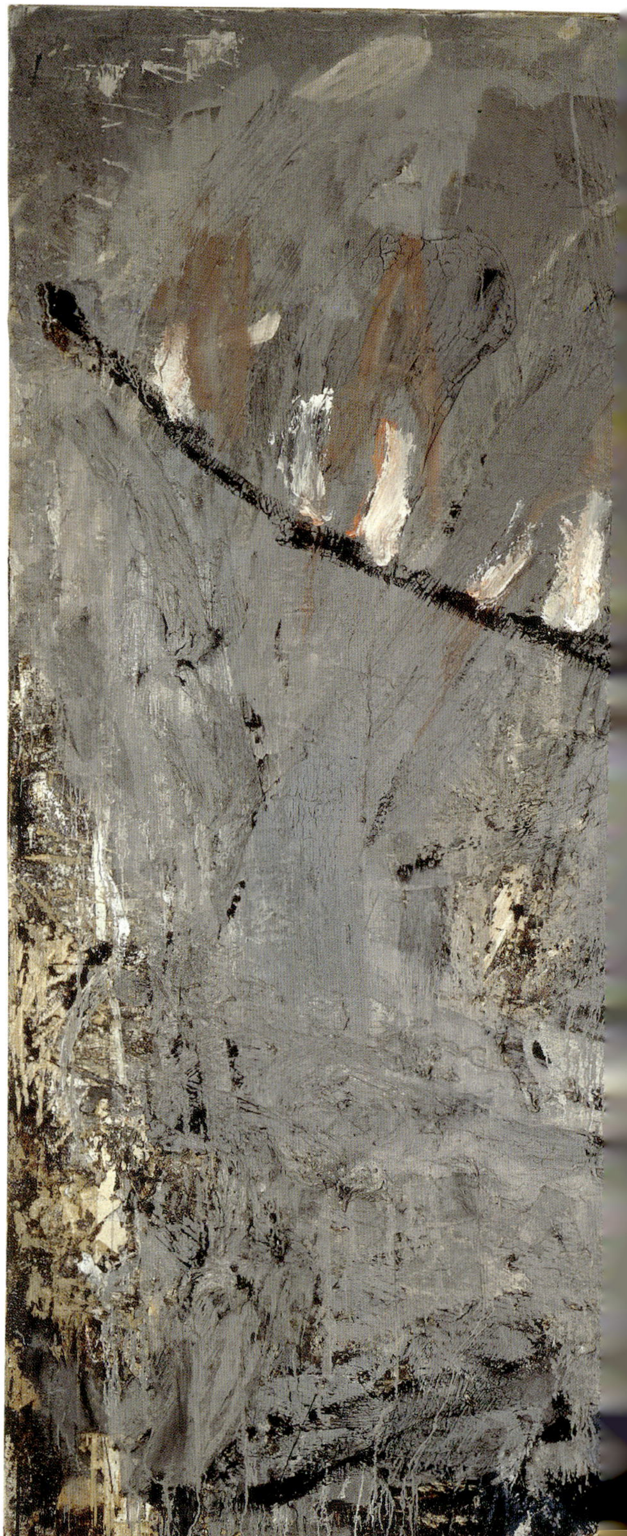

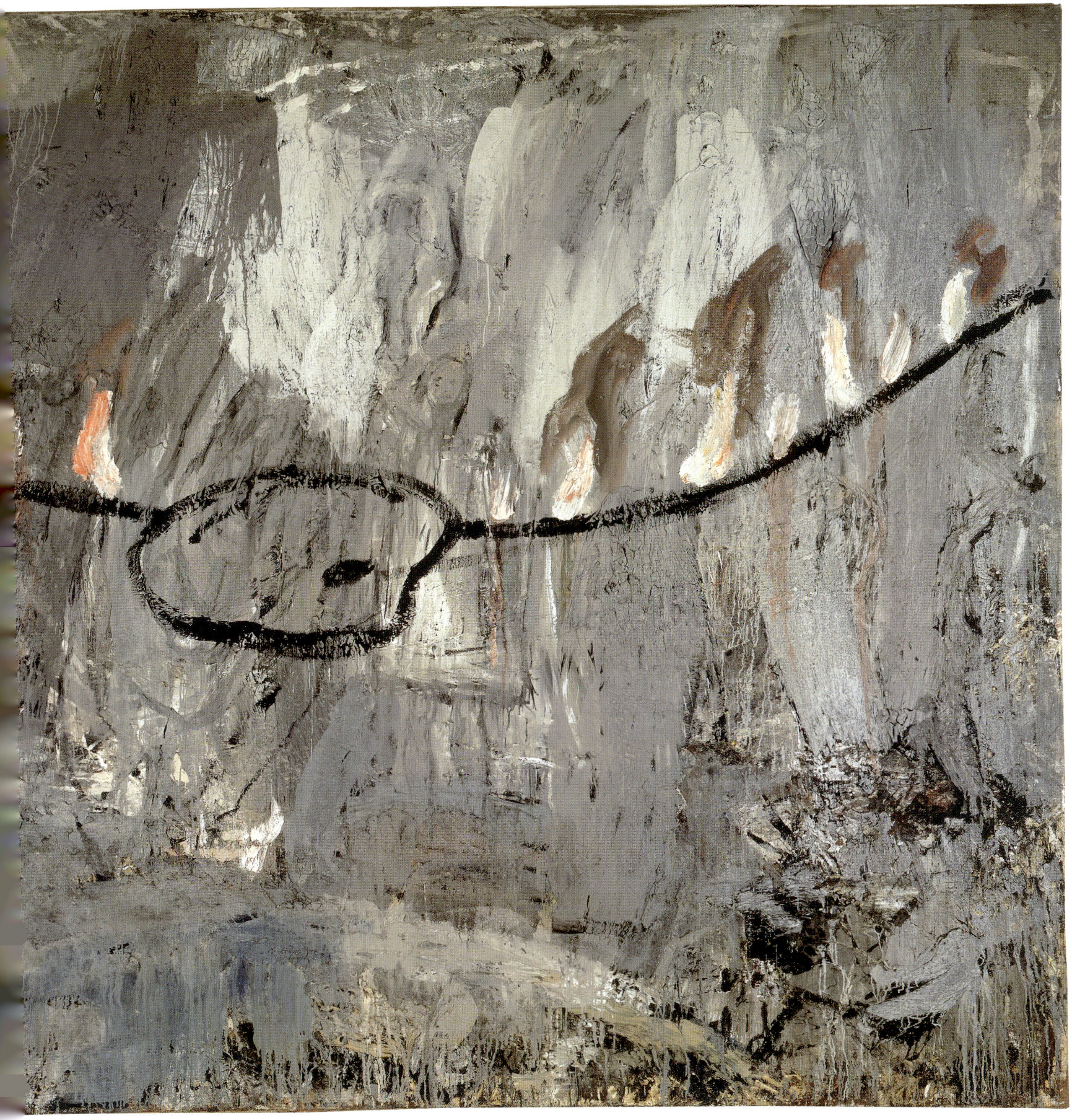

Palette, 1981
Oil and mixed media on canvas
114 × 157½ inches (290 × 400 cm)

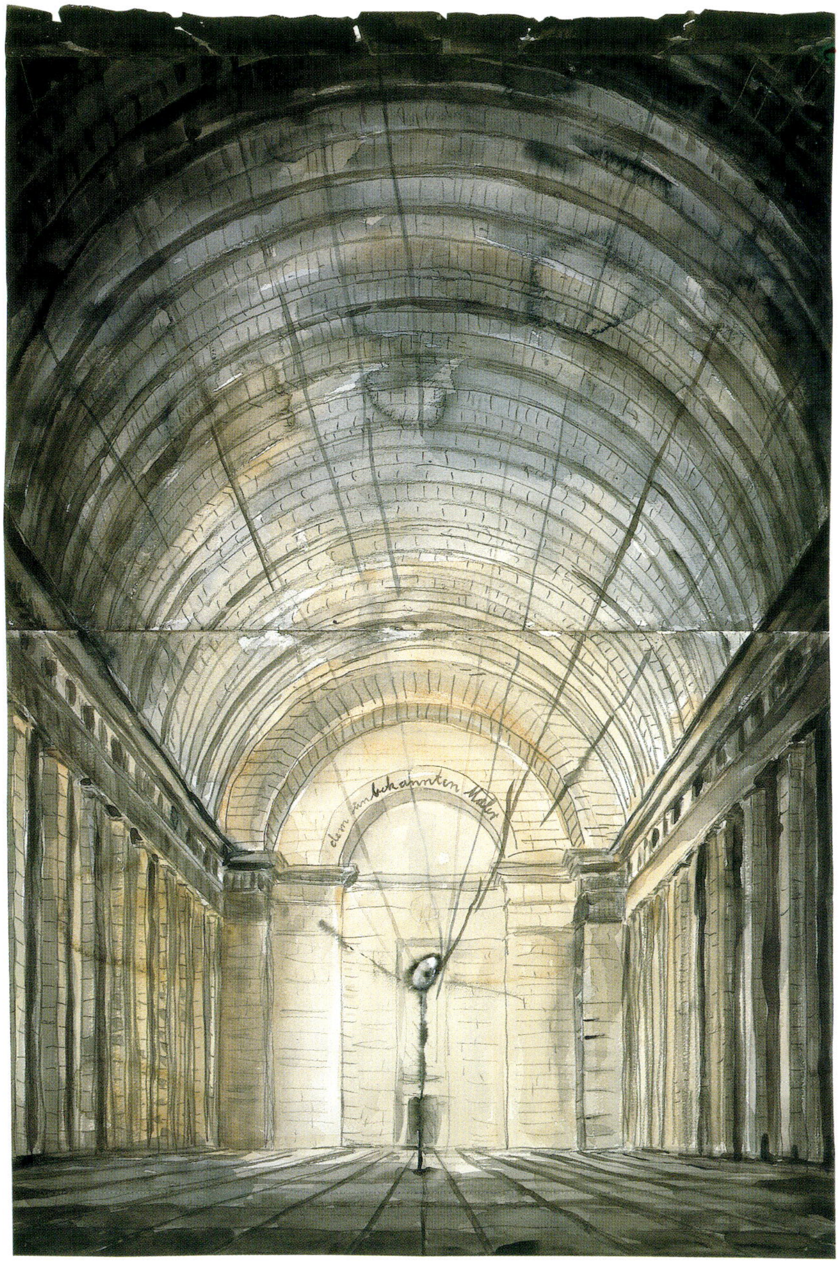

Dem unbekannten Maler (To the Unknown Painter), 1982
Watercolor and pencil on paper
34 5/8 × 21 5/8 inches (88 × 55 cm)

Emanation, 1984–85

Over the years, Kiefer has worked with molten lead to create cloudlike forms that move over the surface of his pictures. The source of these gray metallic eruptions is deliberately ambiguous. Like angels, clouds are often considered symbolic messengers, taking different forms and invoking various meanings.[1] Again, the messages that Kiefer's clouds send are consistent with his philosophy that "everything contains its opposite." Lead is itself an ambiguous material. It is both one of the heaviest and one of the softest materials. Its weight notwithstanding, it is associated with air and the planets. It is poisonous to the human body, but is used to protect us from radiation. It is used to store batteries, protecting them from a loss of energy, but can also be used to employ great forces of energy as a component of explosives and bullets.

Kiefer has titled works with various cloudlike explosions *Ausgiessung (Effusion)*, the German term for the descent of the Holy Spirit. He has also used gestures of lead to portray his version of the concept of *emanation*, an understanding of the creation of the world that is characteristic of Neoplatonism, Gnosticism, and Indian metaphysics. Emanation is described by Plotinus (205–270), the founder of Neoplatonism, as a series of emanations or emergences radiating from the primordial One. From these emanations springs all of creation. This concept is central to the Neoplatonist belief that all realms of existence belong to one vast order.

Kiefer has also titled works *Schweres Wasser (Heavy Water)*, which he sees as a synonym for radiation.[2] For years, Kiefer has been concerned about the proliferation of nuclear weapons facilities and power plants. At the same time, he is fascinated by nuclear fusion as a spiritual allegory. "A nuclear power station is like a spiritual birth, because it doesn't consume anything. Men are not really able to manage it, but nevertheless it's very spiritual." Kiefer will point out that the universe, once known only as heaven, is not only the source of an efflux of light. It is also an immense power station: "Our planet revolves around and is heated by a powerful reactor, the sun. It's one of many reactors that light the way through 'the heavens.'"

1 J. E. Cirlot, *A Dictionary of Symbols* (New York: Philosophical Library, 1983): 50.
2 The artist in an interview with Nan Rosenthal, July 1997. In Nan Rosenthal, *Anselm Kiefer: Works on Paper in The Metropolitan Museum of Art* (New York: The Metropolitan Museum of Art, 1998): 108.

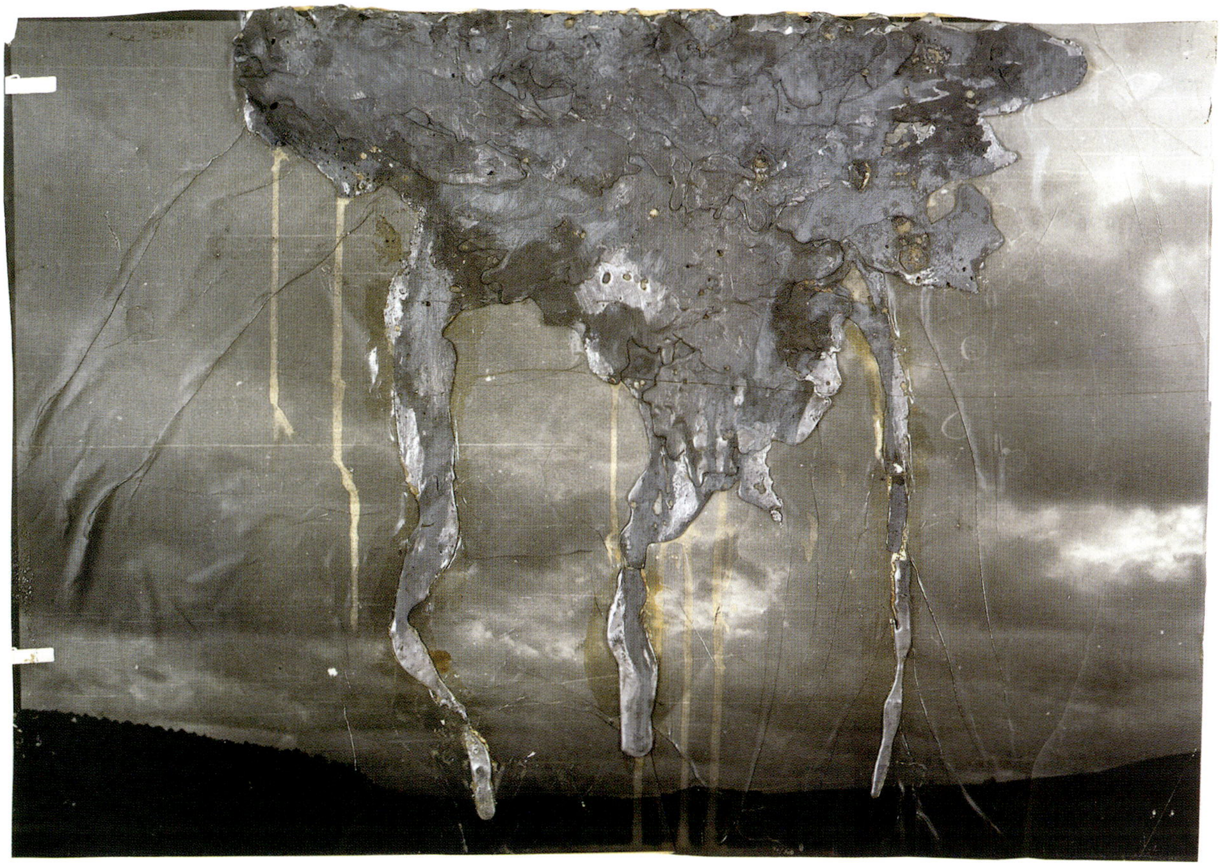

Emanation, 1984–85
Shellac on photograph, mounted on cardboard, with lead
22 ½ × 32 inches (57 × 81 cm)

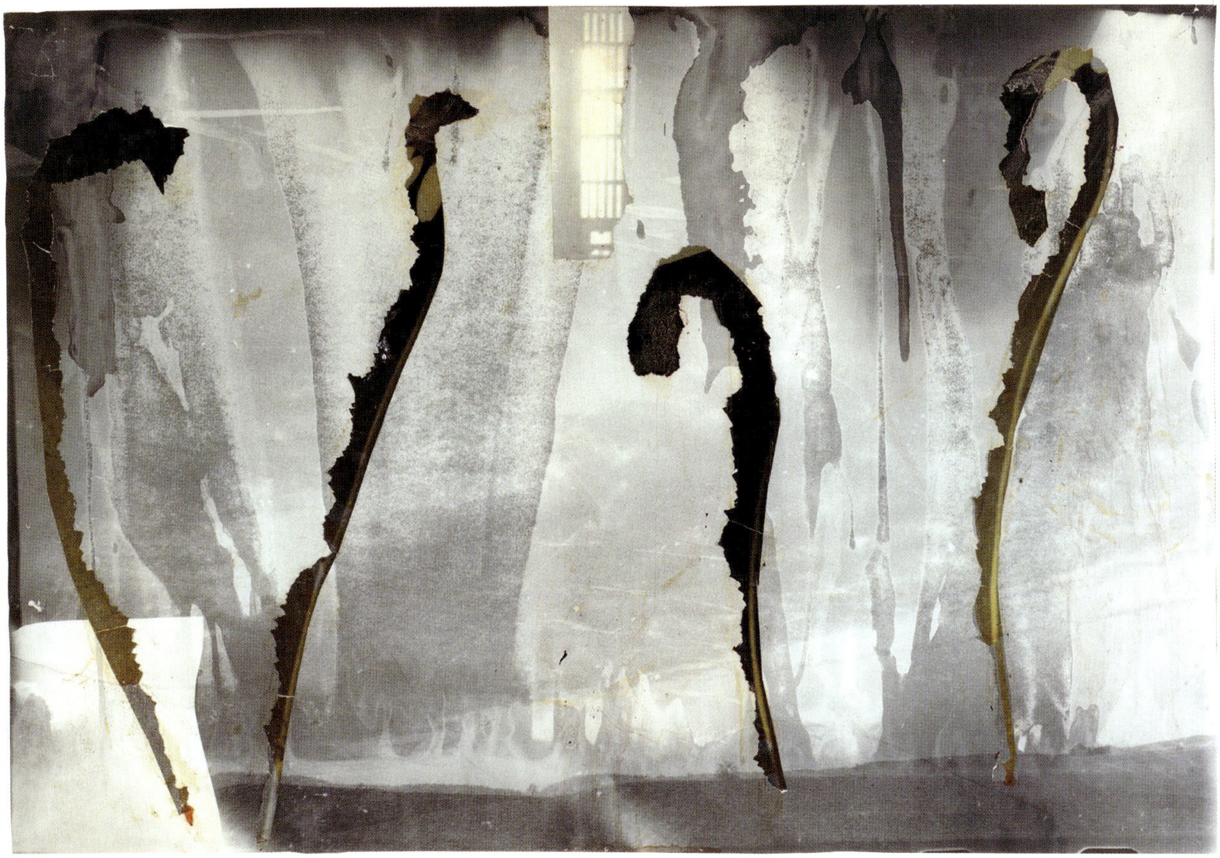

Das Schlangenwunder (The Miracle of the Serpents), 1984–85
Collage and shellac on photographic paper
22 13/16 × 32 11/16 inches (58 × 83 cm)

Die Milchstrasse (The Milky Way), 1985–87

In this epic painting, Kiefer addresses one of the universe's most well-known constellations. According to Greek legend, the Milky Way was created when the child Hercules, half mortal and half god, sucked so violently on Juno's breast that her immortal milk sprayed across the heavens. Playing off Hercules' hybrid character, whose origin is connected to both heaven and earth, Kiefer has created a number of half-human, half-god works that parallel the original myth, yet place it into a more recent context.

As is true of many of Kiefer's works, the viewpoint in *The Milky Way* is one of flying above a broad field that appears to have been burned. The field, which may have been a rural battlefield in World War II, is marked in its center with a deep white gash inscribed with the words *die Milchstrasse*. The tip of a three-dimensional lead funnel attached to the canvas enters this cut, and lead tendrils attached to the funnel's rim extend toward the upper corners of the canvas like delicate wings. The funnel appears to be both sending and receiving light, sucking it from an underground power source and spraying it over the landscape, as well as channeling it from the skies into the open earth. The cone suggests a connector, a funnel in which the heavens are being poured into the earth to regenerate it or, conversely, a megaphone calling from earth to a higher power. The milky golden light that bathes the charred field suggests an alchemical transformation. When lead is burned in alchemical processes, it emits pure white clouds on its surface. *The Milky Way* pictures a transformation from battleground to the promised land of rivers of milk and golden honey.

Kiefer, however, sees a larger metaphor regarding time and our developing understanding of scale within the universe. In *The Milky Way*, one can imagine a flipping of galaxy and ground, and in making the picture Kiefer did exactly that, seeing the cut as what he calls a "puddle" on the ground, reflecting the grand constellation that at one time was considered to be all of the heavens, but now with advanced astronomy is considered itself a puddle in a much vaster universe. With typical irony, Kiefer remarks, "The further we go in space, the more distant heaven becomes."

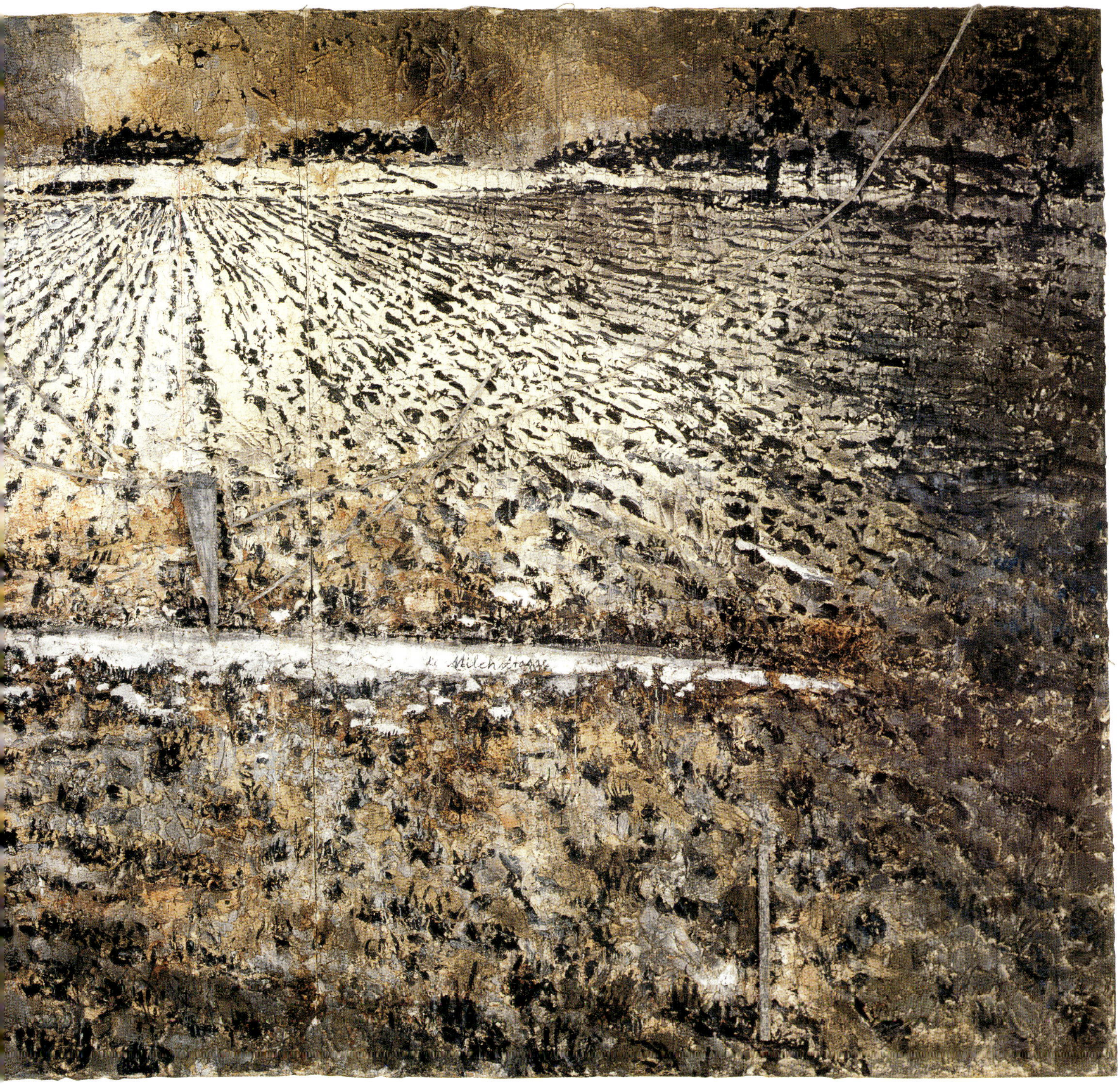

Die Milchstrasse (The Milky Way), 1985–87
Emulsion paint, oil, acrylic, and shellac on canvas with applied wires and lead
overall 150 × 221 ⅝ inches (381 × 563 cm)

Die Ordnung der Engel (The Hierarchy of Angels), 1985–87

In *The Hierarchy of Angels*, the artist recreates the image of a celestial hierarchy using a large airplane propeller, made from sheets of lead, and nine craggy lead rocks. In a text of the fifth century entitled *The Celestial Hierarchy*, which is attributed to Dionysius the Areopagite, angels were divided into nine categories, or choirs, which were grouped into three hierarchies, all navigating in a twisting space between heaven and earth: Seraphim, Cherubim, Thrones; Dominations, Virtues, Powers; Principalities, Archangels, Angels.

Kiefer has said that the propeller brought to mind Dionysius's concept of heaven as a vast spiral in which time and space move in all directions. Delineated by a line that moves inward and outward simultaneously, the spiral holds the macro- and microcosmic in an "ordered" form. The spiral is a symbol of topological distortion, a process common to both art and myth, in which one form can be transformed into another without changing the material content. Large rocks, or "meteorites" as the artist calls them, stand in for angels, suggesting that celestial space and outer space are one and the same. German history may also play a role in Kiefer's choice of symbols. Hitler's grand scheme of domination relied heavily on the growing strength of his air force, and Germany's potential superiority in the skies.

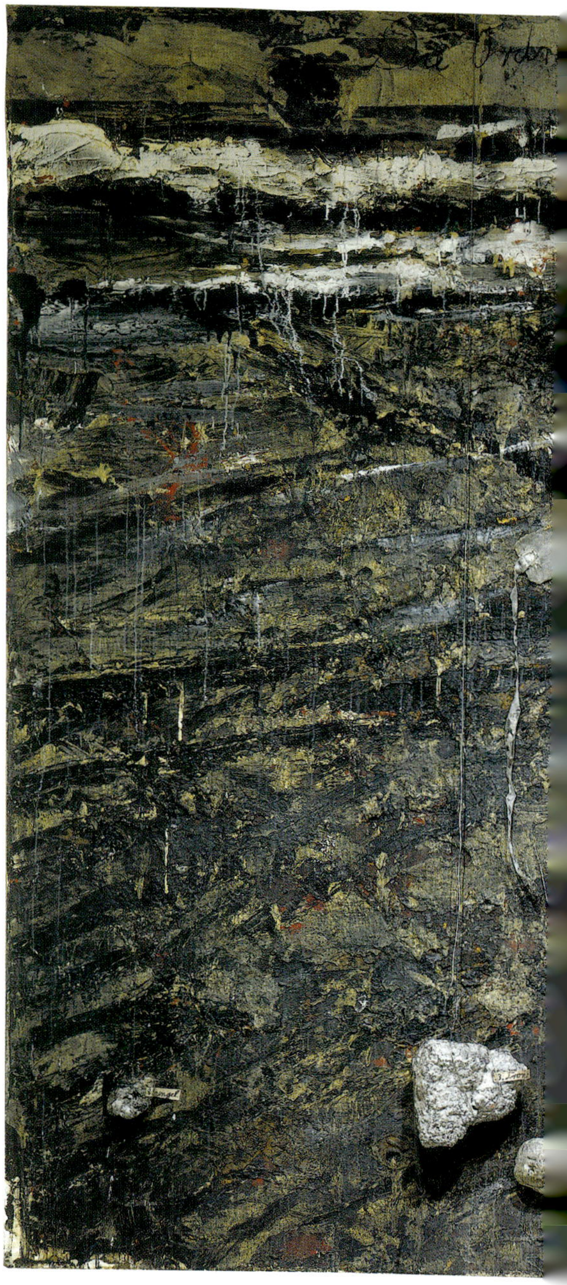

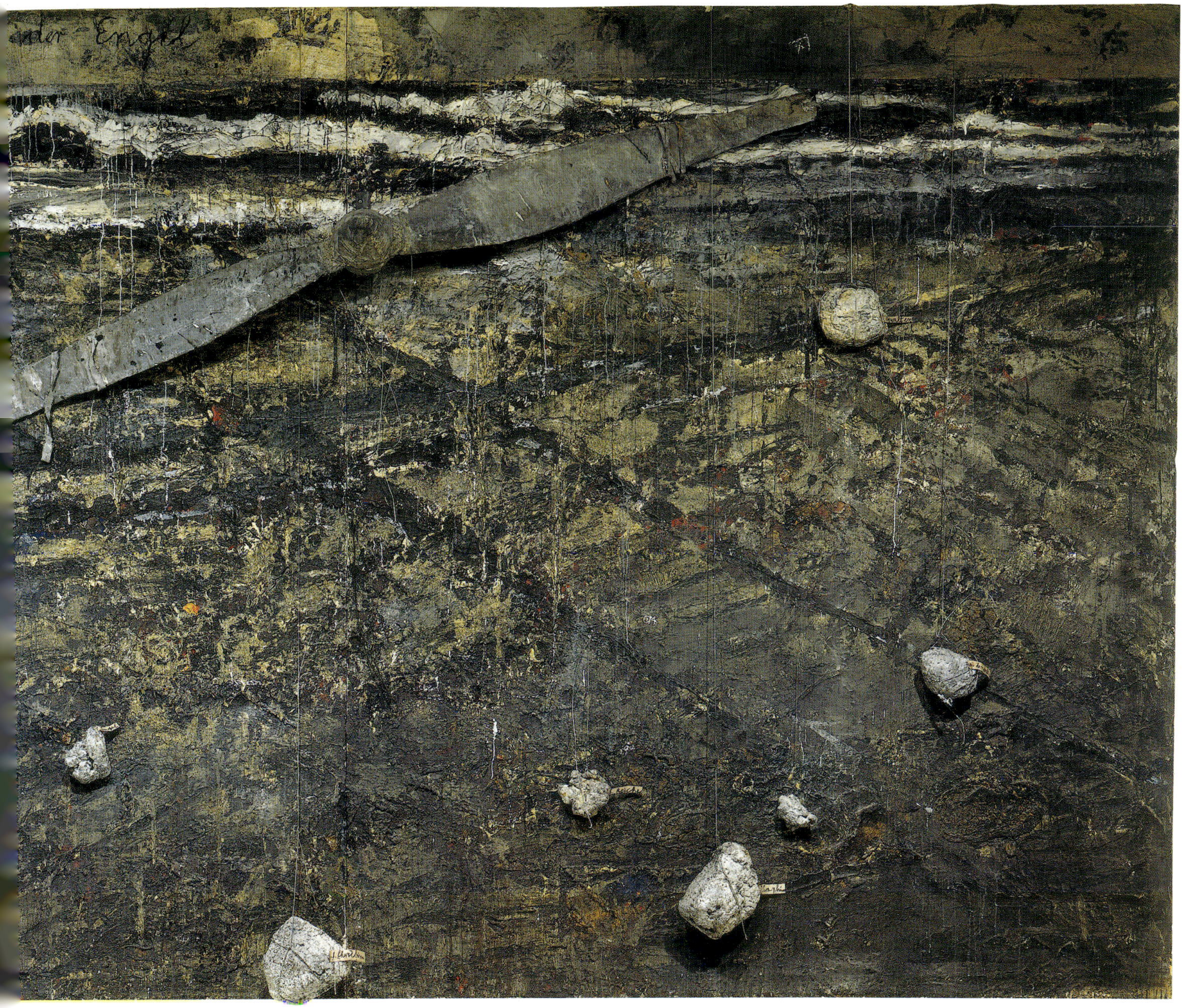

Die Ordnung der Engel (The Hierarchy of Angels), 1985–87
Oil, emulsion, shellac, acrylic, chalk, lead propeller, curdled lead, steel cables, band-iron, and cardboard on canvas
133 ½ × 220 ⅞ × 22 ¾ inches (339.1 × 561 × 57.8 cm)

Johannisnacht (Midsummer Night), 1987–91

"Johannisnacht is a special night in which fields are set on fire and religion bares its roots in ancient mystical acts."
– Anselm Kiefer

The title of this work refers to the evening before the summer solstice, the longest day of the calendar year. In Germany it is celebrated with a ritual of both pagan and Christian significance. Large bonfires and raucous merrymaking are features of this holiday, which was celebrated by the Druids as the wedding of heaven and earth.

Johannisnacht is also known as Saint John's Eve. It takes place the night before the festival celebrating the birth of Saint John the Baptist, who prepared the way for Christ's coming. In this work, in the place of Saint John, Kiefer has inserted a dried fern, which he considers to be an equally important precursor. "Ferns are very important," he remarks. "The first trees were ferns. They are primal. Charcoal and oil are made out of ferns that existed at the beginning of life. There are many stories and folktales about plants having memories. If this is true, ferns could tell us a great deal about our beginnings. Like forests, ferns may contain secret knowledge. But they are complex in relation to Christian symbols of light. They grow in the shade. On the evening of Johannisnacht, the devil goes out into the fields and spreads fern seeds. This creates a certain chaos. Ferns remind us that we also need the darkness."

Johannisnacht has an unfortunate connection to the Third Reich. Operation Barbarossa, Hitler's failed invasion of the Soviet Union, began on June 22, 1941, coinciding with Johannisnacht celebrations. Because Hitler felt the operation would be completed quickly, he failed to prepare the German troops for the brutal Russian winter, causing a huge number of casualties from exposure. Although Kiefer has said that in *Johannisnacht* he intended no reference to Operation Barbarossa, the artist dealt with this and other ill-conceived Nazi military strategies in a number of works of 1975.

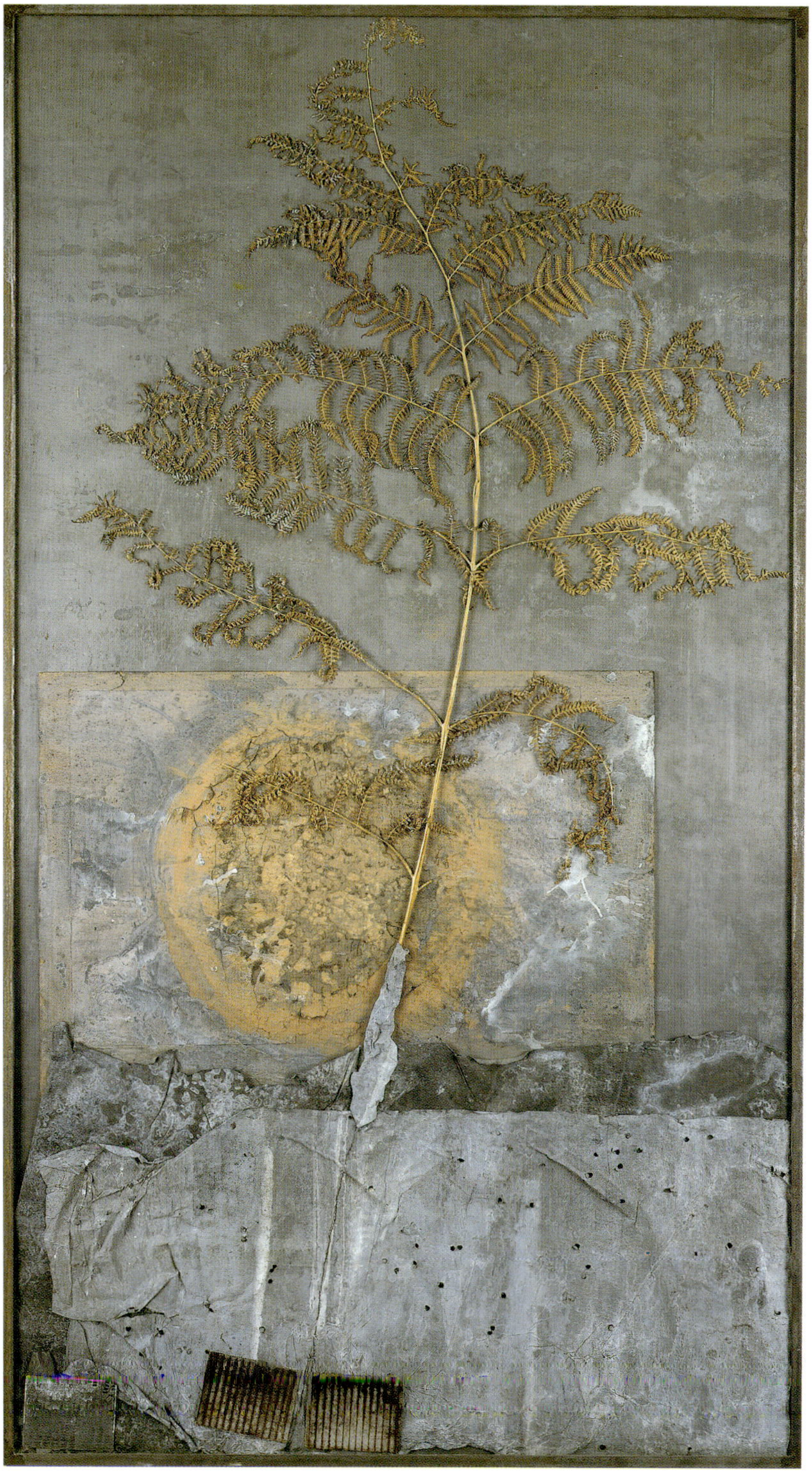

Johannisnacht (Midsummer Night), 1987–91
Acrylic, soil, lead on cardboard, separators, singed spots, and fern on lead in a glazed steel frame
94 ½ × 51 ⅛ inches (240 × 130 cm)

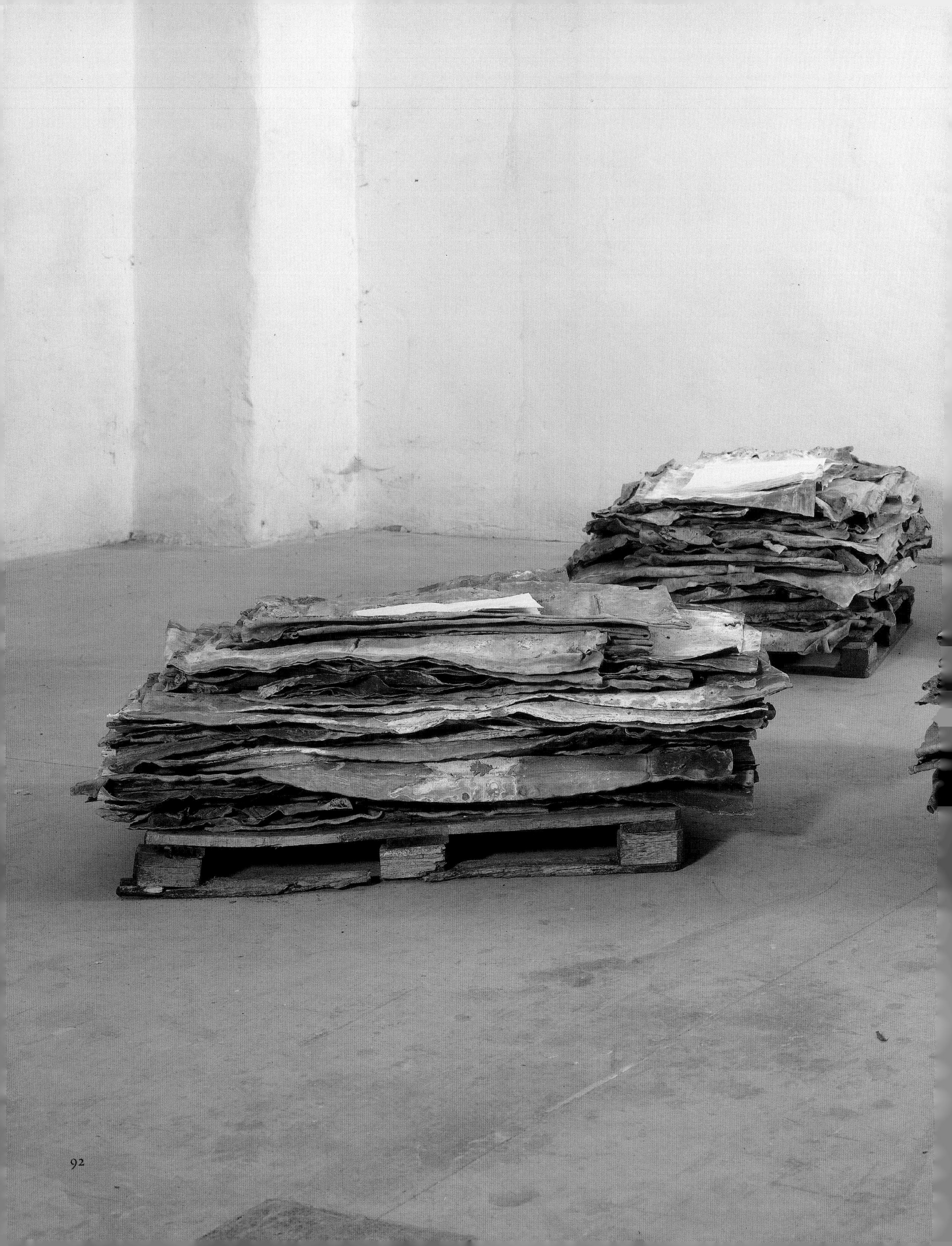

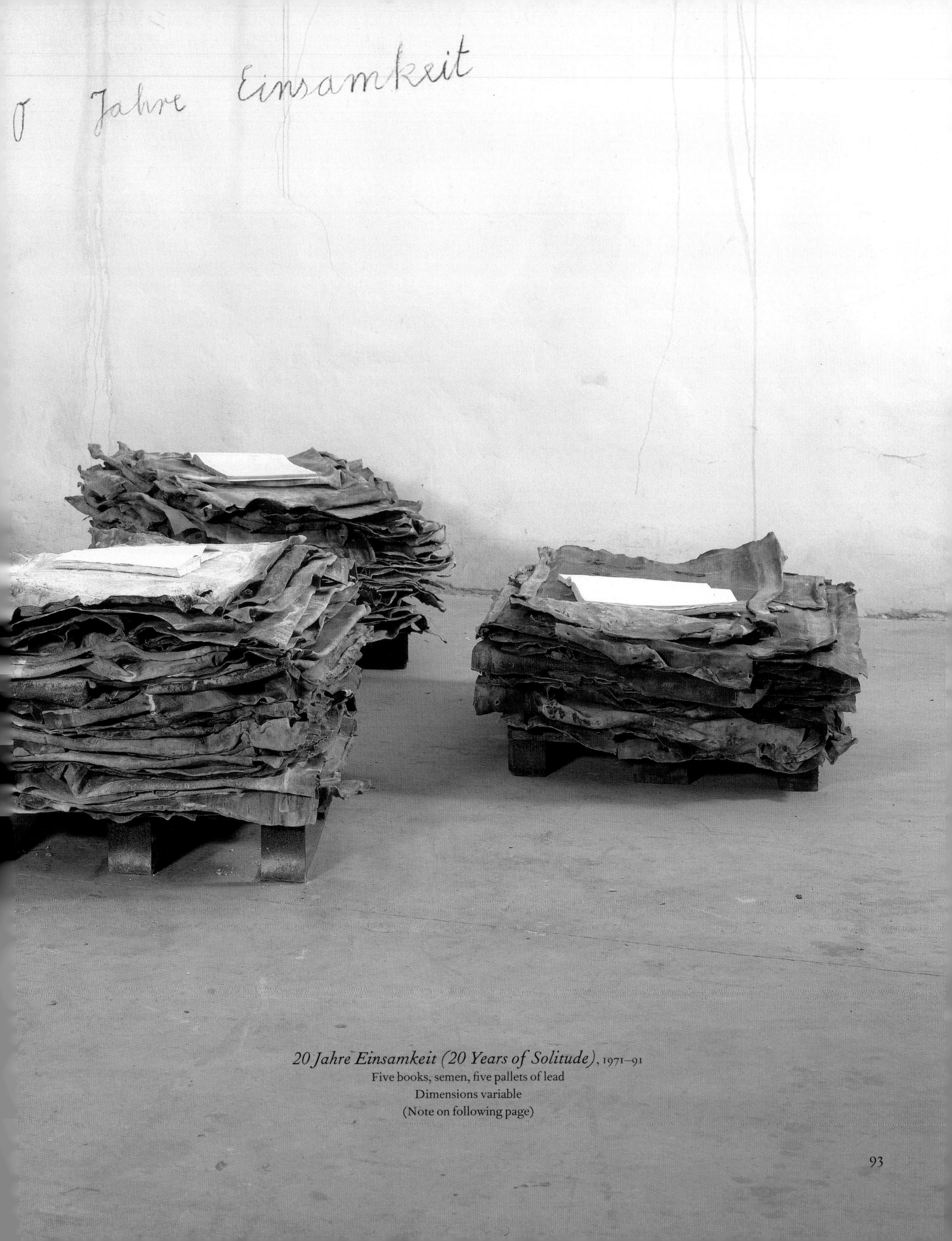

20 Jahre Einsamkeit (20 Years of Solitude), 1971–91
Five books, semen, five pallets of lead
Dimensions variable
(Note on following page)

previous double page:
20 Jahre Einsamkeit (20 Years of Solitude),
1971–91

Not long after the Berlin Wall was dismantled, Kiefer left his homeland, saying simply, "I needed to move. I am not only a German." The artist's restlessness was reflected in a 1993 exhibition he titled *20 Years of Solitude*. The artist gathered parts of the contents of his Mannheim studio and stacked the material in a pile in the Marian Goodman Gallery as if it were refuse. Sticking out of this cultural compost of heaped paintings and sculptural debris were large dried sunflowers. References to growth cycles and slash-and-burn farming were directly applied to the artist's studio. In a separate room, he installed twenty-six small white books, the pages of which were stained with the artist's semen. A room heavy with materials was paired with one of elusive lightness. Together, the pile of earth-encrusted debris and the stained books formed a symbolically methodical statement, yet again creating a dialogue between heaven and earth.

The title *20 Years of Solitude*, written on the gallery wall in Kiefer's now-familiar cursive script, was a reference to the artist's sense of feeling "trapped in the studio and in Germany" after twenty years of continual exhibitions. Kiefer spent the next three years moving between countries (including Mexico, Asia, America, and Central America), exploring different lands and the ancient beginnings of their civilizations. The twenty-six semen-stained books symbolize a refertilization of the imagination through an oblique reincarnation of the artist's first book, *The Heavens* (pages 1–16), in which magazine images of skies are presented as deadpan tropes for a paradise unimaginable. In *20 Years of Solitude*, however, Kiefer is literally making heaven out of himself, as Barnett Newman had described, decades ago, the intentions of the Abstract Expressionists.

Kiefer's ejaculations extend a performative theme in postwar art that ranges from Jackson Pollock's explosive drips to Carlo Manzoni's canned excrement. It would not be lost on Kiefer that his sperm is the heavenly counterpoint to Manzoni's earth. Kiefer has remarked on more than one occasion that a Pollock lies beneath many of his paintings. As Pollock's splattered paint marks challenge the edges of the canvas and thereby suggest a gesture beyond the confines of the painted field, Kiefer's semen sometimes appears to move off the edges of the page. *20 Years of Solitude* explores the metaphorical space between what Kiefer calls "small heavens inside" and those that we project in "another dimension, a place we assign to the gods of our myths and religions."

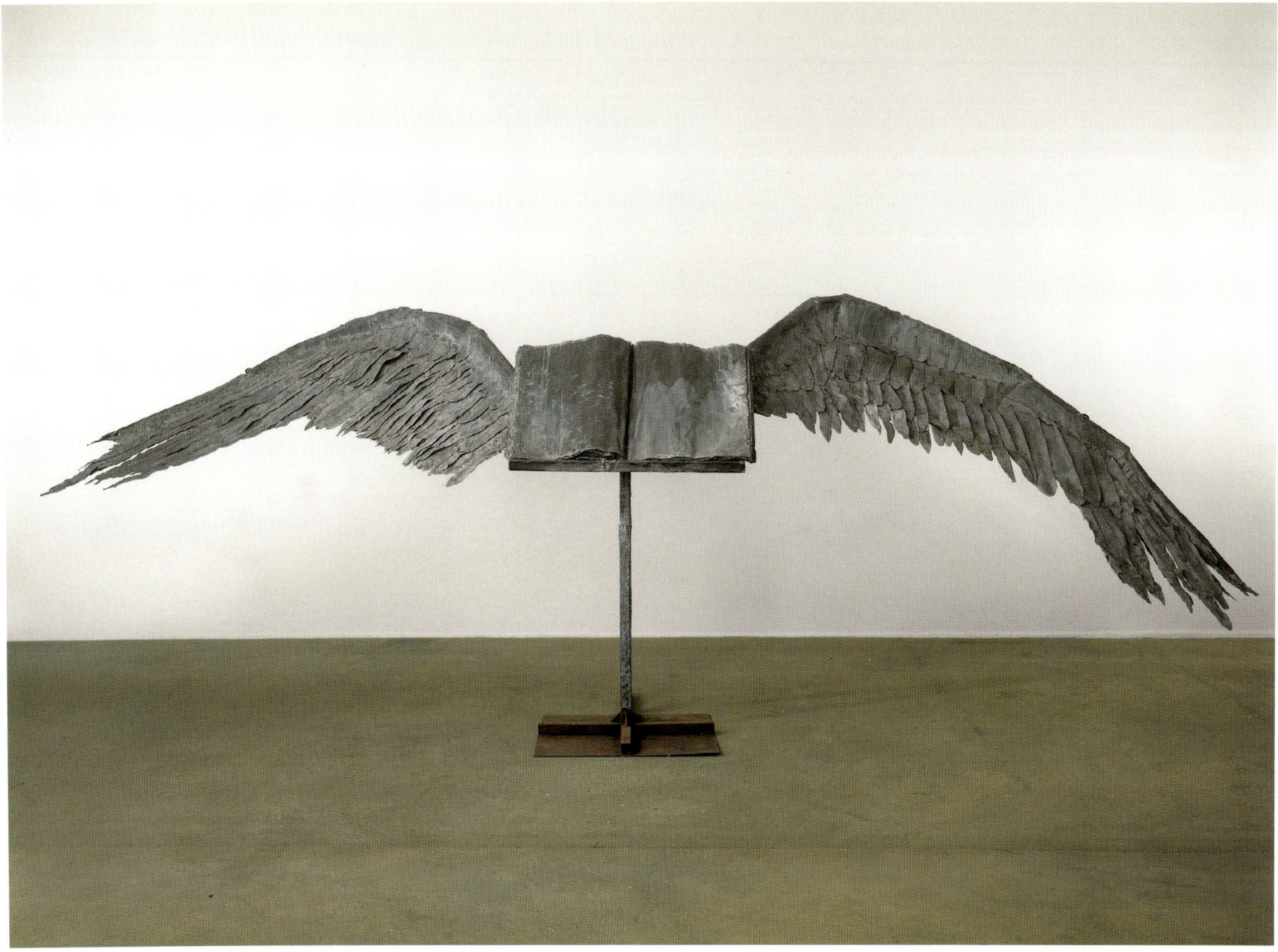

Buch mit Flügeln (Book with Wings), 1992–94
Lead, steel, and tin
74¾ × 208⅝ × 43⅜ inches (189.9 × 529.9 × 110.2 cm)

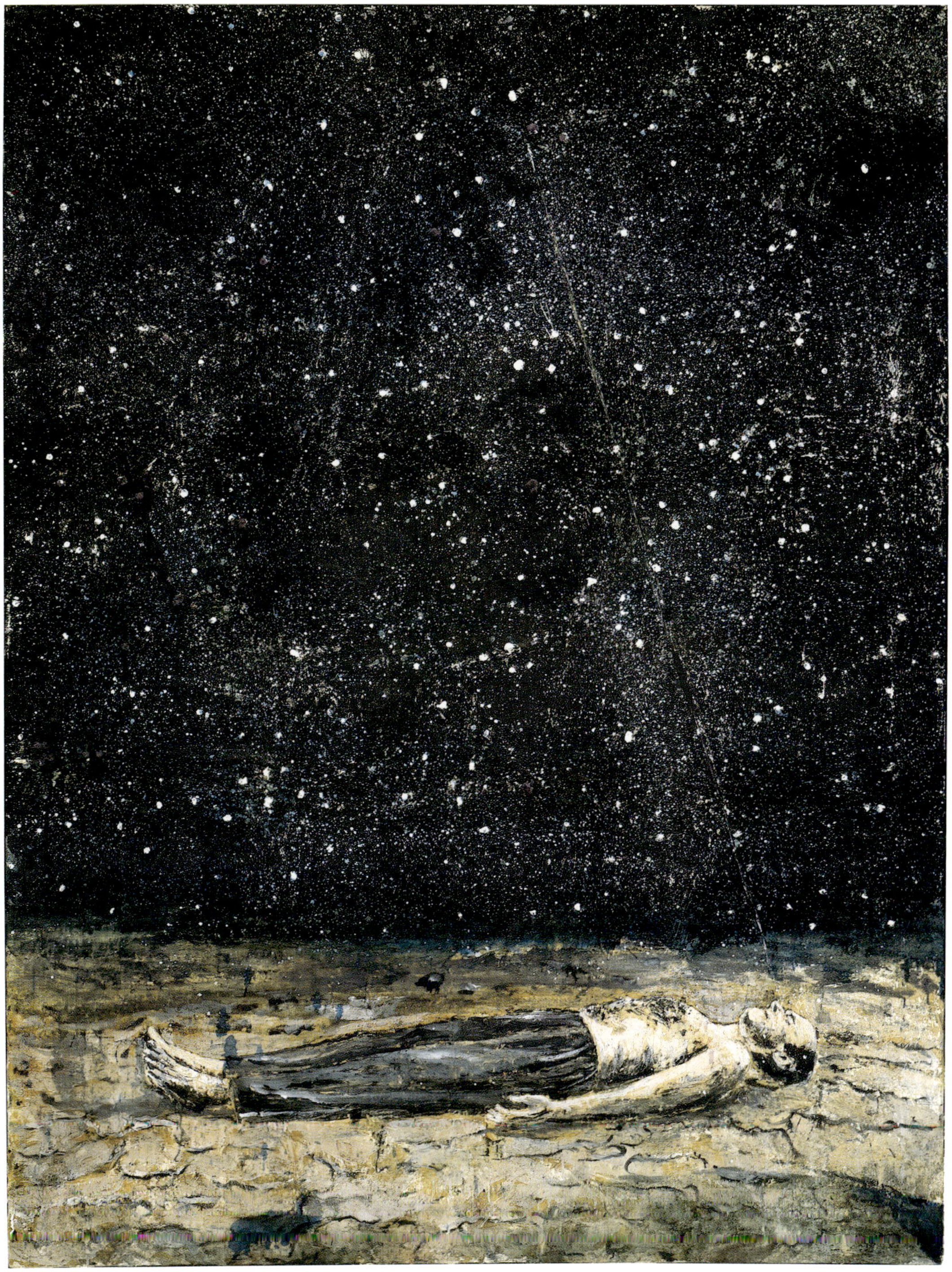

Sternenfall (Falling Stars), 1995
Oil on canvas
90 ½ × 67 inches (230 × 170 cm)

Dein und Mein Alter und das Alter der Welt (Your Age and Mine and the Age of the World), 1996

Für Robert Fludd (For Robert Fludd), 2003

Hermes Trismegistus (Thrice-greatest Hermes), generally considered the father of the so-called "hermetic" arts, proposed the visual relationship and indivisible connection between the microcosm and the macrocosm in the statement "As above, so below."[1] This principle is found in many of the world's religions and is the root of all Gnosticism and mystical art and belief.

The mystical philosopher-scientist Robert Fludd (1574–1637) elaborated on this concept, declaring that everything on earth has its equivalent star in heaven.[2] One of the best-known representatives of Rosicrucianism, Fludd was a Renaissance man who attempted to merge Gnostic belief, Christianity, the kabbala, and the discoveries of modern science into a cohesive picture of the universe. In the book *For Robert Fludd* (pages 138–143), Kiefer has juxtaposed painted poppies and star maps, creating a visual parallel to Fludd's poetic statement. Various pages of the book suggest rich fields of poppies growing over a vast cosmos, or the cosmos being revealed behind a dense curtain of poppies.

The painting *Your Age and Mine and the Age of the World* also contains a reference to Fludd, in the form of sunflowers and seeds, which Kiefer has used to suggest planets creating a canopy over the earth. A cosmic elaboration on Vincent van Gogh's paintings of sunflowers, completed not far from Kiefer's Barjac studio, the work also brings to mind the giant sunflowers Kiefer cultivates on his property. The viewpoint of the painting is that of a person lying on the ground looking up as the sunflowers loom above. Sunflower seeds are embedded in the paint, evoking distant stars, but they are black. Again we are reminded that the stars we admire are actually remnants of planets that have long since burned out.

Kiefer further refers to the ineffable qualities of time in the title of this work, which is taken from a poem by the celebrated modern Austrian writer Ingeborg Bachmann. Alongside Günter Grass and Paul Celan, Bachmann was part of the loosely formed postwar German literary association known as Gruppe 47, which was active from 1947 to 1977. The full line, taken from Bachmann's poem "The Game Is Over," is

Your age and mine and the age of the world
Cannot be measured in years.[3]

1 See Alexander Roob, *The Hermetic Museum: Alchemy and Mysticism* (Cologne: Taschen, 1997): 8.
2 Ibid., 501.
3 In *Songs in Flight: The Collected Poems of Ingeborg Bachmann*, Peter Filkins, trans. (New York: Marsilio Publishers, 1994): 111–13.

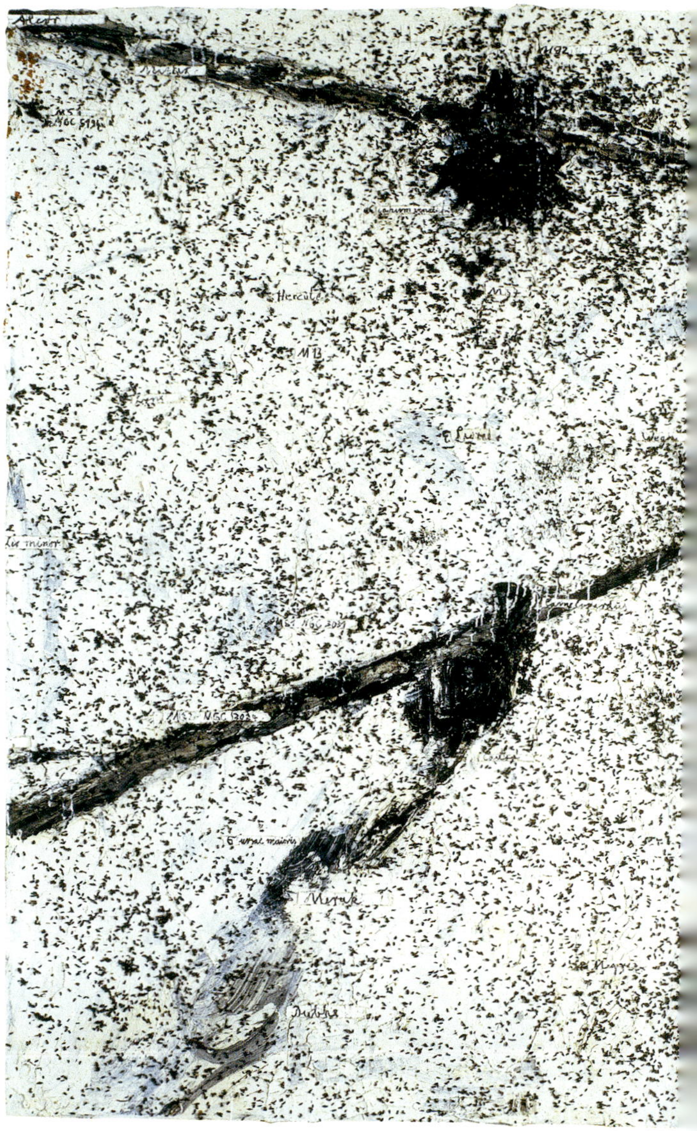

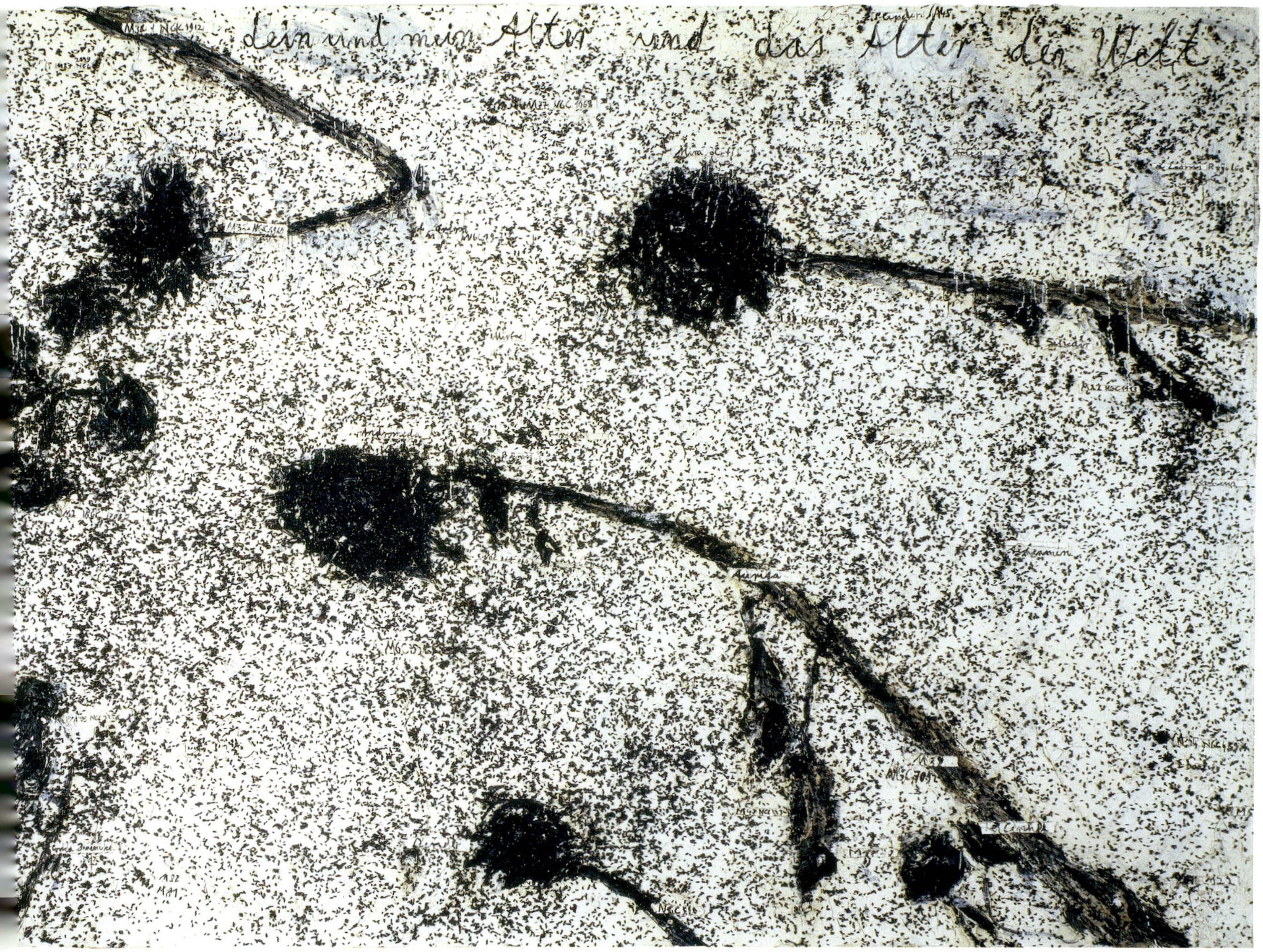

Dein und Mein Alter und das Alter der Welt (Your Age and Mine and the Age of the World), 1996
Emulsion, acrylic, shellac, and sunflower seeds on canvas
109 ⅜ × 218 ¾ inches (280 × 560 cm)

Merkawa, 1996

The title *Merkawa* refers to the ancient chariot described by kabbalistic mystics that operates between earth and seven heavenly palaces. Meditations on this theme appear in many of Kiefer's works. In the book *Merkawa*, Kiefer envisions the journey beginning from the gritty floor of his studio. From holes in the floor, which he has numbered one to seven, he has painted washes of white light or smoke, which float through the ceiling. The first page of the book shows a brick wall with a broken window, revealing a night sky within. This image is followed by pages of black fields with flecks of white paint indicating distant galaxies.

Just when we suspect that Kiefer's book is en route to the edge of heaven, he shatters the image, and starry points of light morph into splinters of broken glass. Kiefer has over the years scattered broken glass within paintings and around sculptures. Like lead, glass has a history and evocative qualities that work their way through the artist's allegorical journey, attracting many references. The etymology of *glass* involves the definition "to shine." Glass is a transmitter of light, and, constructed through high heat and fusion, it is a distant cousin to stars. When Kiefer shatters large plates of glass and spreads the shards over a broad area, he suggests a reference not only to the Big Bang theory of the origin of the universe, but also to the kabbalistic concept of Tsim Tsum, in which the primordial light was concealed in order to make room for humankind.

For a German born at the end of World War II, glass has a dark past that is not so distant, relating to the infamous *Kristallnacht* (Night of Broken Glass), in which the Nazi regime instituted a night of terror against the Jewish population. In the Jewish sections of German cities, every pane of glass that was in any way related to Jewish culture—including windows of synagogues, businesses, and private homes—was shattered. The sharp and shiny edges of Kiefer's glass bear the weight of recent history, turning the starry heaven into a night of mourning.

The middle section of *Merkawa* contains tiny dresses that are generically cut, as if issued by a prison. They are covered with ash and dust, apparently belonging to lost victims of a catastrophe, perhaps the Holocaust. The dresses may also be related to the artist's longtime interest in the legendary Jewish figure Lilith. Kiefer at least partially identifies Lilith with the role of the artist. In many of the artist's early photographs, he wears a dresslike garment. Like the artist, Lilith is a rebel, as well as a seeker of a higher power, operating in an impure space between the mortal and the divine. In the kabbala, Lilith, like lead, is associated with the planet Saturn. Those with a melancholic character, a disposition often associated with artists, are called "Lilith's sons."

Merkawa, 1996
Book, 32 pages. Mixed media
41 1/8 × 32 1/4 × 3 7/8 inches (104.5 × 81.9 × 9.8 cm) (bound volume)

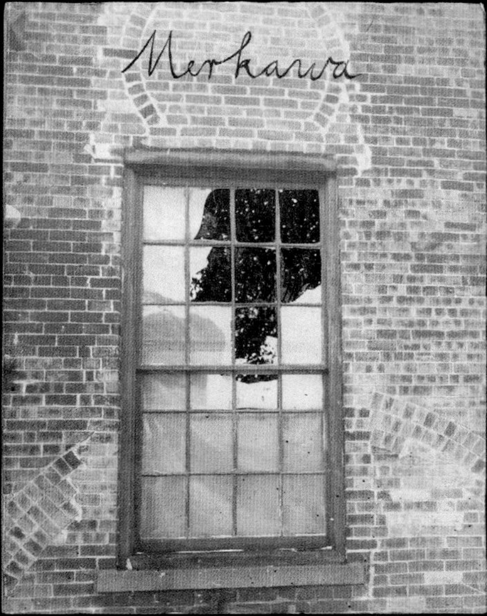
Merkawa

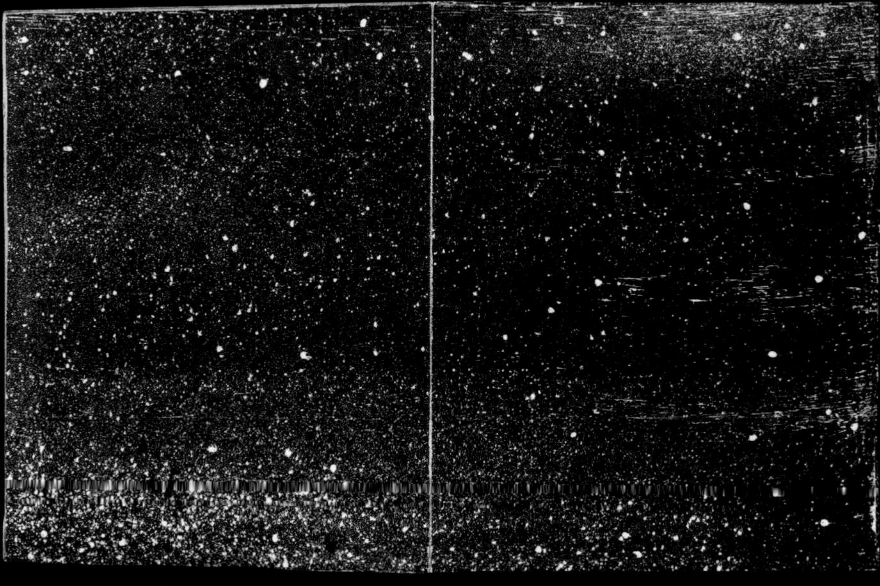

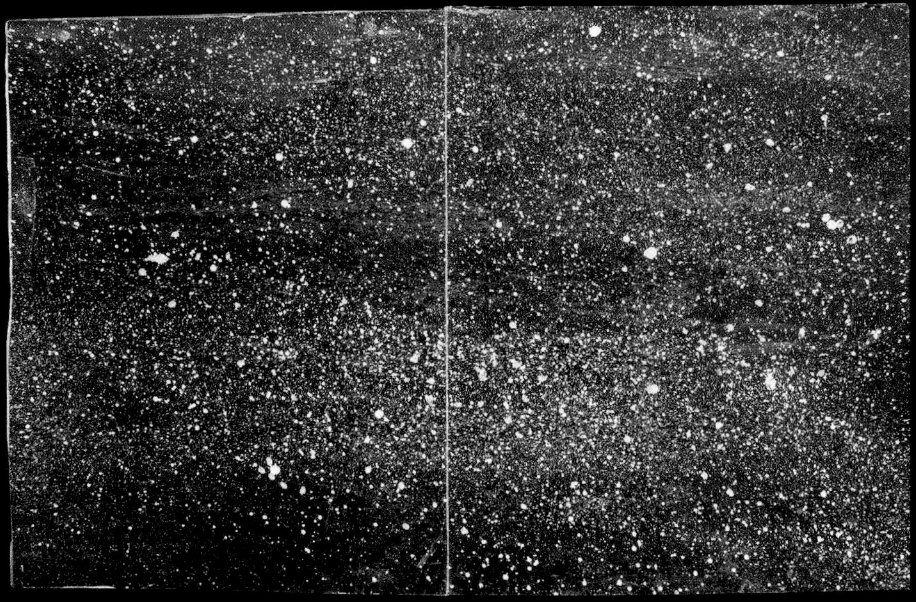

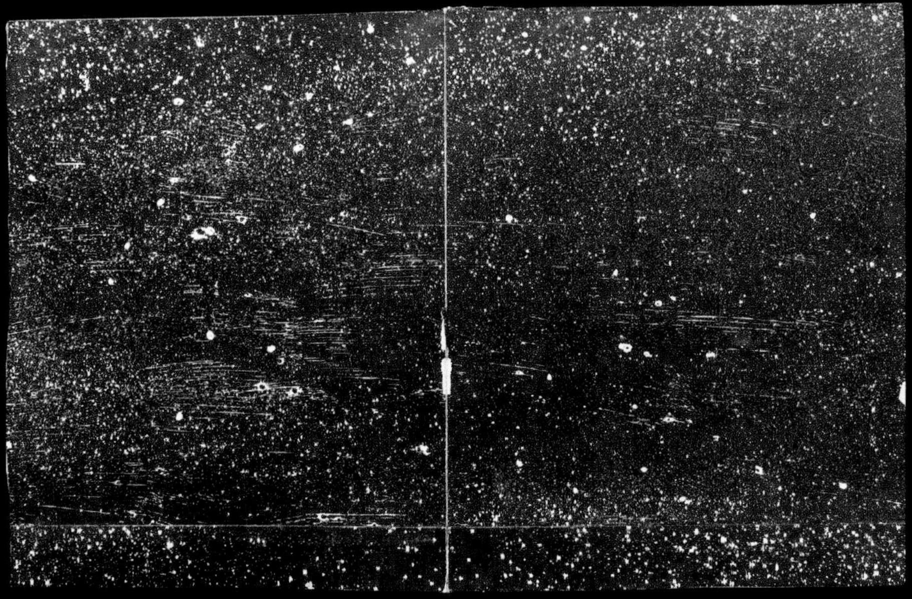

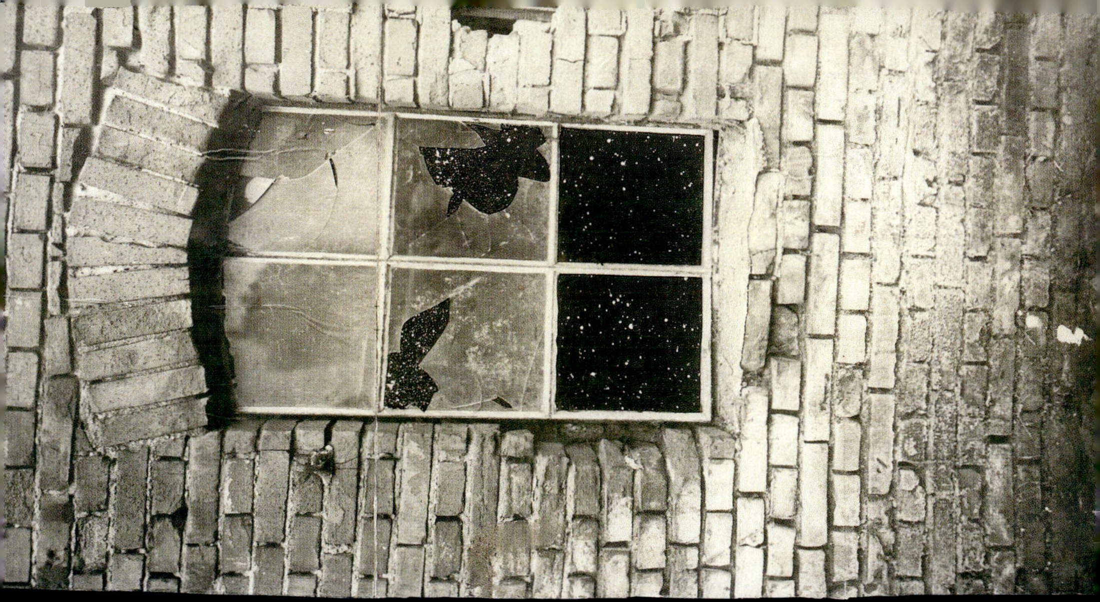

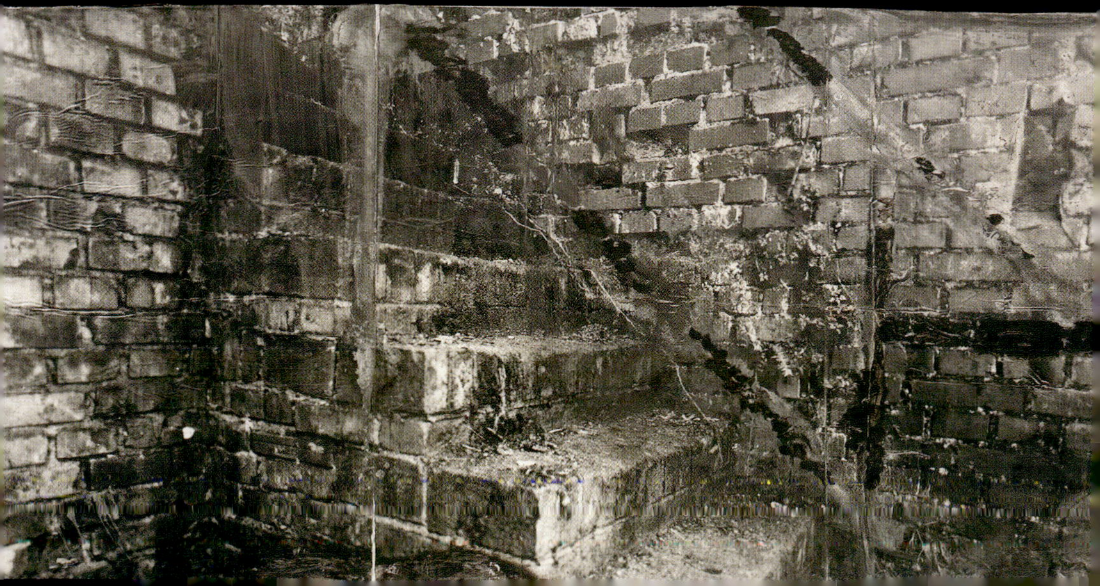

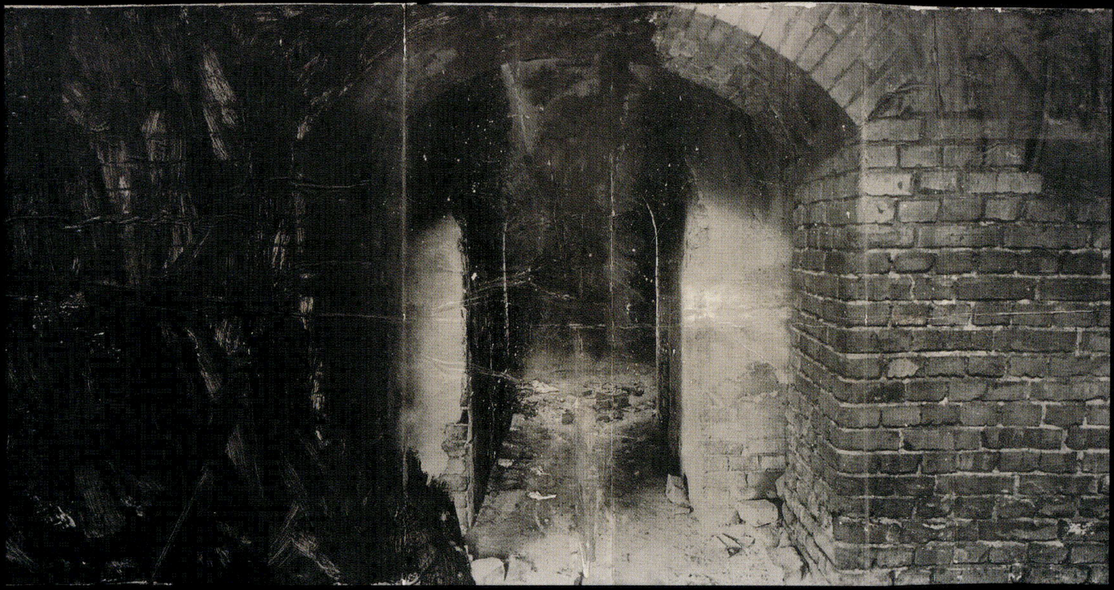

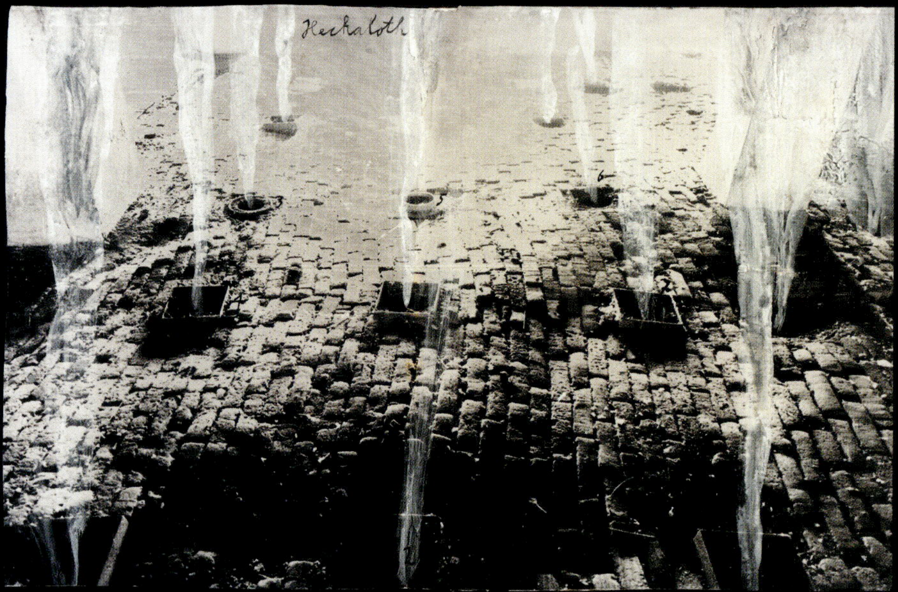
Hechaloth

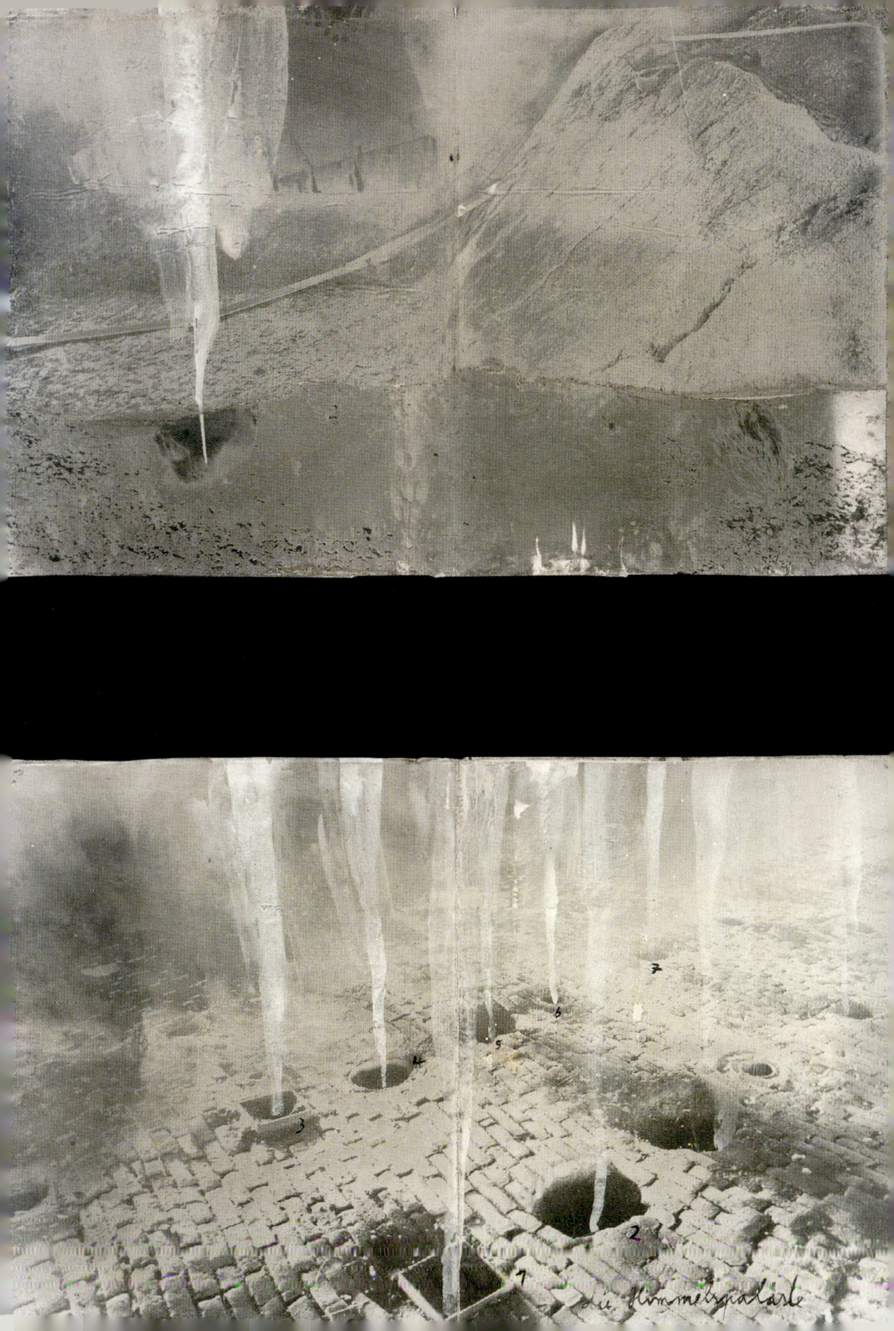

1
2
3
4
5
6
7
die Himmelspaläste

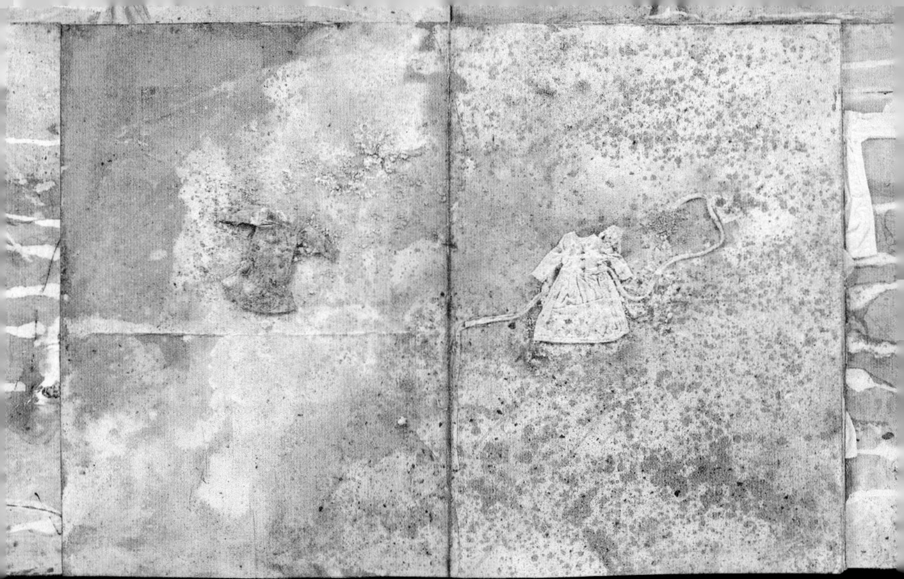

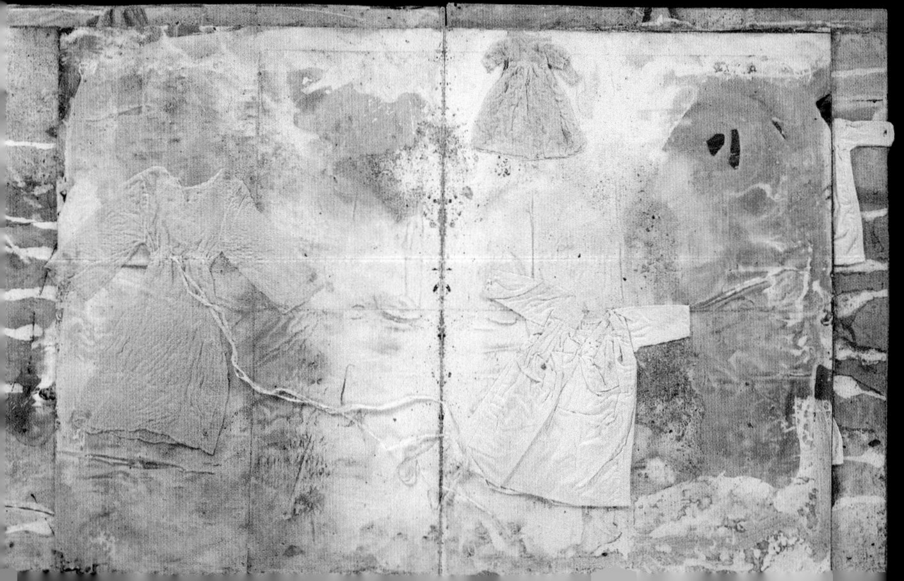

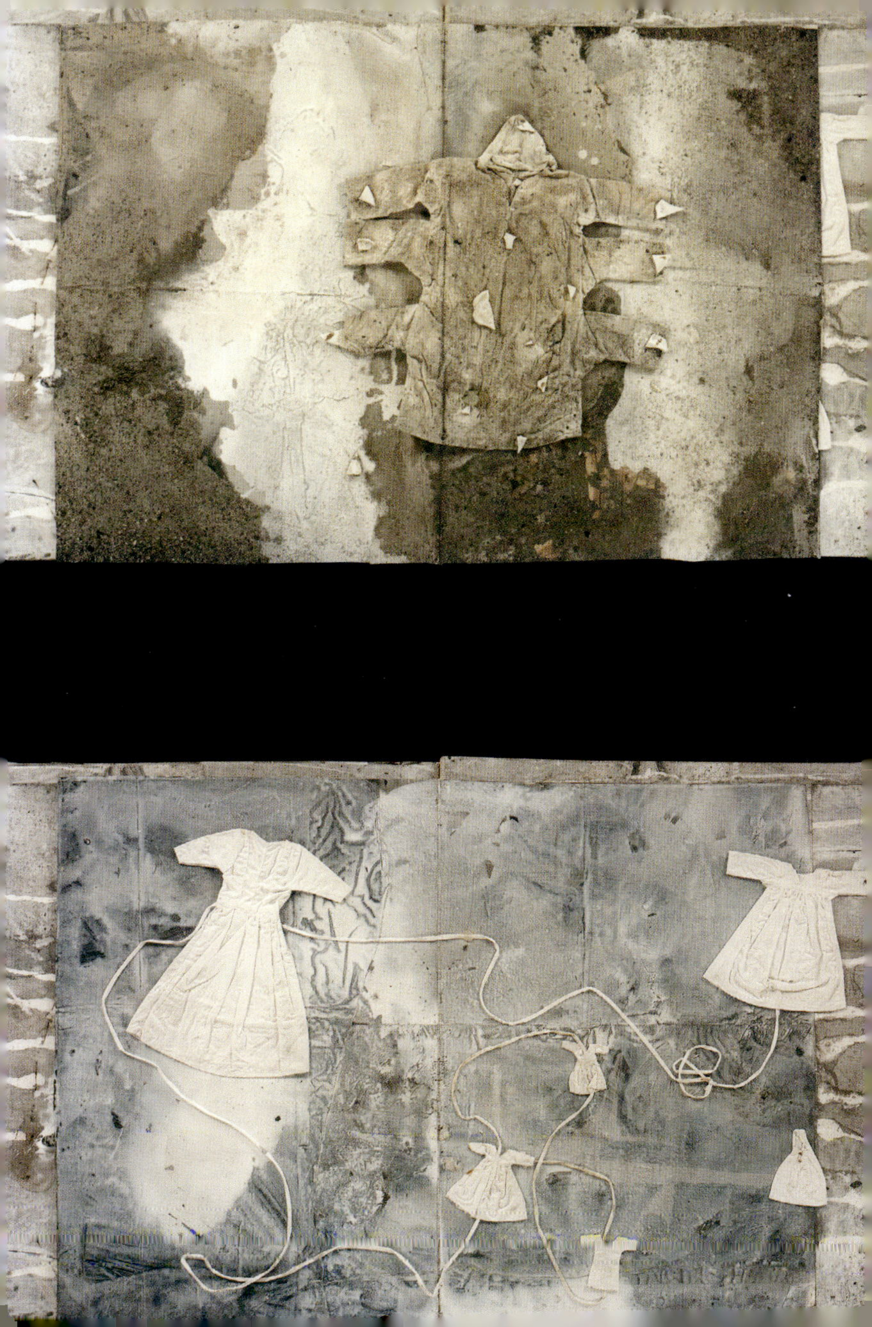

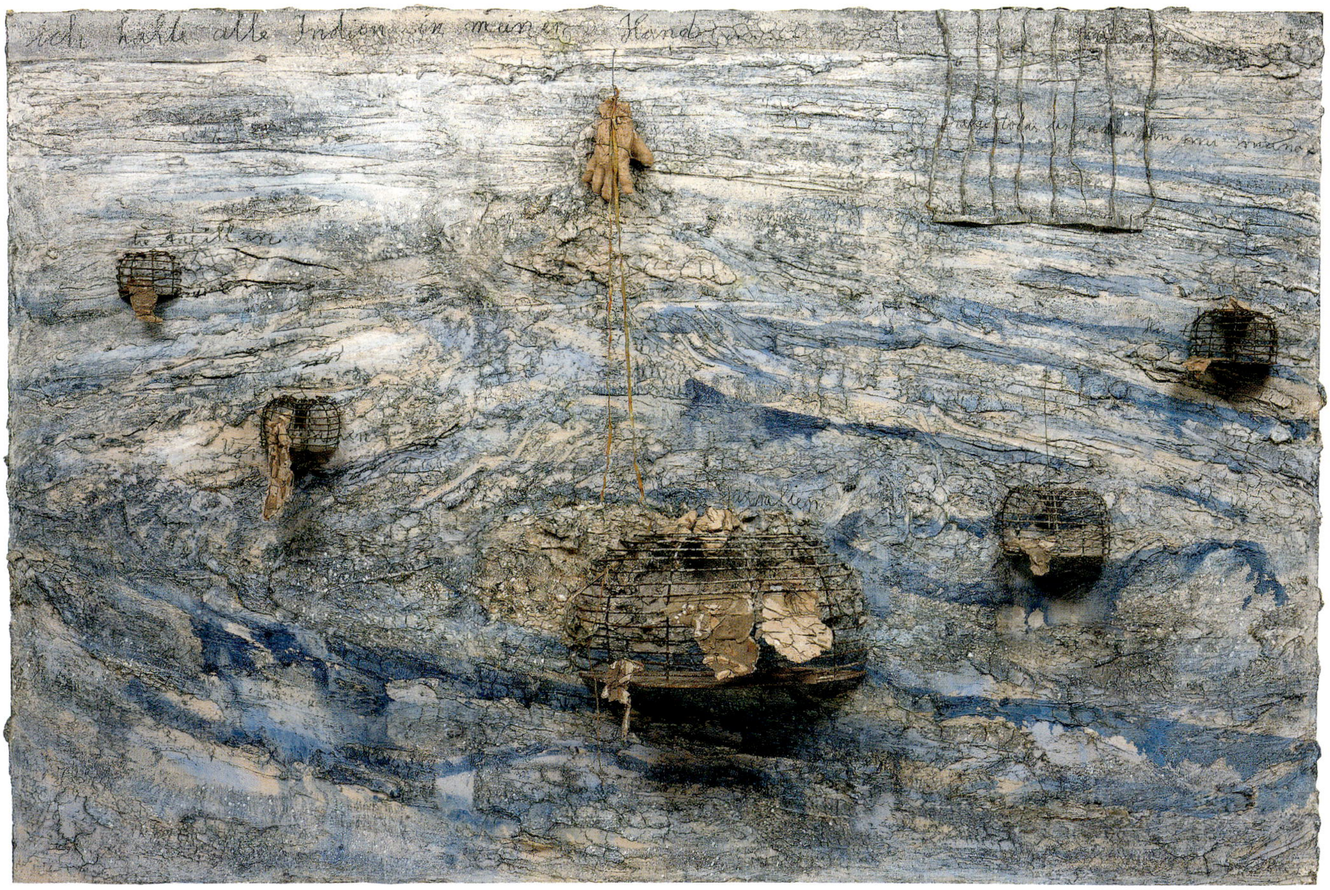

Ich halte alle Indien in meiner Hand (I Hold All Indias in My Hand), 1996
Oil, emulsion, and acrylic on canvas with wire cages
74¾ × 110¼ inches (190 × 280 cm)

Papst Alexander VI: Die goldene Bulle
(Pope Alexander VI: The Golden Bull), 1996

Throughout his career, Kiefer's work has reflected his interest in architecture as an emblem of political and transcendental ambitions. Within the wide-ranging complex of architectural symbolism, one of the most profound and fundamental structures is the mountain–temple, exemplified by the Babylonian ziggurat, the Egyptian pyramid, the Buddhist stupa, and the American *teocalli*, or stepped pyramid. Such structures aspire to the symbolic transcendence of the mountain, an ancient symbol of the connection between heaven and earth.

If such monuments are central to the mythic or religious goals of a culture, they can also be a reflection of human pretension and greed. Kiefer's mid-1990s images of ancient Mexican pyramids represent the site of a fusion of spiritual transcendence and bloody sacrifice. *Pope Alexander VI: The Golden Bull* depicts a colossal pyramid with a line of gold streaming down its surface. Kiefer's pyramid swells to fill almost the entire picture plane, reaching through the edges of the canvas. Radically foreshortened, it has the presence of an immense man-made mountain. The sky rains a dark, thick emanation.

Although the structure is a composite of a number of pyramids the artist saw during his travels in Mexico and Central America, in his eyes it represents the grand Pyramid of the Moon at Teotihuacán, one of the greatest and most infamous Aztec monuments. It was from this structure that human sacrifices were presumably offered, leaving a trail of blood down the steps of the pyramid to the Street of the Dead.

Alexander VI was Pope at the time of Christopher Columbus's discovery of the New World and the driving force in the search for gold there. The term "golden bull" refers to a papal decree with a golden seal. The Pope's ambitions for church and country were veiled by his professed desire to bring Christianity and law to the natives of the New World. In Kiefer's paradoxical worldview, gold and blood mark a trail between heaven and earth.

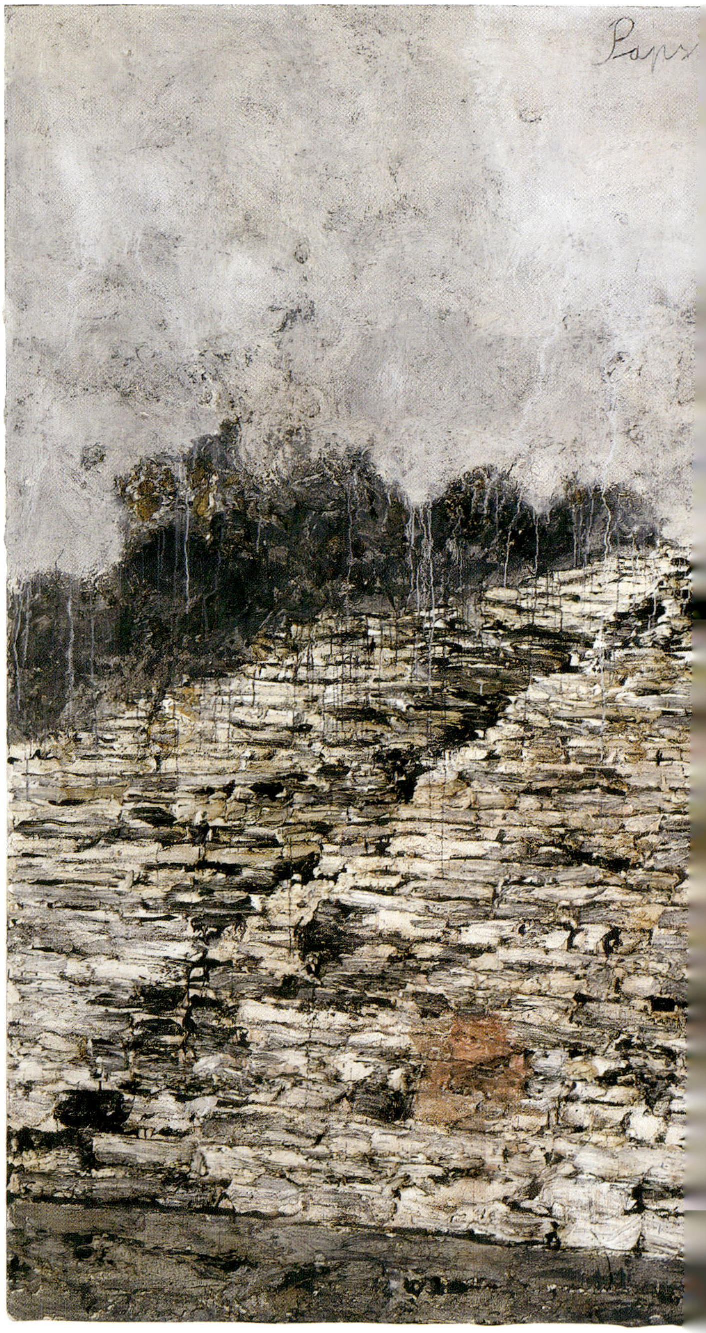

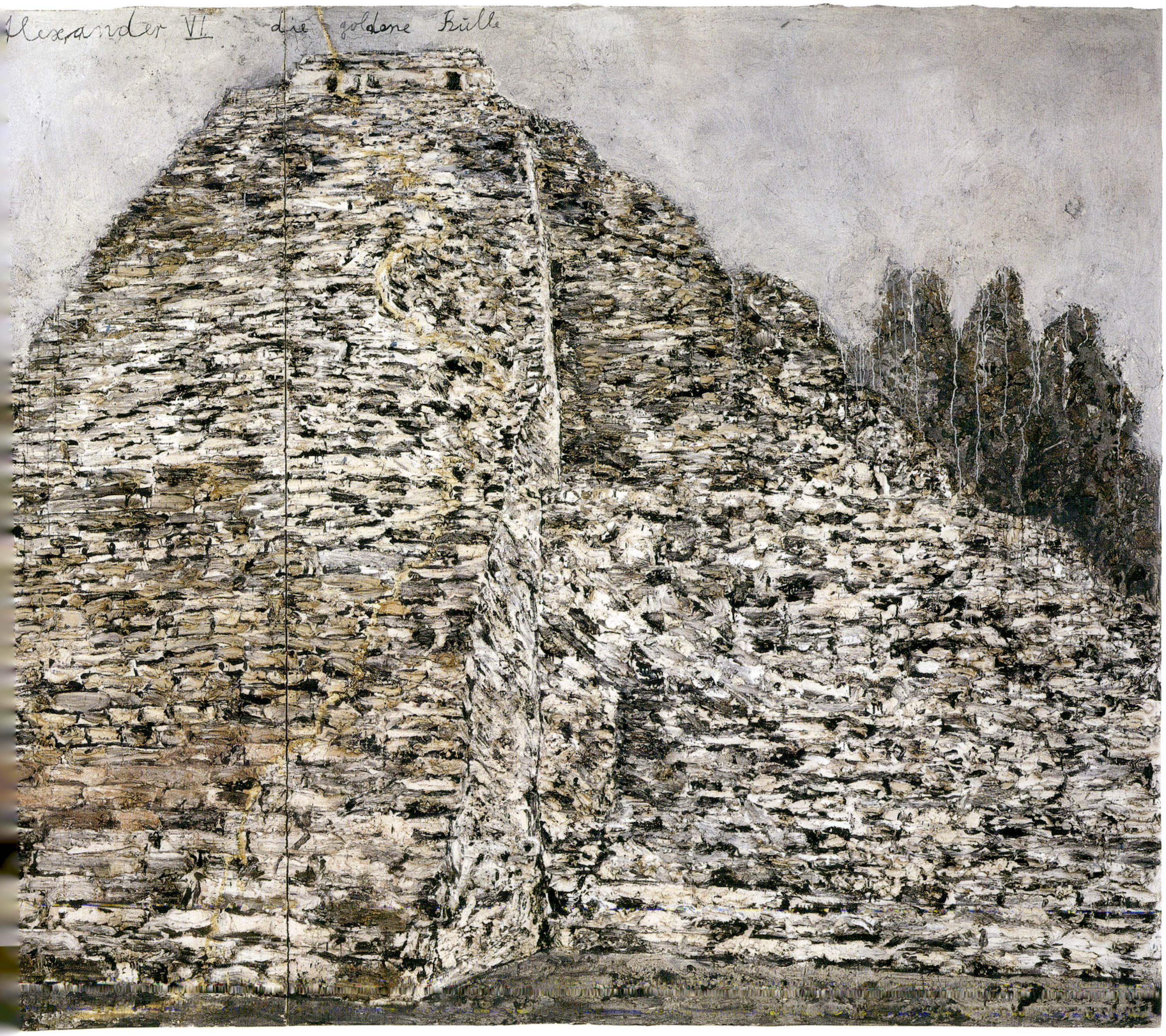

Papst Alexander VI: Die goldene Bulle (Pope Alexander VI: The Golden Bull), 1996
Emulsion, acrylic, and gold leaf on canvas
130 × 218 ¾ inches (330.2 × 555.6 cm)

Die Aschenblume (Ash Flower), 1983–97

In this monumental painting, Kiefer uses an architectural image—a Nazi ceremonial hall designed by Albert Speer—to suggest the possibility of transformation. Begun in 1983 and not completed until 1997, this transformation is physical and symbolic. A layer of ash nearly obliterates the building, suggesting a large grey stone. Given Kiefer's interest in symbolic play, this work contains a reference to the *ashlar*, an important emblem in alchemy and many other esoteric traditions. The ashlar is a simple, square-cut building stone, which represents the goal of spiritual perfection.

The colossal space of Speer's room is empty, except for the intrusion of a tall, dried sunflower plant Kiefer has attached directly to the surface of the painting. "The ash is the result of a great fire," the artist has said, "yet the ash fertilizes the ground. The huge, dried flower is placed upside down—its seeds pouring into the ash to regenerate." Kiefer suggests a space in a moment of transition, in which new images can grow from the brittle goals of the Third Reich. As Kiefer has said, "There is no point in destroying the building. Its memory could do more harm than the bricks it is made of. It's better to transform the space—to create a space for something new. It's like an open book waiting for the next chapter."[1]

The word *Aschenblume*, meaning "ash flower," is taken from a 1952 poem by Paul Celan entitled "I Am Alone." Celan's evocative image has resonated in different ways in Kiefer's works. In a painting of the same title from 2004 (page 145), a powerful eruption takes place high above the surface of the earth. In the center of this explosive form is a grid—an attempt to measure or give rational form to the chaos.

1 The artist in conversation with the author, April 10, 2001.

Die Aschenblume (Ash Flower), 1983–97
Oil, emulsion, acrylic paint, clay, ash, earth, and dried sunflower on canvas
149⅝ × 299¼ inches (380 × 760 cm)

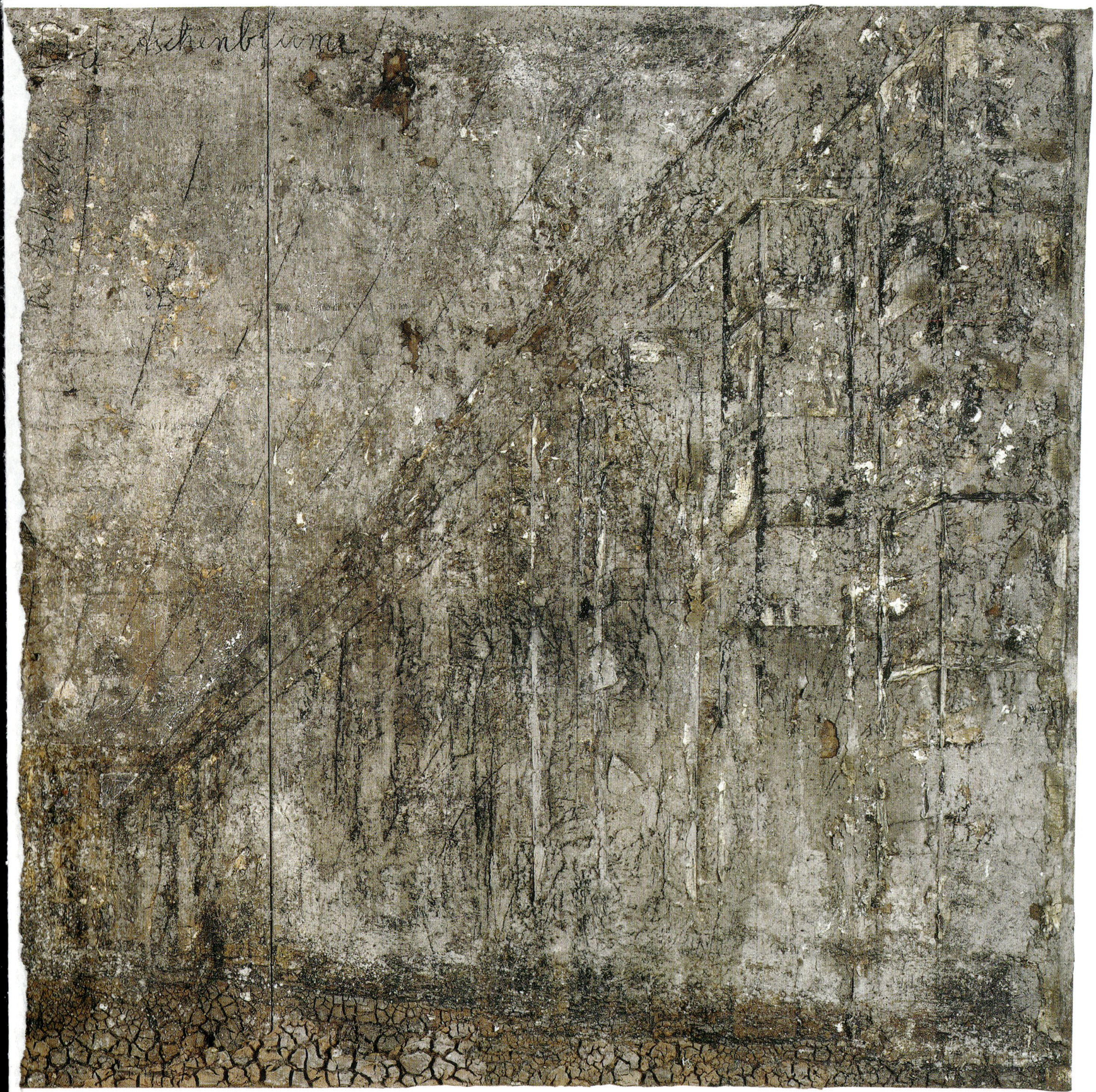
Aschenblume

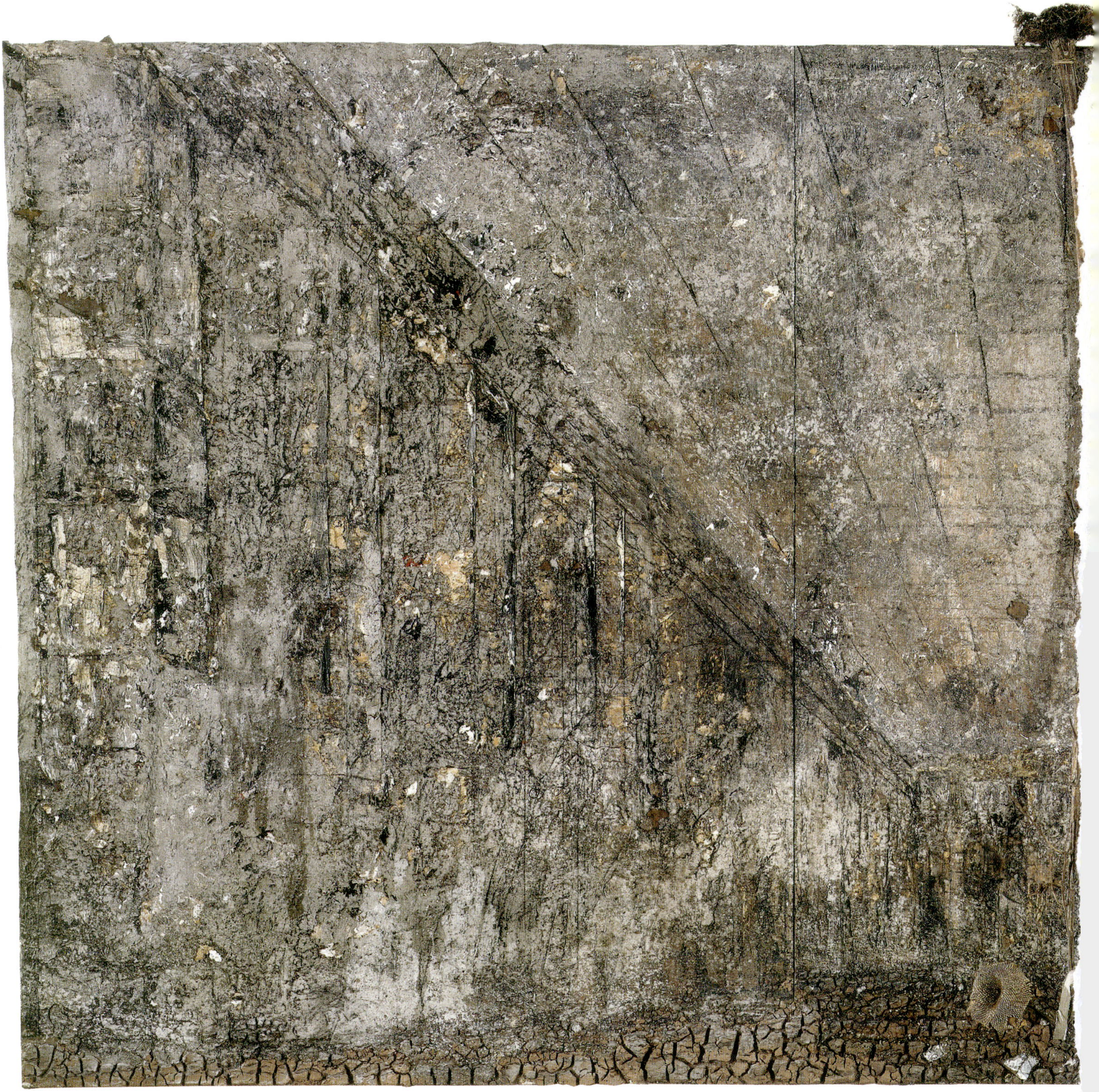

The Secret Life of Plants, 2001

Kiefer is interested in the plant as a symbol of the earth's beginnings, and he has commented that ancient forests and plants "may contain secret knowledge." He alludes to this in the title of this work, a more than six-foot-high book of lead that stands upright, its pages fanning out in all directions.

The title is that of a book by Peter Tompkins and Christopher Bird first published in 1973, which explores the sentience of plants and proposes that plants, whose cells are as connected to the cosmos as those of any person, may be able to provide answers to the mysteries of the world that science cannot. This idea is a twentieth-century version of the mystic Robert Fludd's assertion that every plant on earth has its equivalent star in the heavens. Kiefer's book, which contains fields of stars, likewise belongs to the lineage of Fludd's thoughts on the microcosm and the macrocosm.

Here, the book becomes both seed and universe. Using his signature material, lead, Kiefer materializes the ancient concept of the universe as an immense book. On the dark pages, he has drawn the stars' NASA identification numbers along with lines connecting them, suggesting a system of arrangement and alignment that belies logic and explanation. As part of an indefinable macrocosm, Kiefer's universe experiences the entropic pressure of its own gravity. The weight and malleability of the lead cause the star-flecked pages to gently give way under their own weight, evoking a collapsing universe.

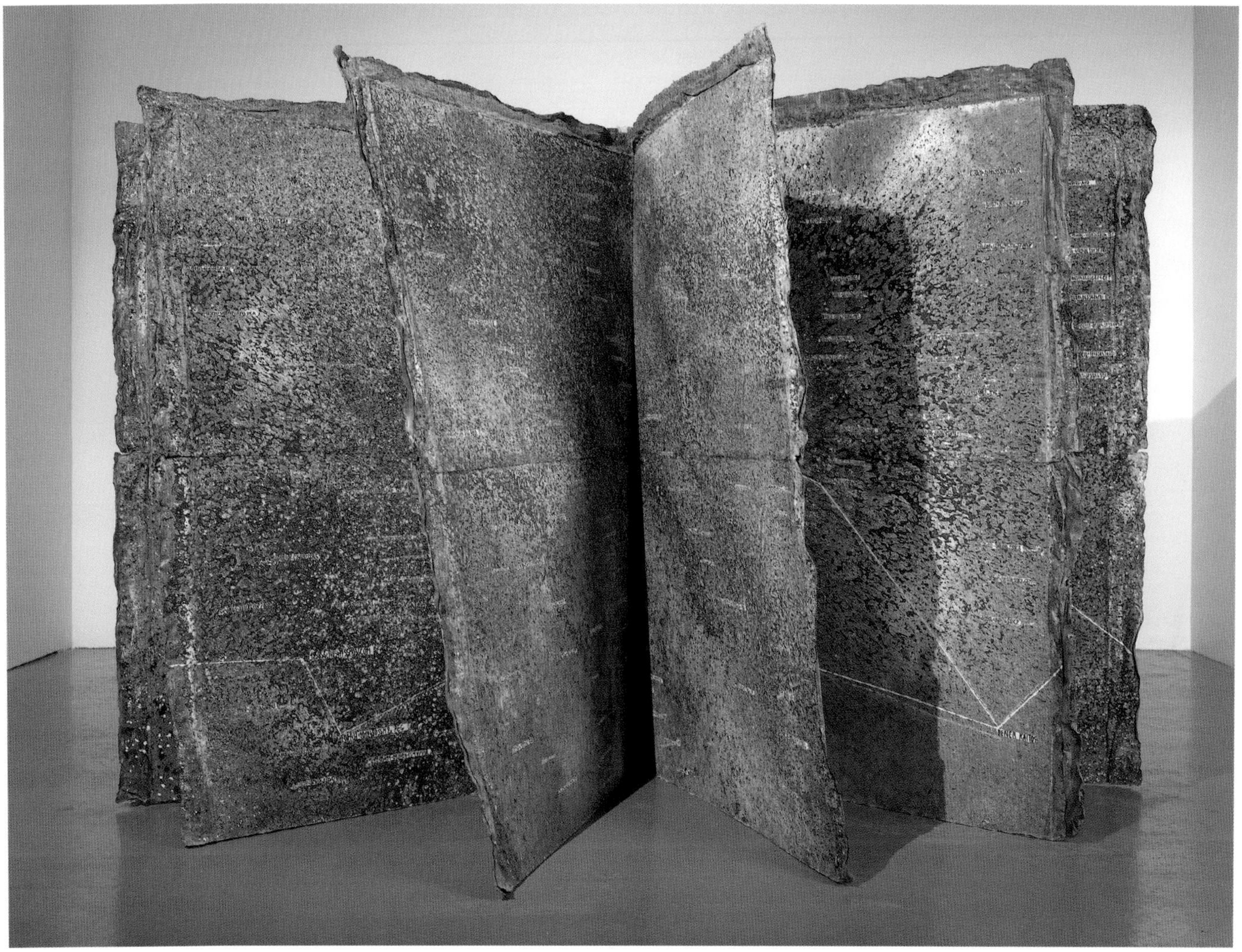

The Secret Life of Plants, 2001
Paint and mixed media on lead
122 inches (309.9 cm) diameter; 79 × 58 inches (200.7 × 147.3 cm) each page

Die Himmelspaläste (The Heavenly Palaces), 2002

Sefer Hechaloth, 2002

Die Himmelspaläste (The Heavenly Palaces), 2004

The ancient Hebrew book known as the Sefer Hechaloth describes an ascent through seven heavenly palaces to the *Hechaloth*, the palace in which the wise will be united with God. This metaphor for the journey towards gnosis predates the kabbala, but belongs to the same Jewish mystical tradition. The Sefer Hechaloth contains a description of the *merkaba* (or *merkawa*), a chariot that carries the seeker on the journey. Depicted in Eastern religions, this throne-chariot was also described in a fiery vision by the biblical prophet Ezekiel. This journey has been ritually practiced by mystics and is symbolized in countless ways throughout history. It is eventually incorporated into the kabbalistic Tree of Life.

Regarding the Hechaloth, Kiefer has said, "The palaces of heaven are still a mystery . . . I am making my own investigation." To the surface of many of the artist's works related to this theme, he has attached metal shelves or cages containing symbolic objects. The metal shelves attached to the surface of *Sefer Hechaloth*, 2002, form a staircase leading to the top of the painting. They hold burned books. Above the shelves, along with the title of the work, the artist has written *Merkaba*. The immense work *The Heavenly Palaces*, 2002, depicts a cavernous hall with massive pillars holding up a ceiling made of stars spiraling through an infinite universe, which dwarfs even this monumental building.

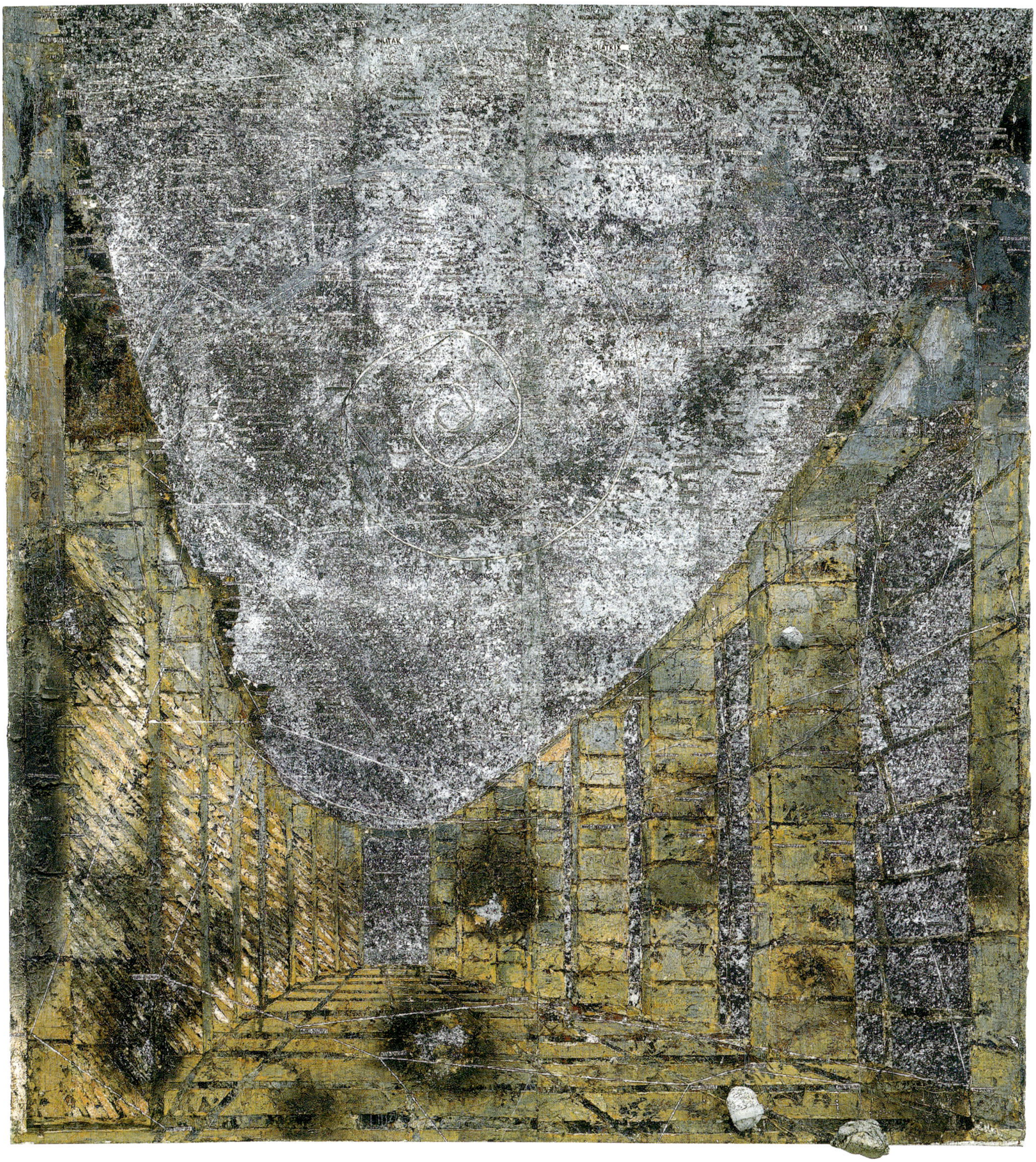

Die Himmelspaläste (The Heavenly Palaces), 2002
Oil, emulsion, acrylic, and lead objects on lead and canvas
248 × 212 ½ inches (630 × 540 cm)

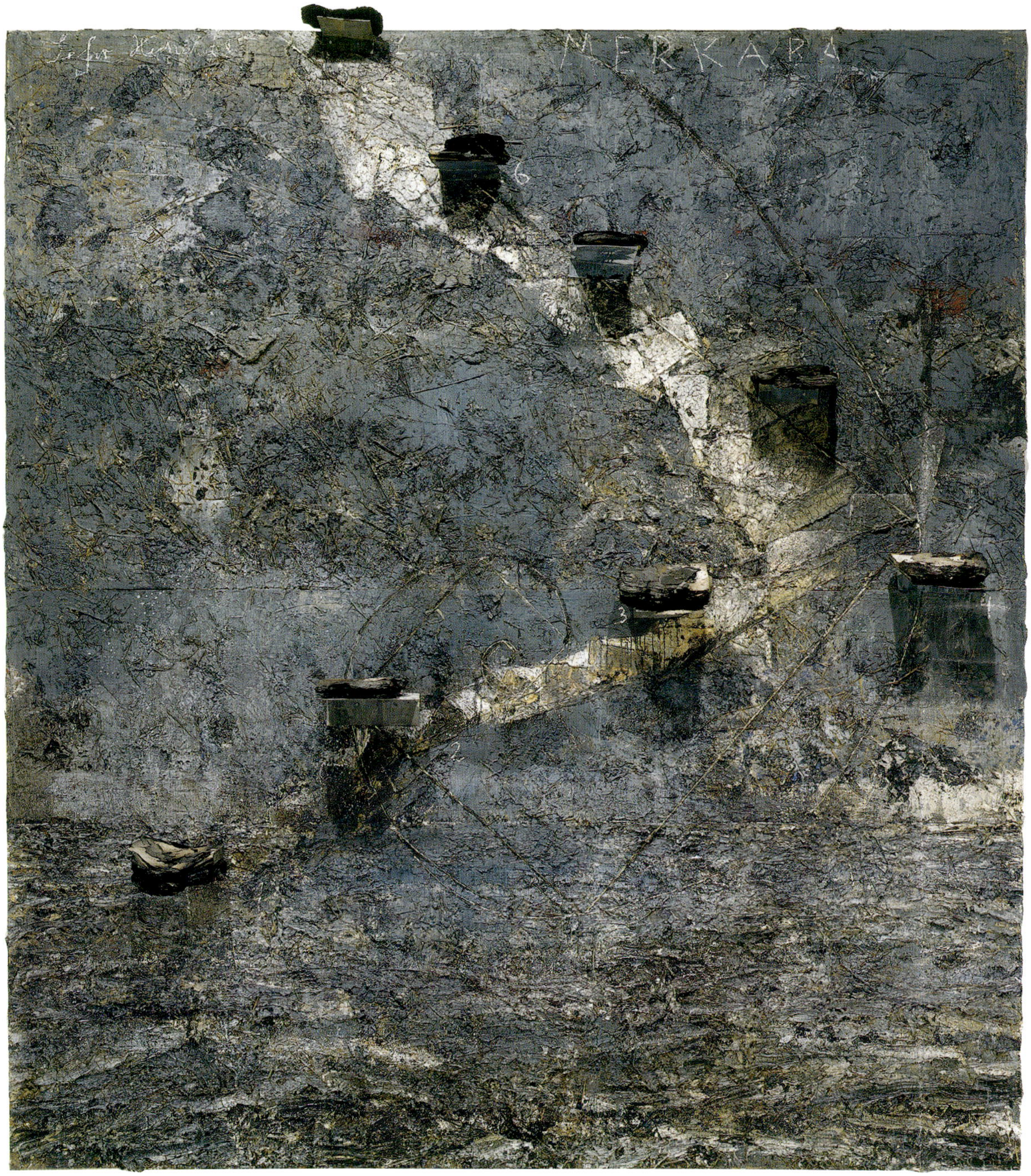

Sefer Hechaloth, 2002
Oil, emulsion, acrylic, metal shelves, and burned books on canvas
147 ½ × 130 inches (375 × 330 cm)

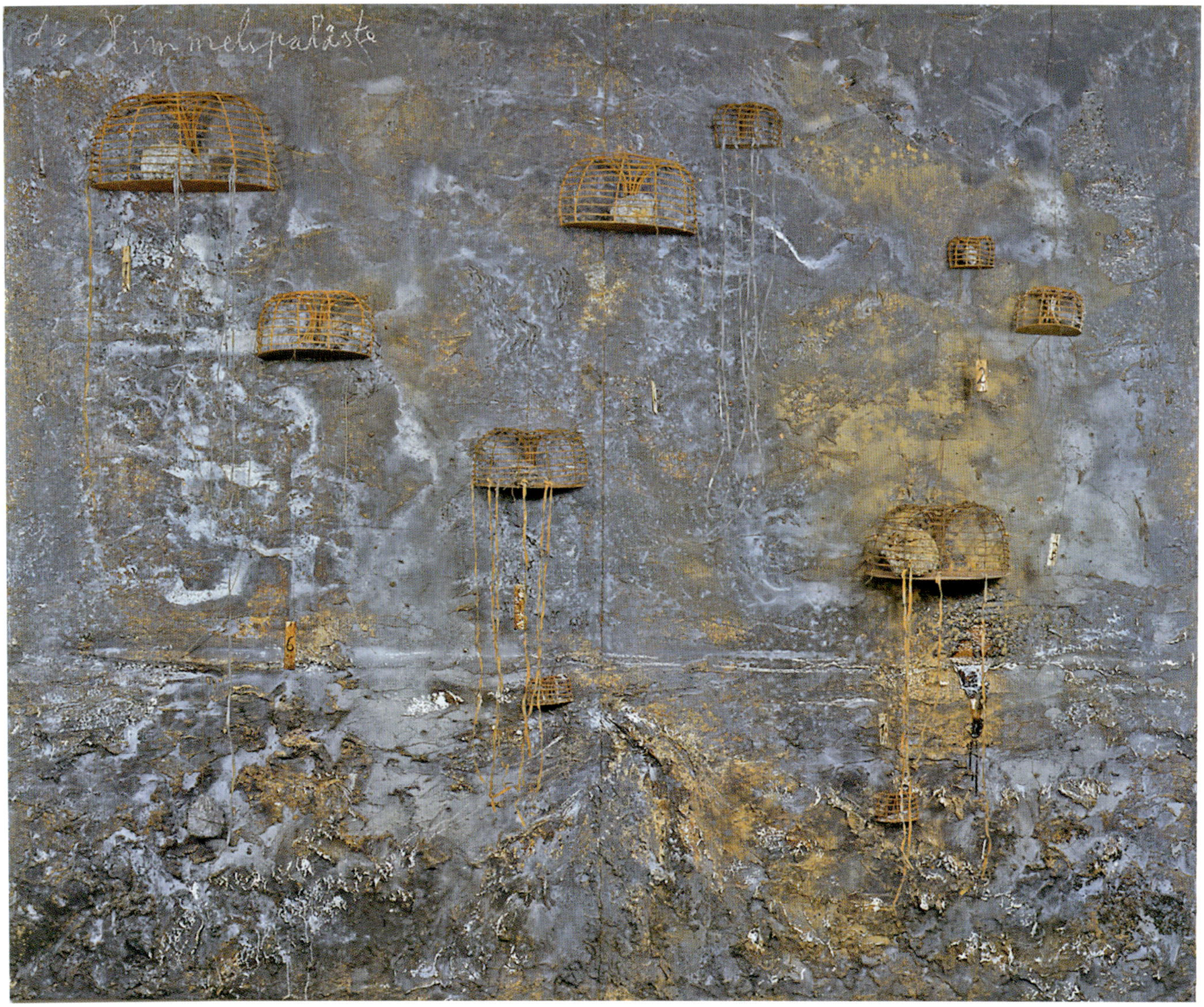

Die Himmelspaläste (The Heavenly Palaces), 2004
Oil, emulsion, and acrylic on canvas with wire cages
110¼ × 130 inches (280 × 330 cm)

In a recent group of gouaches, Kiefer freely interprets mystical literature using photographs of oceans, cliffs, industrial sites, and his sprawling Barjac studio complex as a backdrop. To the photographs he has added collaged photographic fragments of different formed and found objects that he has distributed around his property. Chief among these are long stretches of concrete stairs the artist makes and then breaks into pieces, which he stacks in various configurations.

Kiefer often numbers the stairs in ascending and descending order, one through seven, relating to the seven heavenly palaces described in the ancient Jewish book called the Sefer Hechaloth. These works carry an echo of the artist's statement about the Hechaloth: "It is about finding symbols that move in all directions." Staircases generally offer a clear path from one place to another. Kiefer's stairs—which lead in all directions, often simply into the sky—may be a wry caution about taking metaphors literally.

In the gouaches, the concrete remnants rise from murky underground atmospheres, float over ocean surf, support lead pages, and form poignantly awkward wings. In some of the photographs, Kiefer has formed the broken stairs into tank-like configurations. This may be a reference to an Israeli tank with the paradoxical name Merkava ("chariot"), a reminder that a military group has taken the venerated name of a tool for enlightenment and applied it to a tool for destruction.

The titles of some of these works refer to the Sefer Hechaloth and the kabbala; *Asijah* is the kabbalistic term for the material world. The titles also have geographic implications. The Lorelei is a cliff on the bank of the Rhine with a rich mythological history. It is described in a thirteenth-century legend as the place where Siegfried hid the golden ring of the Nibelungs. This treacherous passage is also the setting for a traditional German folk song based on a poem by Heinrich Heine. A caution against being seduced by beautiful, golden visions on high, it describes a golden-haired maiden whose bewitching song lures sailors to their death.

Like the *Attic* works of the 1970s, these gouaches exemplify Kiefer's inclination to use his personal workspace as a living, changing staging ground for an investigation of our conflicted world and what we call heaven.

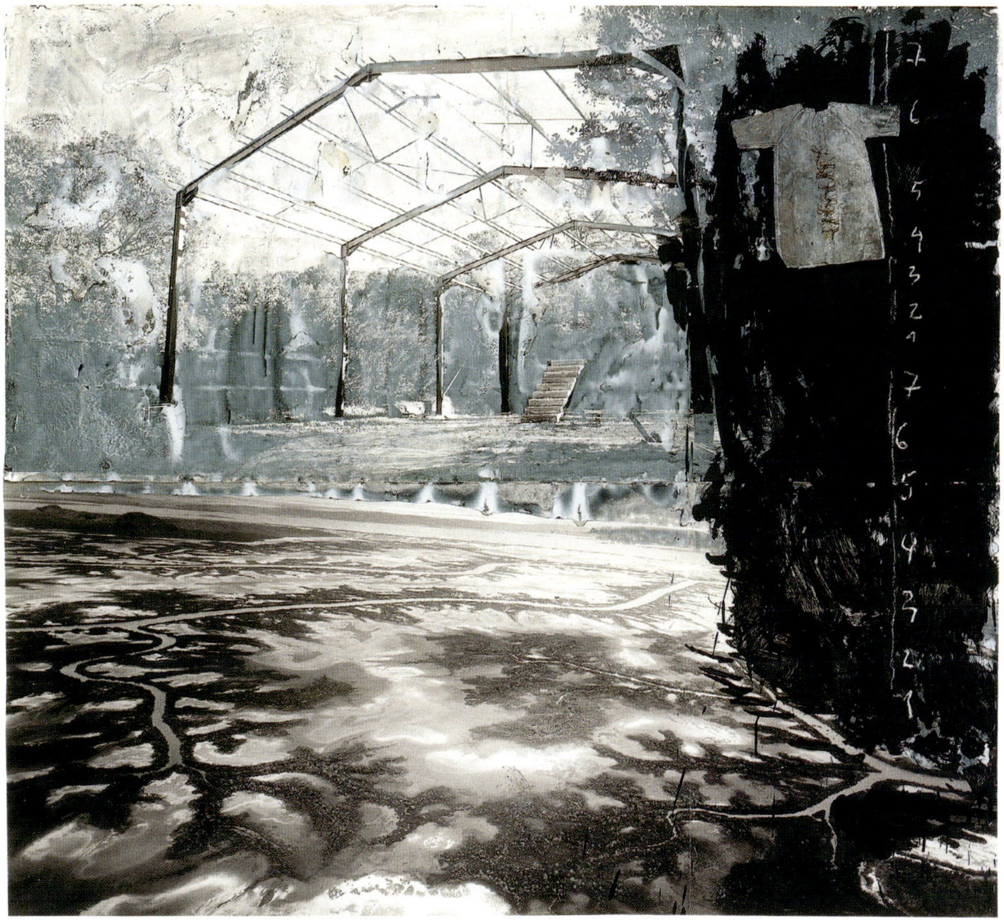

Asijah, 2003
Gouache on photo paper
46 ⅜ × 50 inches (117.7 × 126.8 cm)

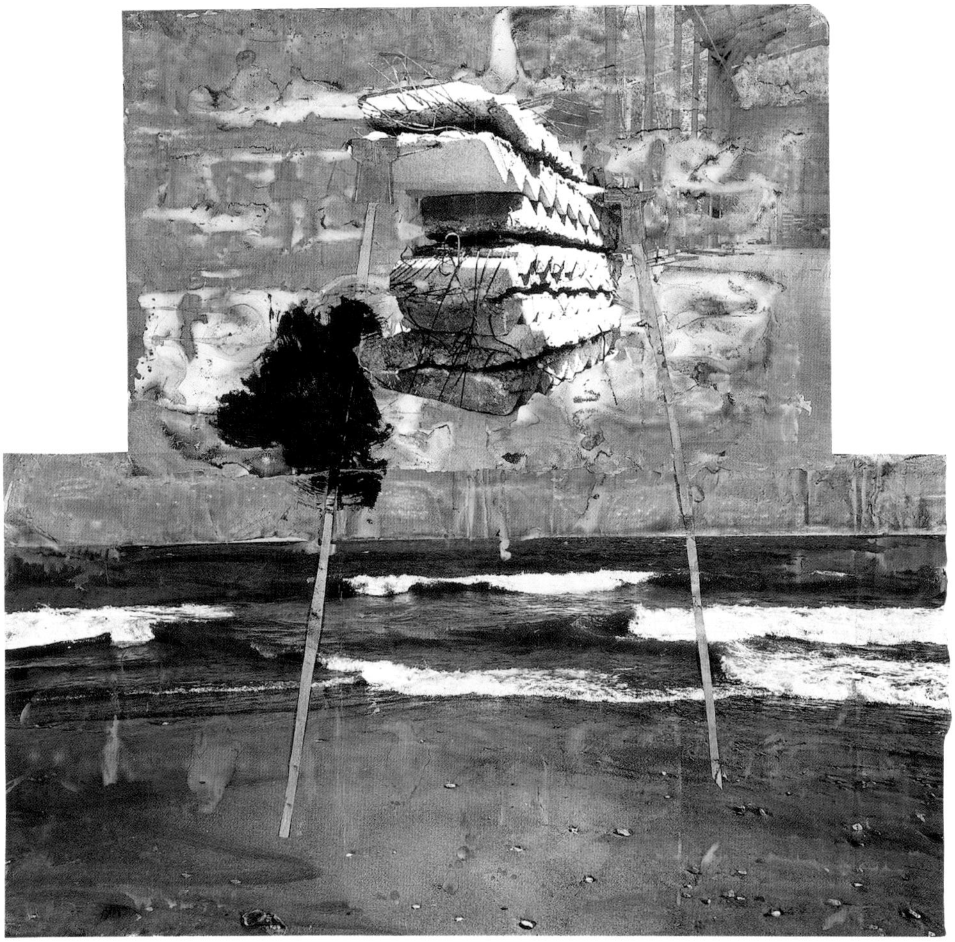

Asijah, 2003
Gouache on photo paper
46 ¼ × 46 ⅝ inches (117.5 × 118.5 cm)

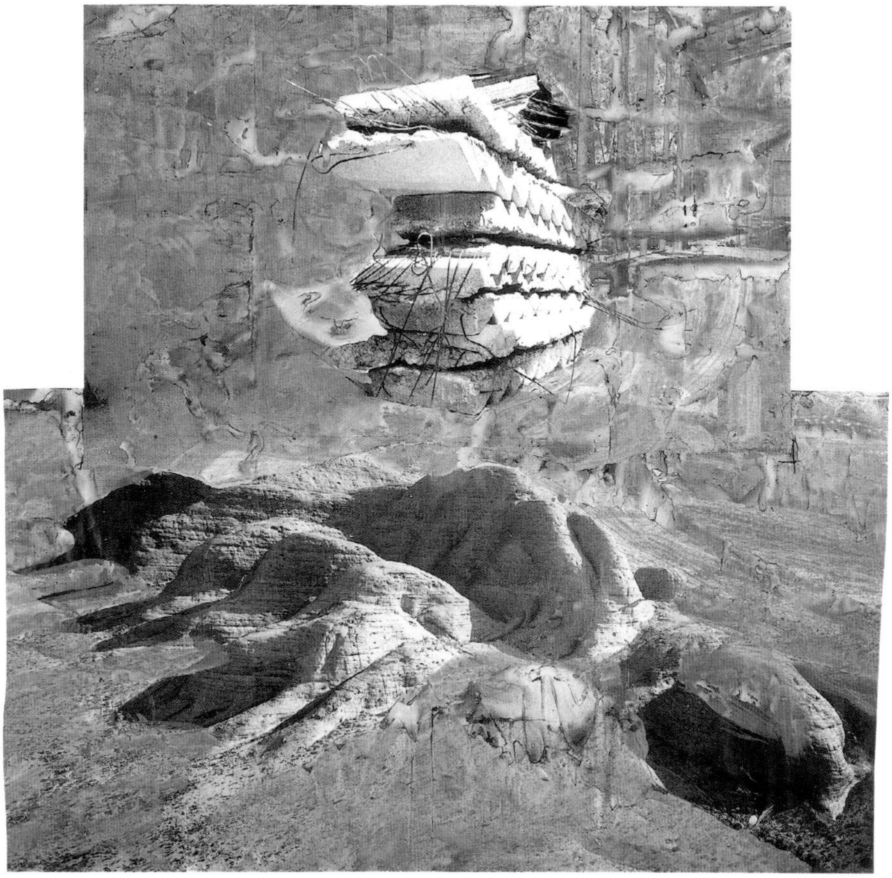

Benija, 2003
Gouache on photo paper
43 ½ × 43 ⅜ inches (110.5 × 110 cm)

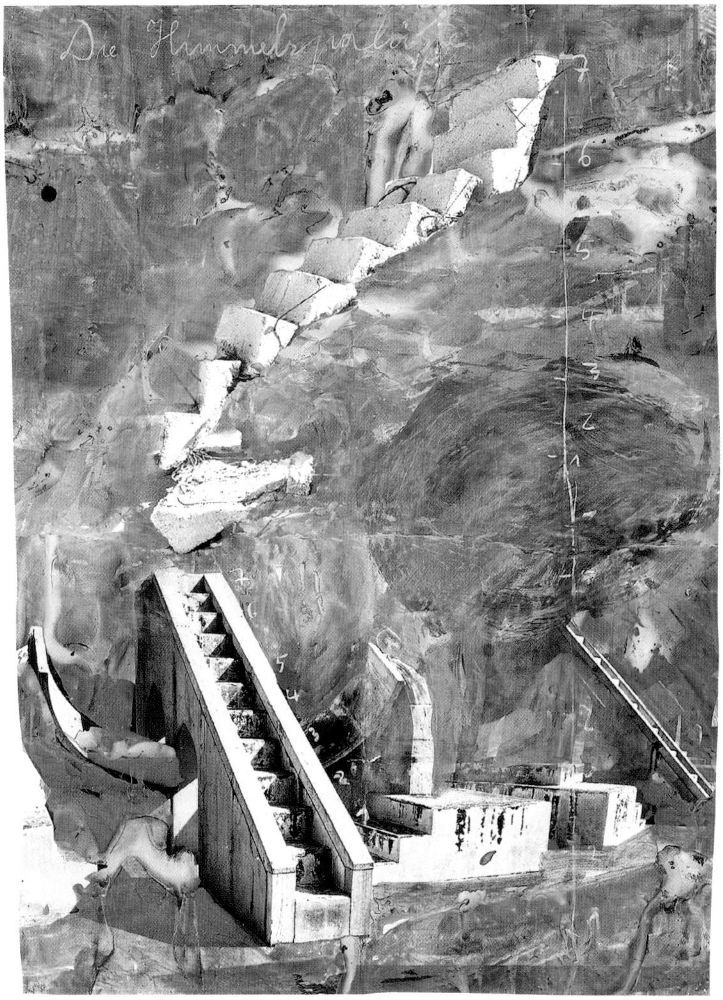

Die Himmelspaläste (The Heavenly Palaces), 2003
Gouache on photo paper
44¼ × 31¼ inches (112.5 × 79.3 cm)

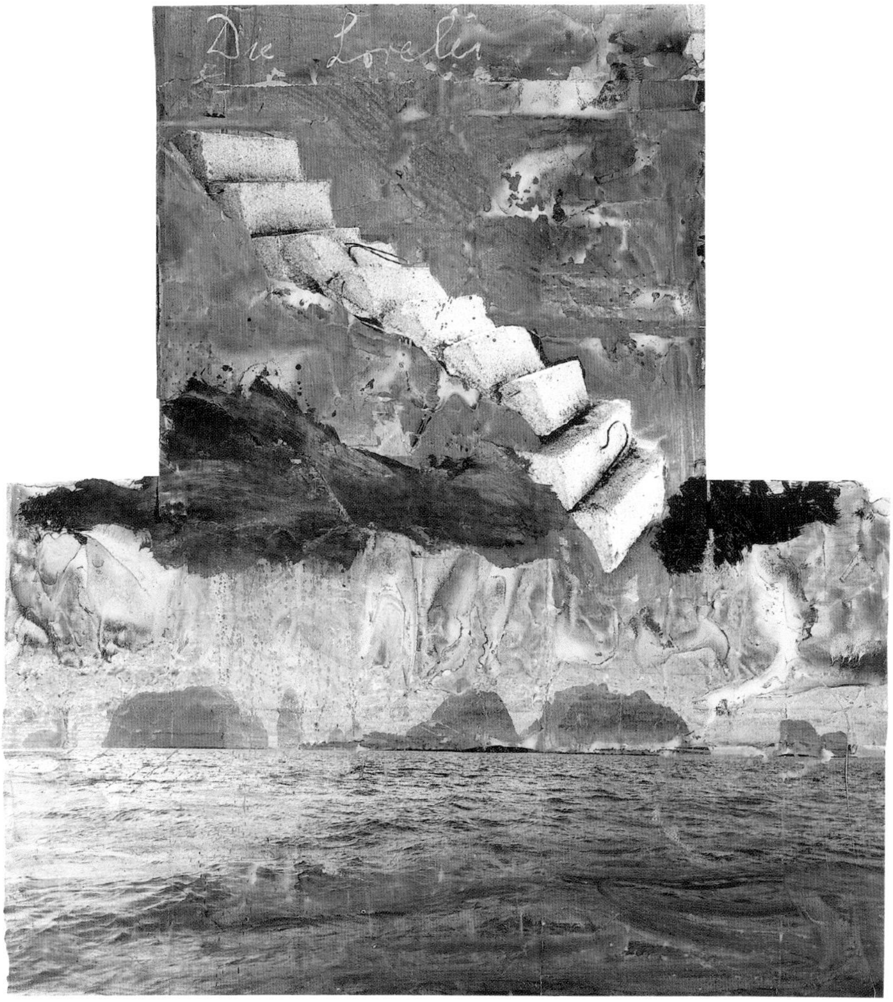

Die Lorelei, 2003
Gouache on photo paper
46 1/8 × 40 5/8 inches (117.3 × 103.3 cm)

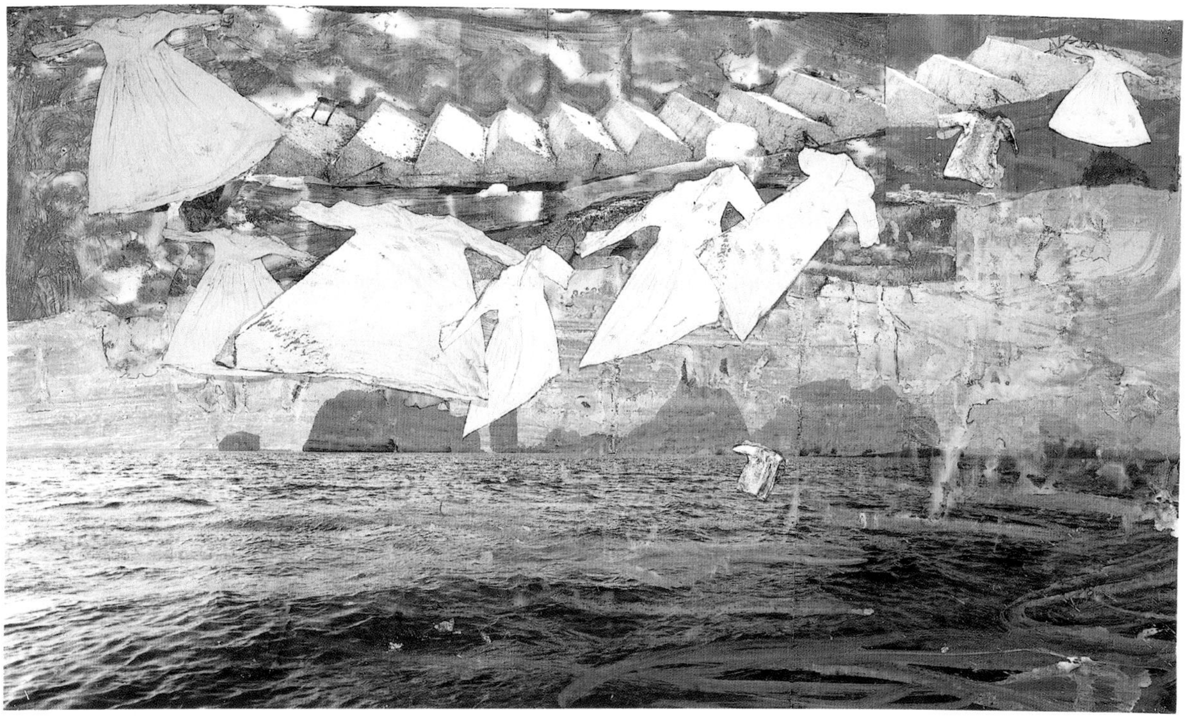

Hexen, 2003
Gouache on photo paper
30⅛ × 49¾ inches (76.5 × 126.3 cm)

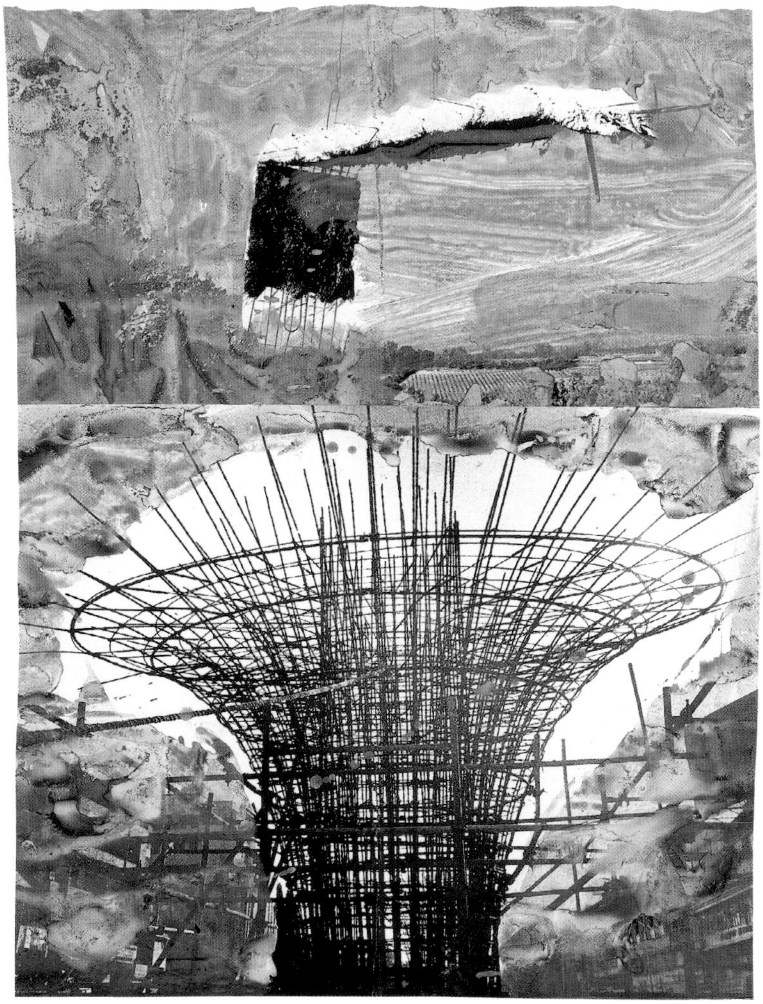

Nagpur, 2003
Gouache on photo paper
41 ¾ × 30 ¾ inches (106 × 78 cm)

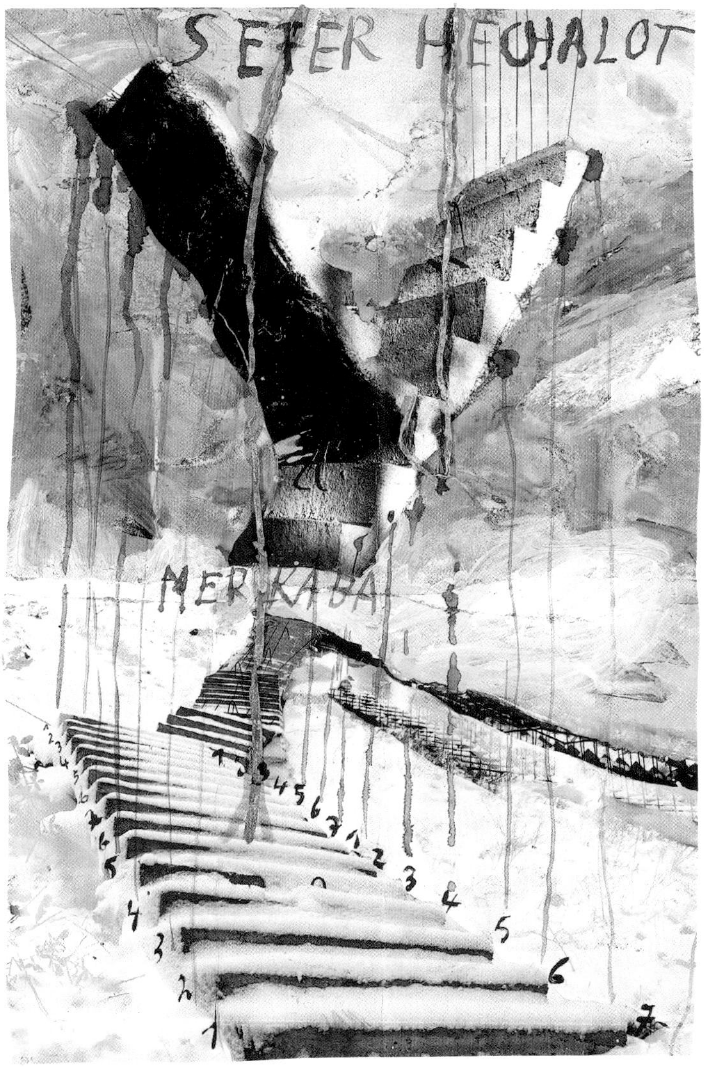

Sefer Hechaloth, 2003
Gouache on photo paper
44 ⅞ × 29 inches (114 × 73.5 cm)

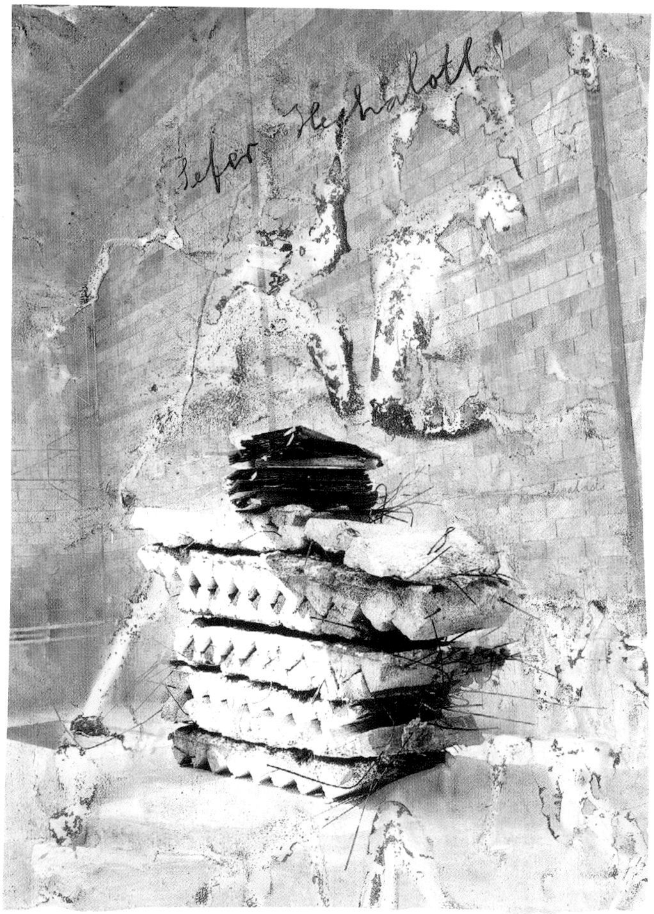

Sefer Hechaloth, 2003
Gouache on photo paper
32 ½ × 22 ⅞ inches (82.5 × 58 cm)

Am Anfang (In the Beginning), 2003

Melancholia, 2004

In both of these works, a three-dimensional geometric form hovers above a vast, desolate space. *Am Anfang*, a seascape, suggests a visualization of the creation story described in the first verses of Genesis: "In the beginning God created the heaven and the earth. And the earth was without form, and void; and darkness was upon the face of the deep. And the Spirit of God moved upon the waters." In *Melancholia*, the geometric form is emitted from a cloud of lead suspended over a murky desert.

This polyhedron appears in Albrecht Dürer's well-known and enigmatic *Melencolia I* of 1514, an engraving that depicts an angel surrounded by symbolic objects. Its title refers to one of the four humours of medieval physiology, which was thought to cause deep and lasting sadness if present in excess in the body. Melancholy has traditionally been associated with Saturn, the god of contemplation, and also with creativity, alchemy, and lead. Although the melancholic/Saturnine temperament is known as one of brooding or sullenness, it has also been revered as enabling a state in which profound self-knowledge becomes possible. Saturn in this context came to represent the contemplative life and the search for that which was most secret.

The polyhedron, which appears in many of Kiefer's works and is encountered variously lying and hanging in his studio, may appeal to Kiefer on several levels. Similar forms have been used throughout the history of hermetic art to represent the alchemical philosopher's stone, or *lapis*, the key to the Great Work and the highest expression of the human spirit. The form in Dürer's *Melencolia I* has been described as a model of a tool the artist created in order to enable himself to more accurately represent the material world. This allegory, then, uses the mastery of visual perception to represent gnosis, or mastery over earthly illusions. For Kiefer, the polyhedron may be an emblem of the key to perfect understanding.

In *Am Anfang* and *Melancholia*, Kiefer pits the rational architecture of the mind against the potentially unformed nature of the cosmos, imagining one explanation for our origin. He has said, "It is the artist's job to imagine the most impossible things. These are not answers. They are just possible entries into hidden things."

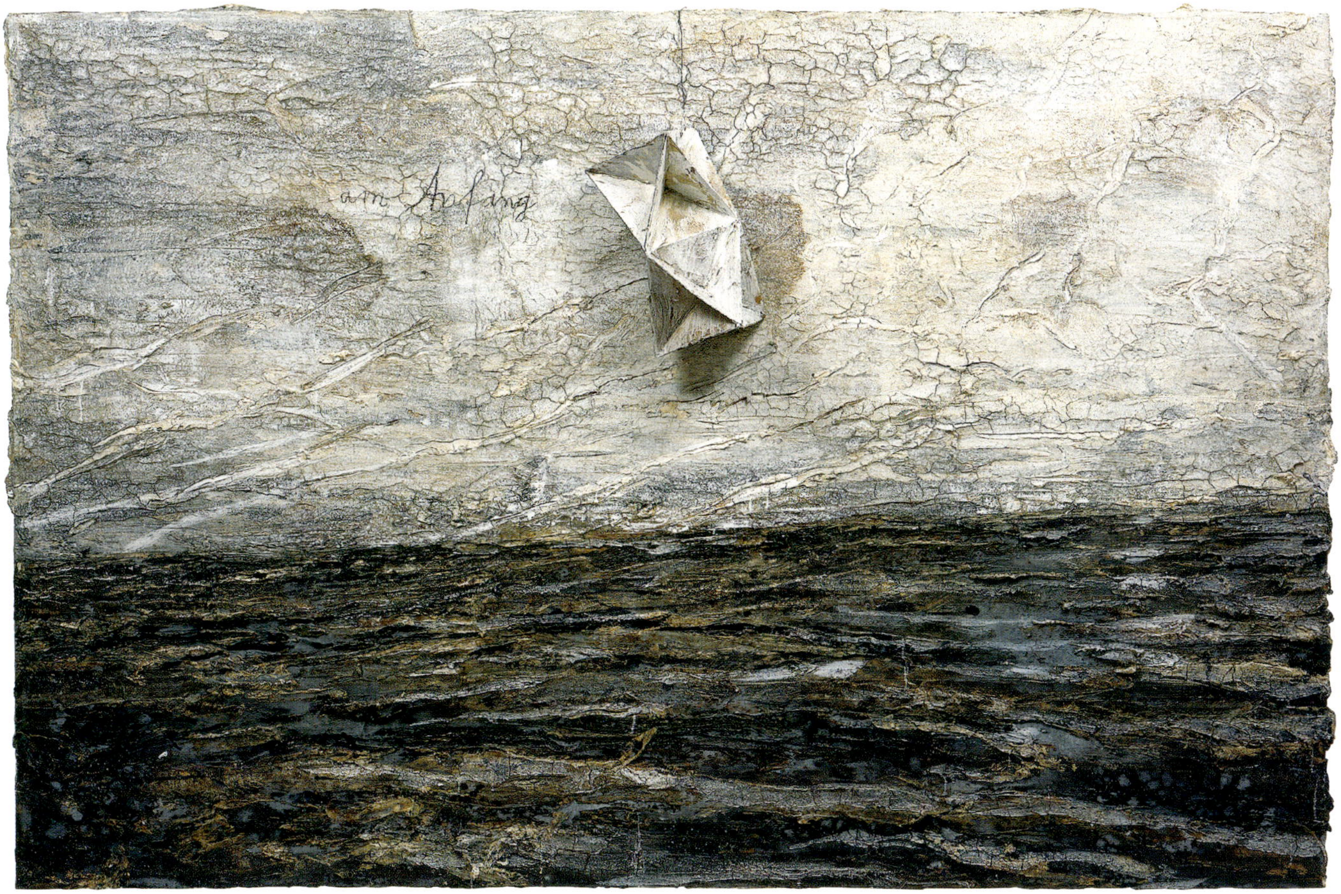

Am Anfang (In the Beginning), 2003
Oil, acrylic, and emulsion on canvas with polyhedron
74 ¾ × 110 ¼ inches (190 × 280 cm)

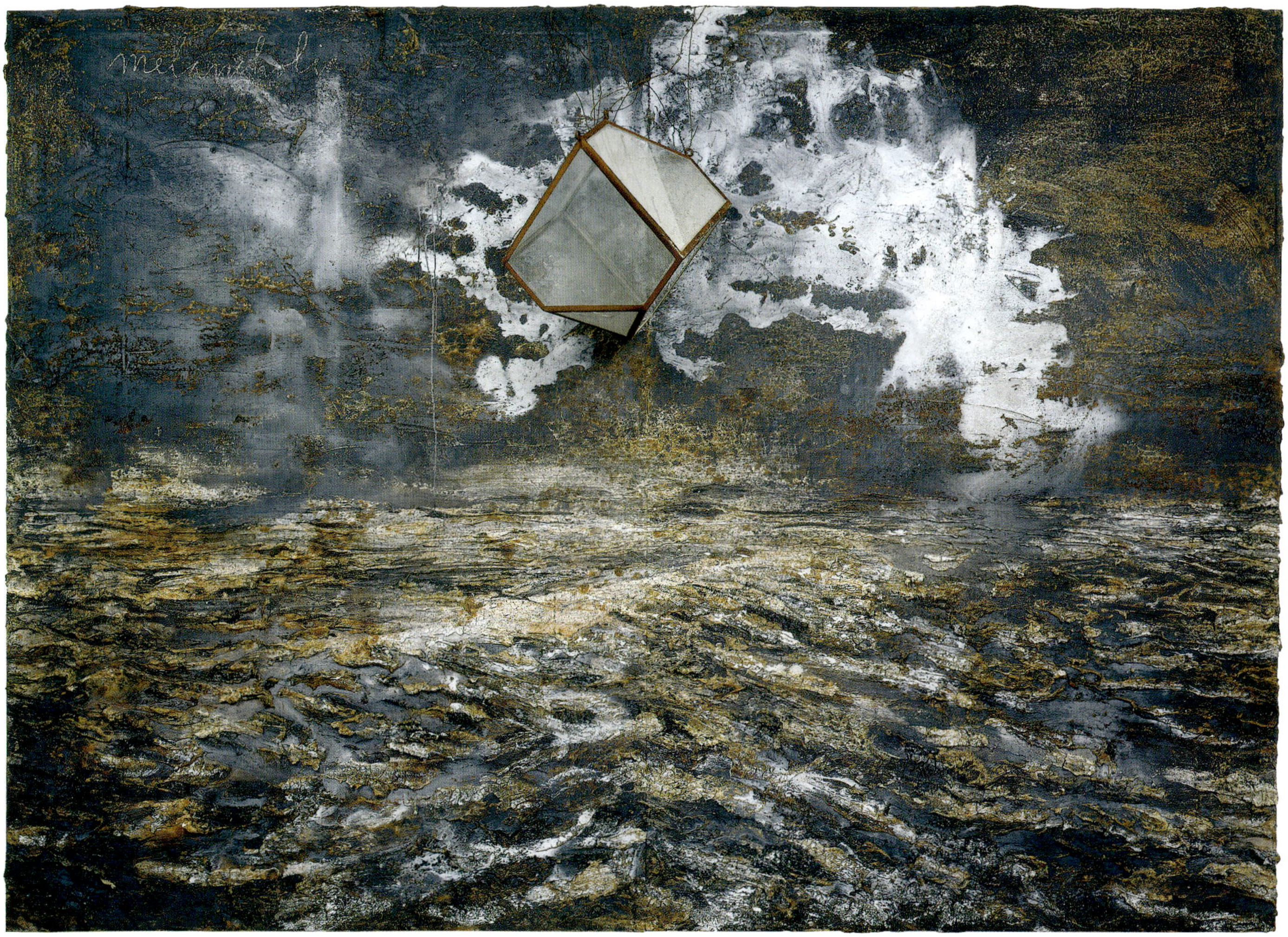

Melancholia, 2004
Oil, acrylic, and emulsion on canvas with glass polyhedron
110 ⅝ × 150 ⅜ inches (281 × 382 cm)

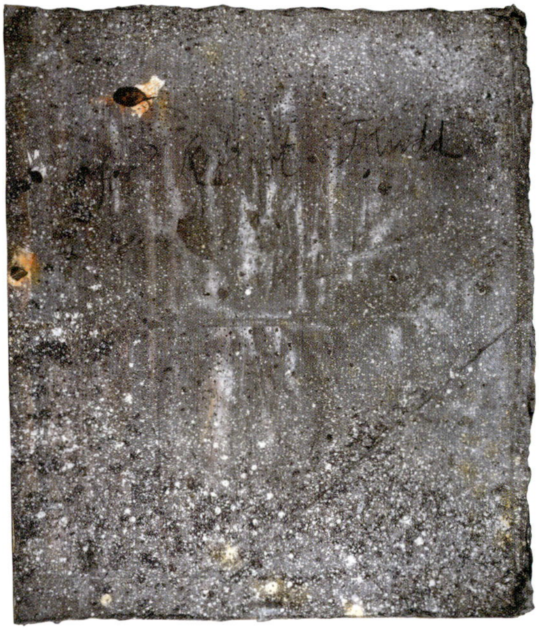

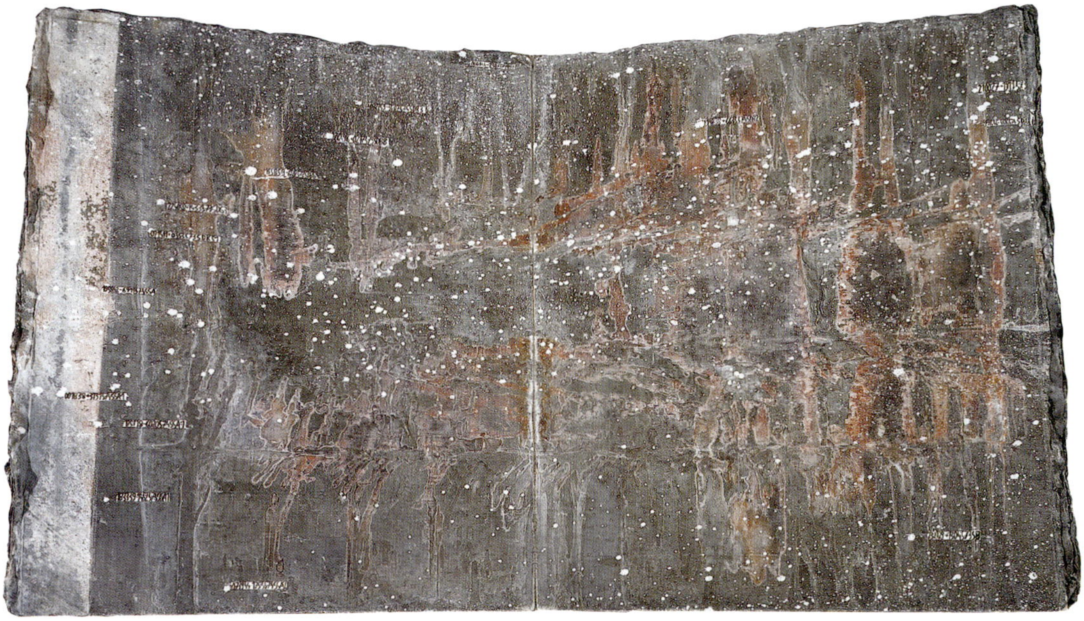

5|6

Für Robert Fludd (For Robert Fludd), 2003
Book, 28 pages. Lead and paint
41 × 32¼ × 3½ inches (104 × 82 × 9 cm) (bound volume)

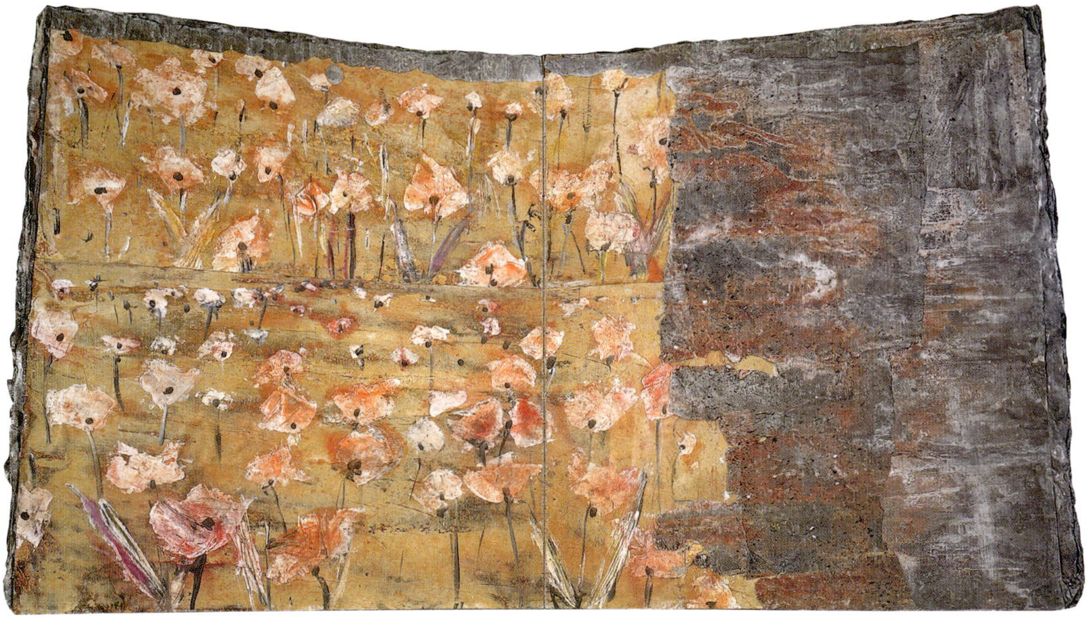

7|8

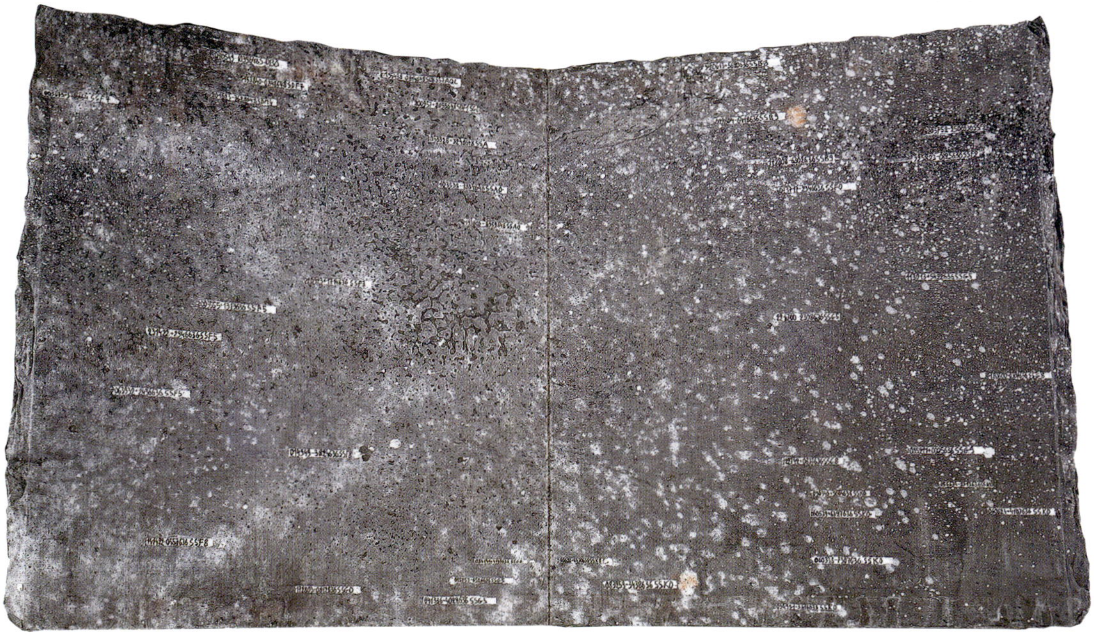

11|12

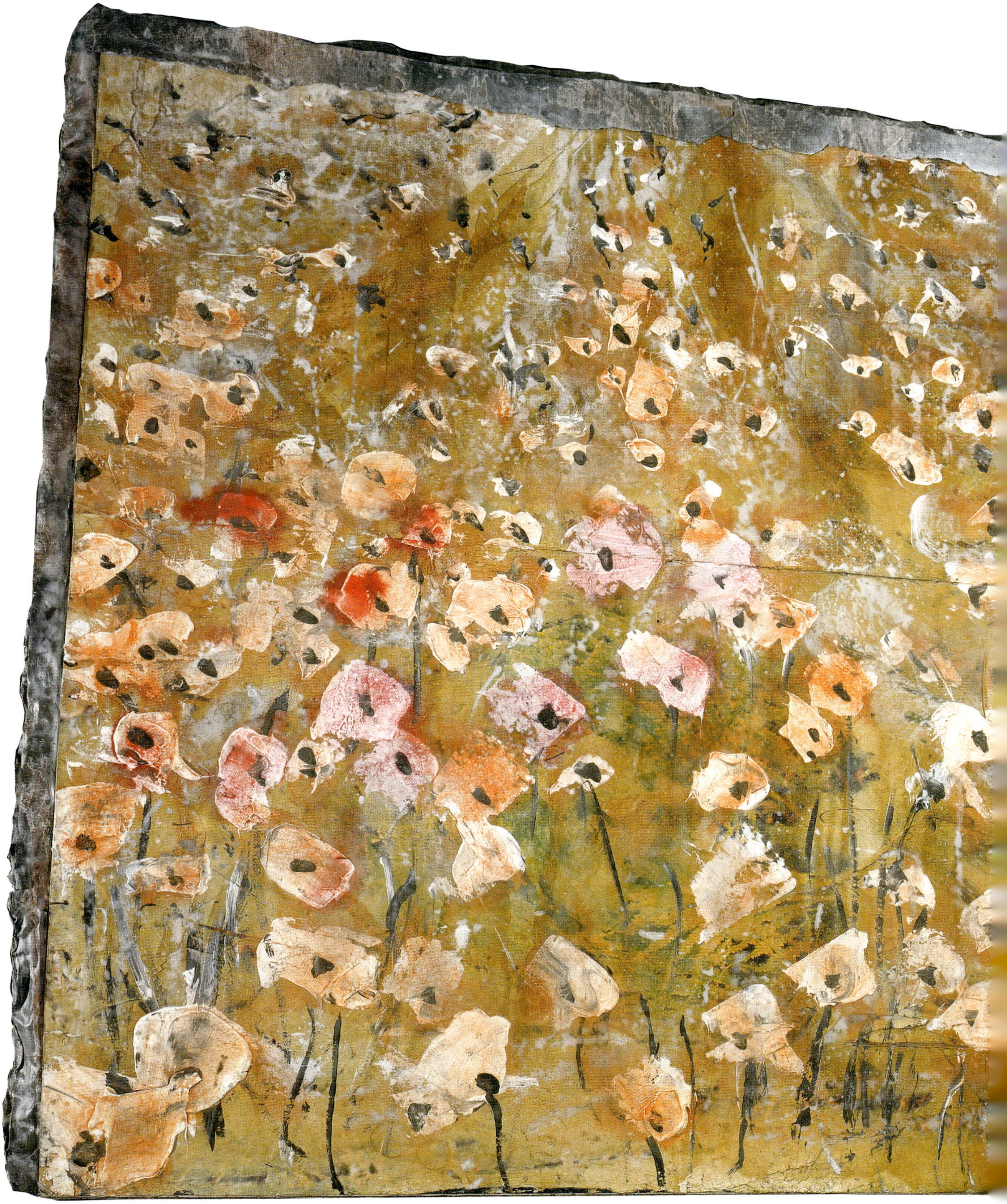

13 | 14

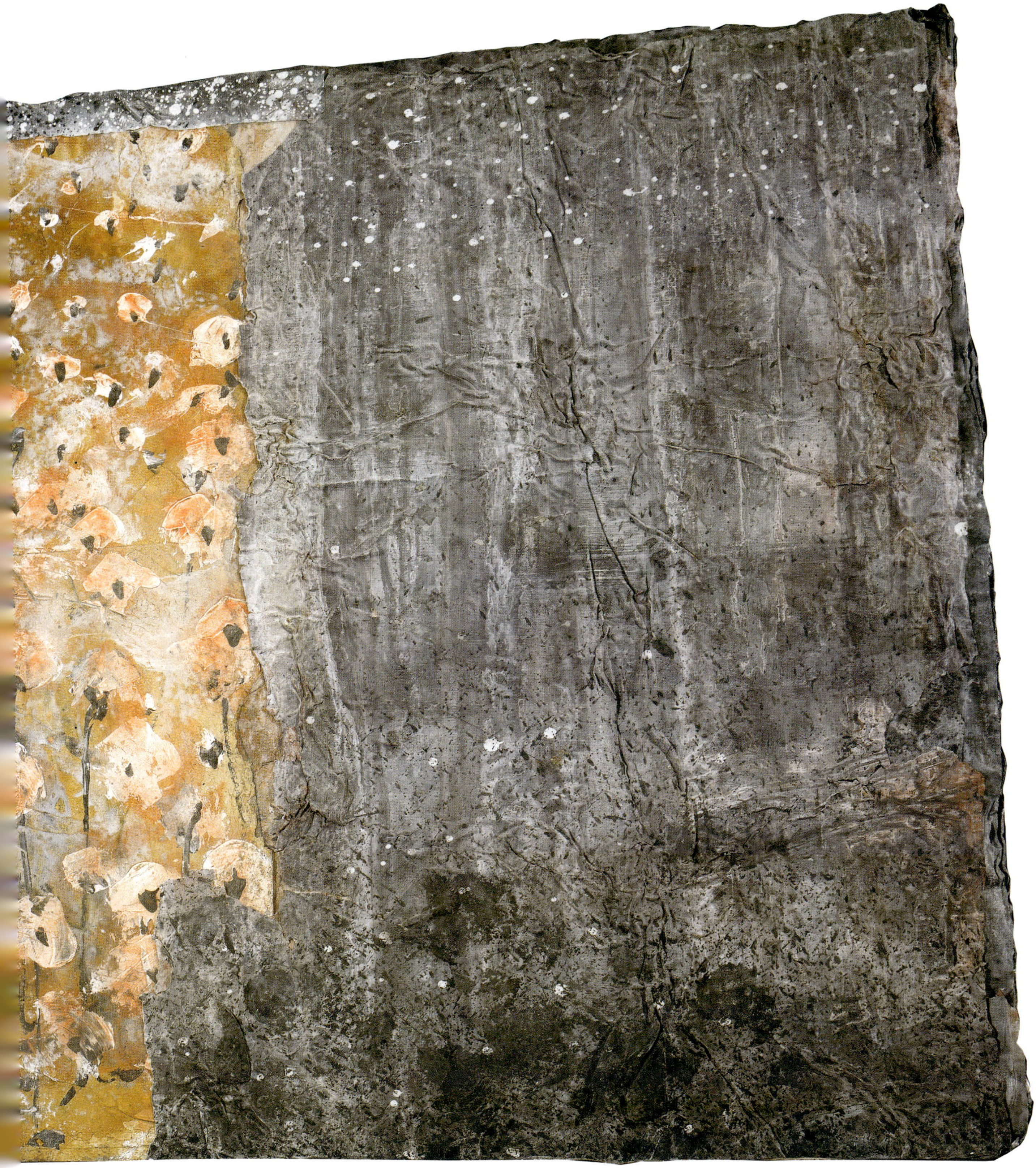

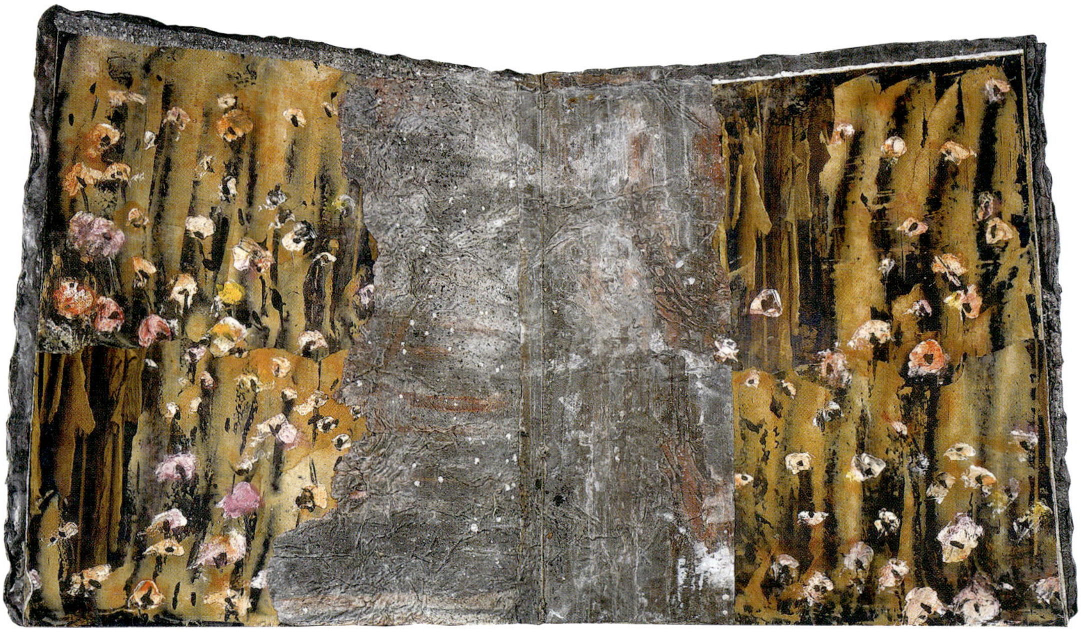

19 | 20

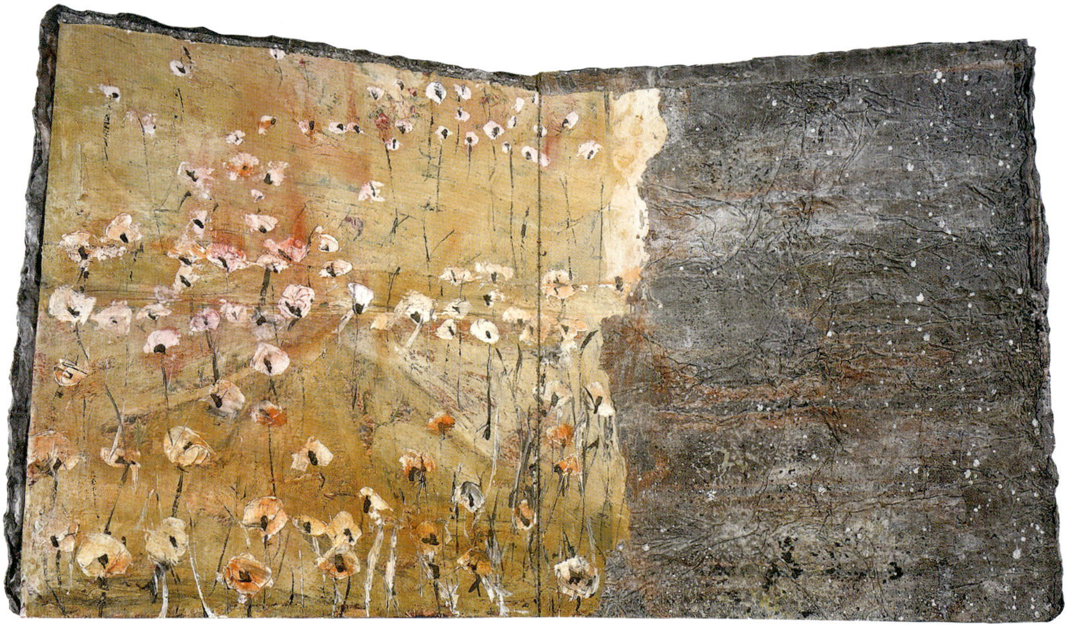

21 | 22

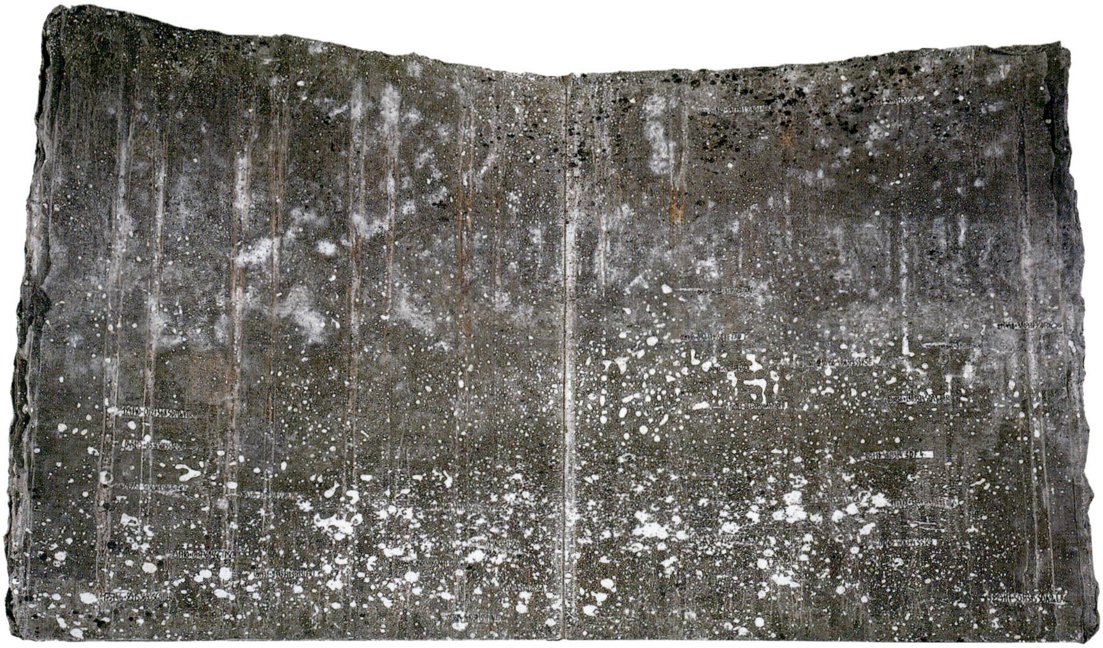

23 | 24

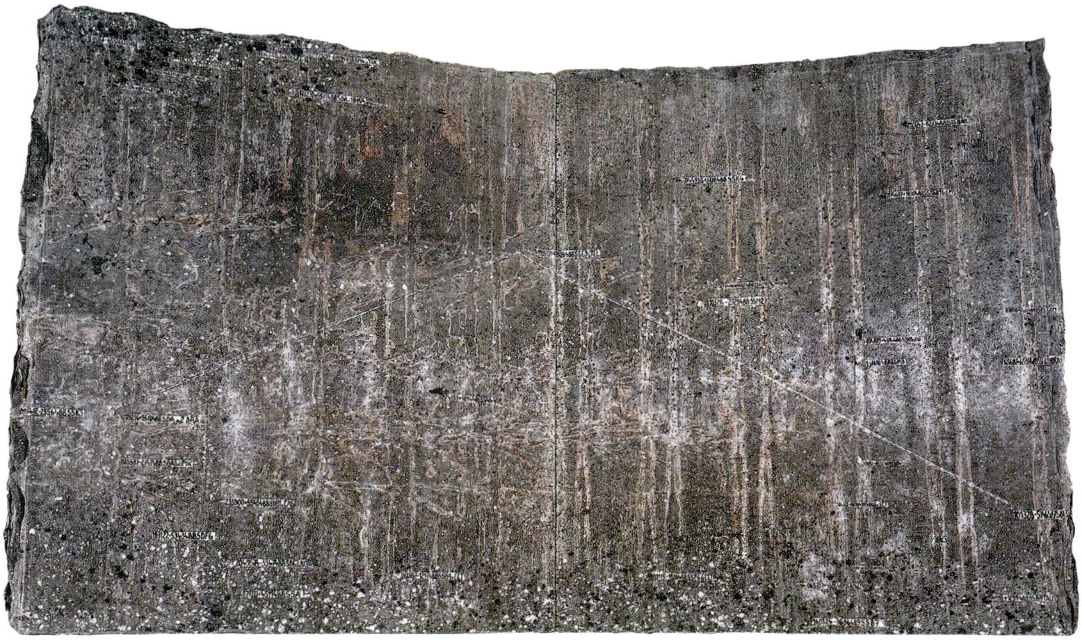

25 | 26

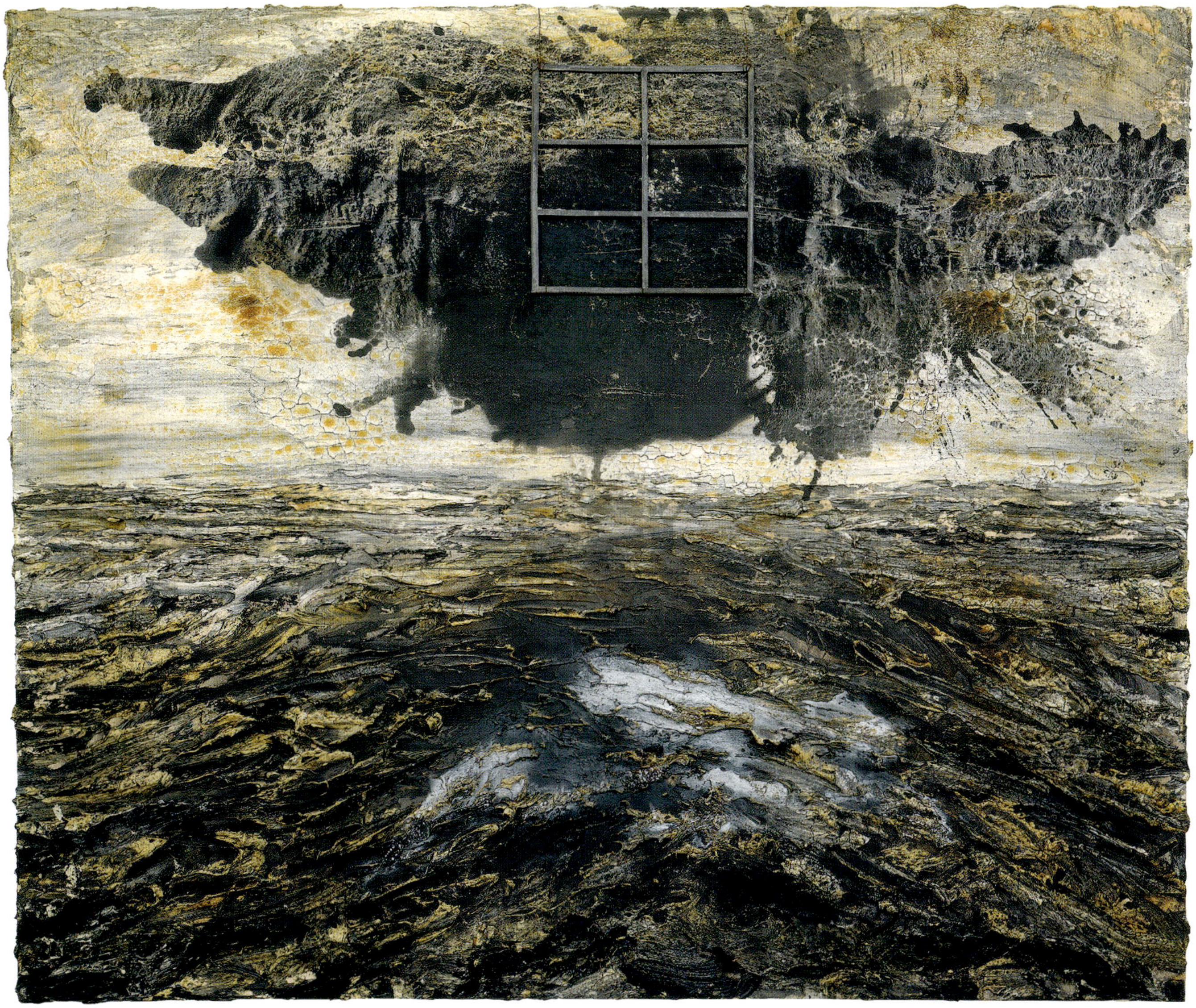

Aschenblume (Ash Flower), 2004
Oil, acrylic, and emulsion on canvas
95 ⅝ × 110 ⅞ inches (243 × 281.5 cm)

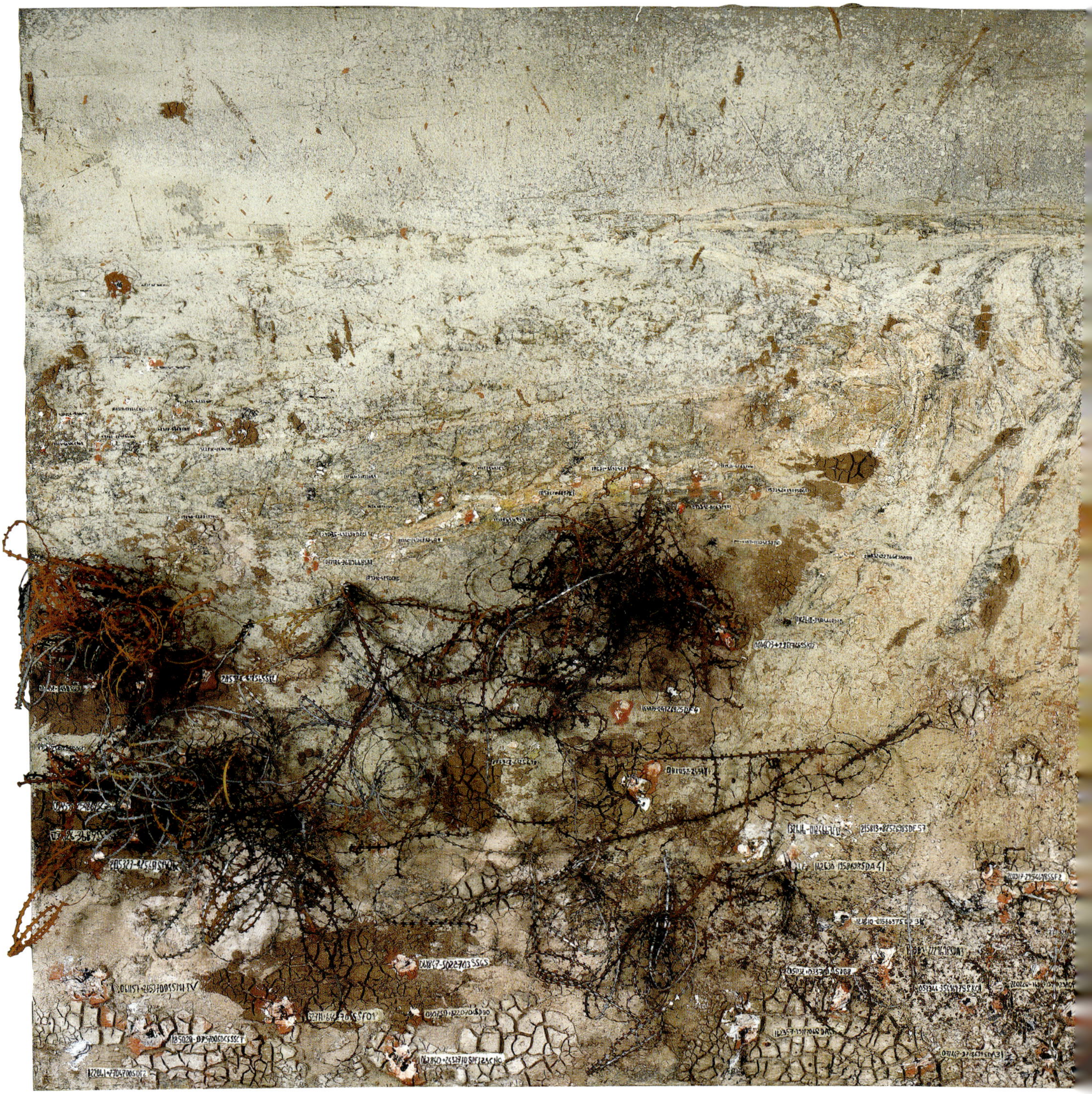

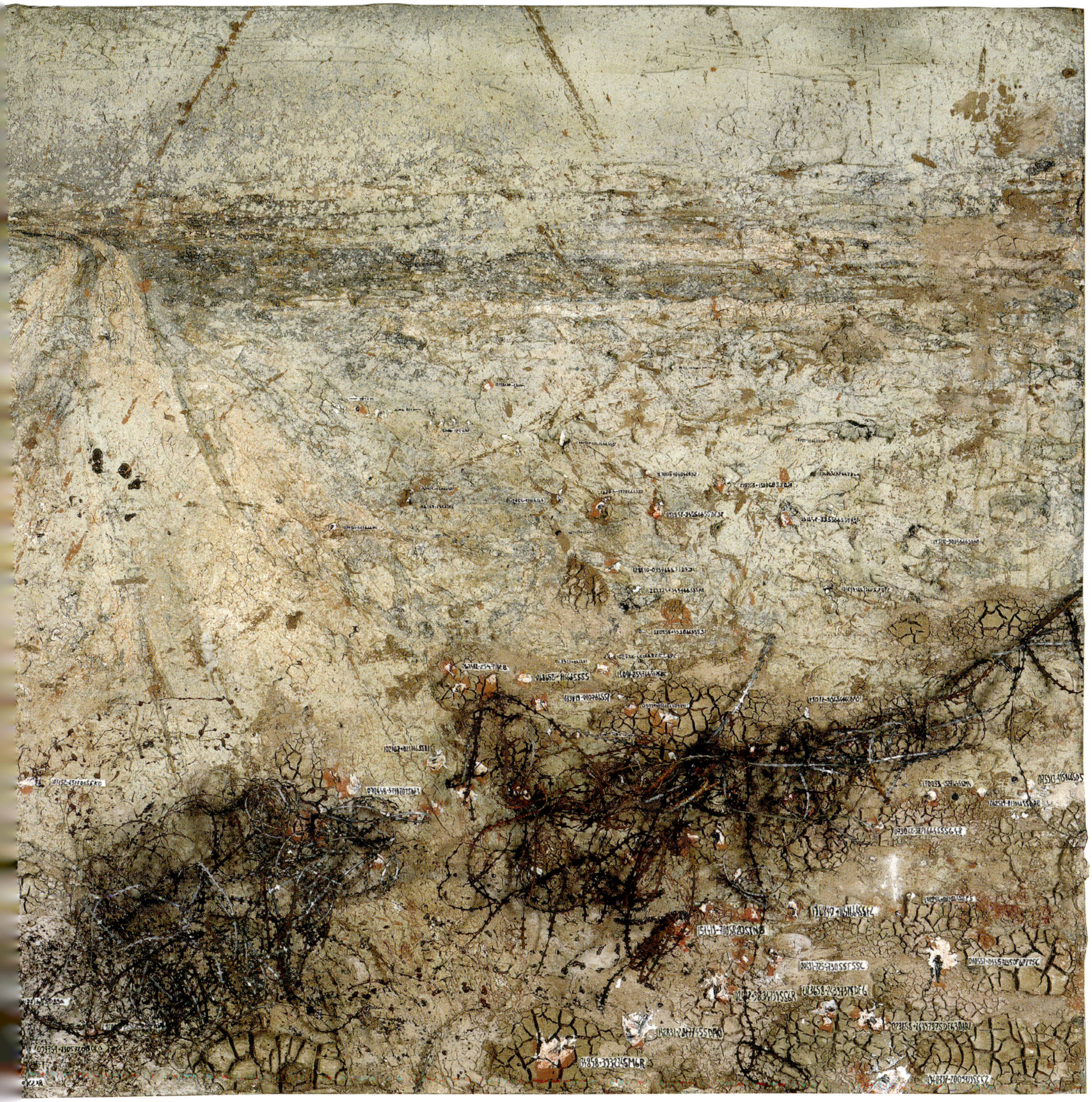

Himmel auf Erden (Heaven on Earth), 1998–2004
Oil, emulsion, and acrylic on canvas with barbed wire
110 ¼ × 220 ½ inches (280 × 560 cm)

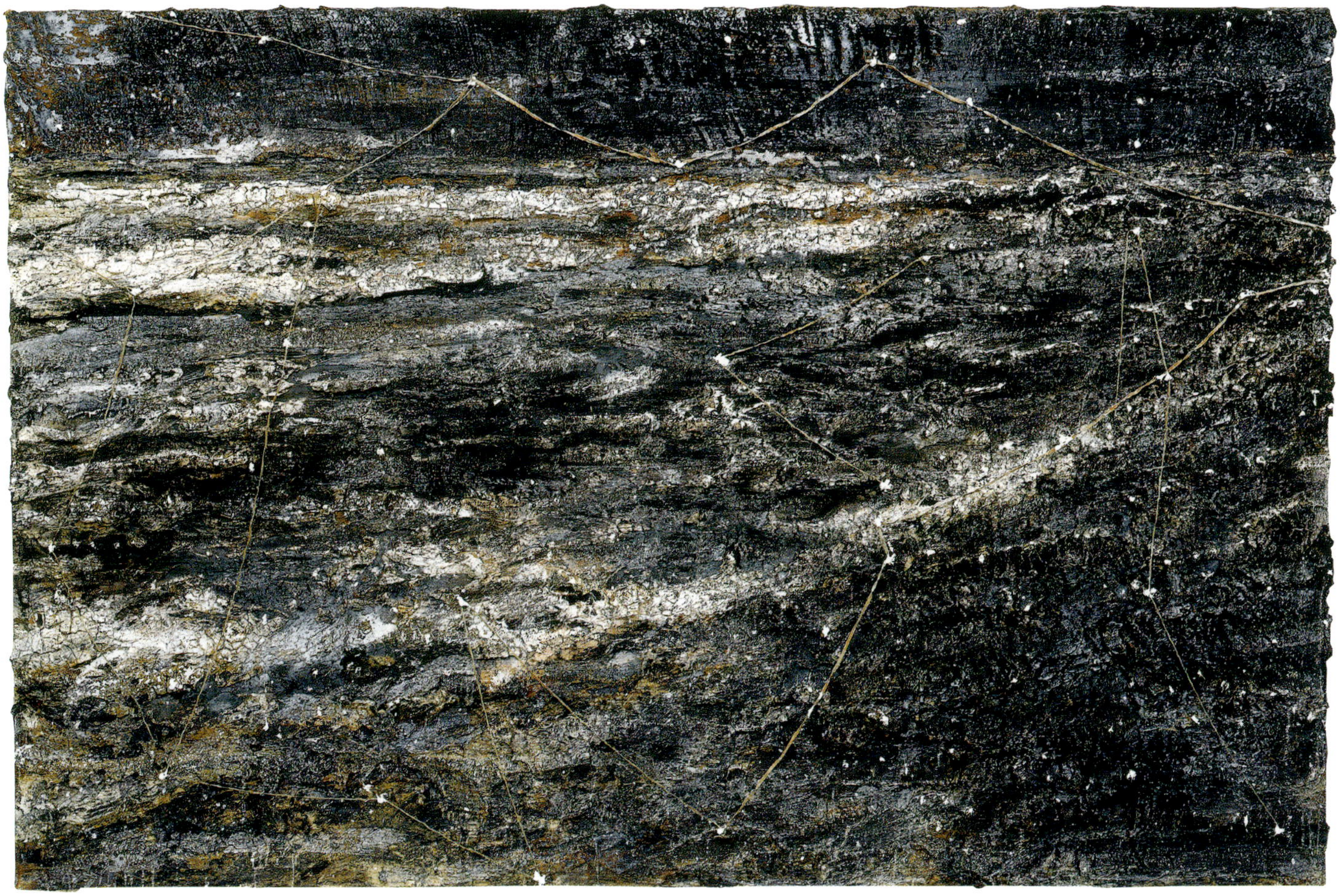

Voyage au bout de la nuit, 2004
Oil, acrylic, and emulsion on canvas with metal strips
75 × 111 ⅜ inches (190.5 × 283 cm)

Burda Moden 92, 2005
Elektra, 2005
Rorate Caeli, 2005
Sefer Hechaloth, 2005

Kiefer explores layers of reality and perception in four recent books that investigate the relationship between the earth and the stars. The pages of *Elektra* and *Rorate Caeli* are covered with dried earth and plants, bringing to mind the evolution of bookmaking; the first books were clay tablets, and later, paper was made of plants and trees.

The earth books are an imaginary suggestion of a new world, evoking the very beginning of the material world as described in the second book of Genesis: "These are the generations of the heavens and of the earth when they were created, in the day that the Lord God made the earth and the heavens, And every plant of the field before it was in the earth, and every herb of the field before it grew: for the Lord God had not caused it to rain upon the earth, and there was not a man to till the ground. But there went up a mist from the earth, and watered the whole face of the ground. And the Lord God formed man of the dust of the ground, and breathed into his nostrils the breath of life; and man became a living soul."

Rorate Caeli is the title and refrain of a Catholic hymn that uses rain in the desert as a metaphor for Christ's coming to earth and returning to heaven. Further connecting the earth books with the heavenly realms, *Elektra* takes its title from one of the brightest stars in the Pleiades (Seven Sisters) star cluster.

The new star books likewise connect heaven and earth. In *Burda Moden 92* a female figure floats, or is "buried," in the cosmos. She is surrounded by lines, which are connected to form geometric shapes that suggest star maps or cracks in the earth. *Sefer Hechaloth* depicts metal tunnels into the sky. Onto the starry pages of this book Kiefer has superimposed photographs of the long metal tunnels in Barjac that connect his living quarters to his studio. He has created an echo of *Resurrexit* (page 61), which depicts the wooden staircase leading to the artist's attic studio, whose door is closed. Here, the tunnels lead to open space. Sometimes cut or photographed at oblique angles, they suggest a vortex in the cosmos. Titled for the mystical Sefer Hechaloth, which has enduring resonance for Kiefer, this book depicts one of many imaginary bridges he has created between the artist's studio and the heavens.

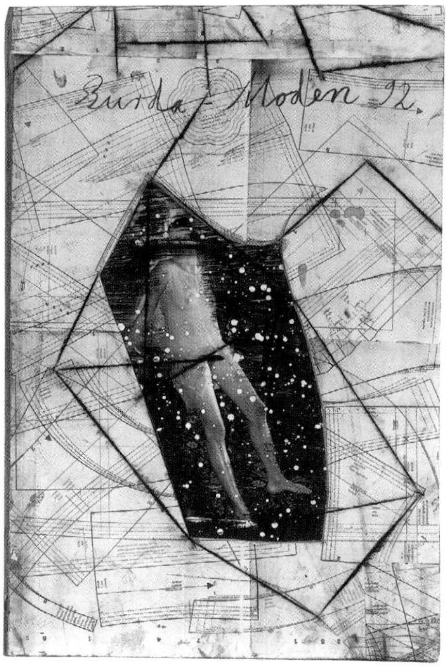

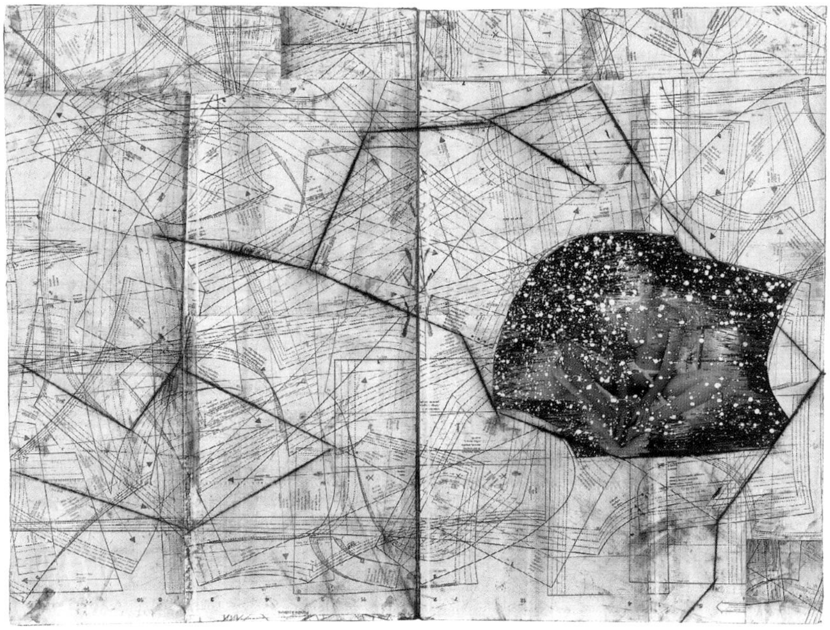

12 | 13

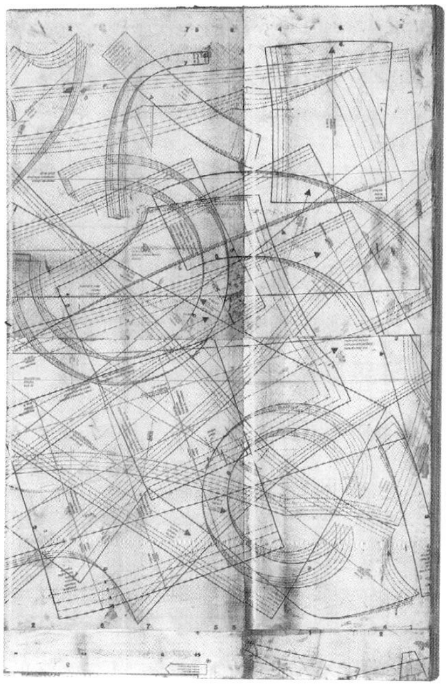

20 | 21

Burda Moden 92, 2005
Book, 21 double pages. Photographs and paper on cardboard
31⅞ × 20½ × 2¾ inches (81 × 52 × 7 cm) (bound volume)

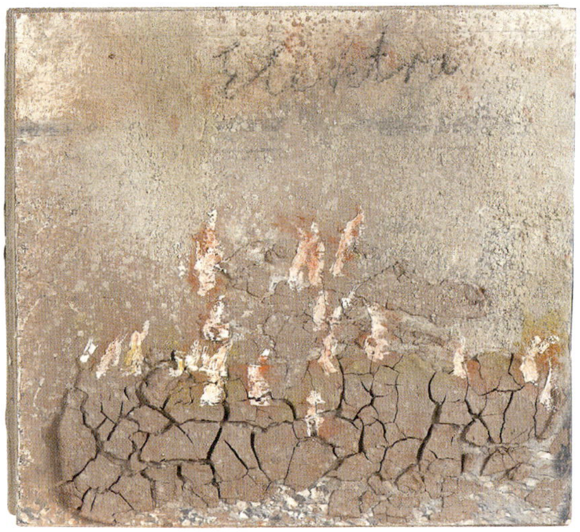

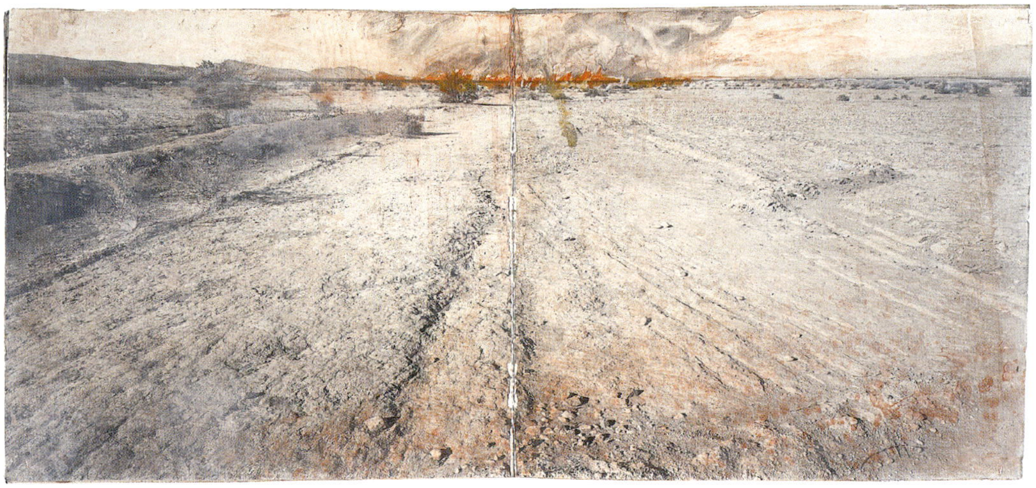

6 | 7

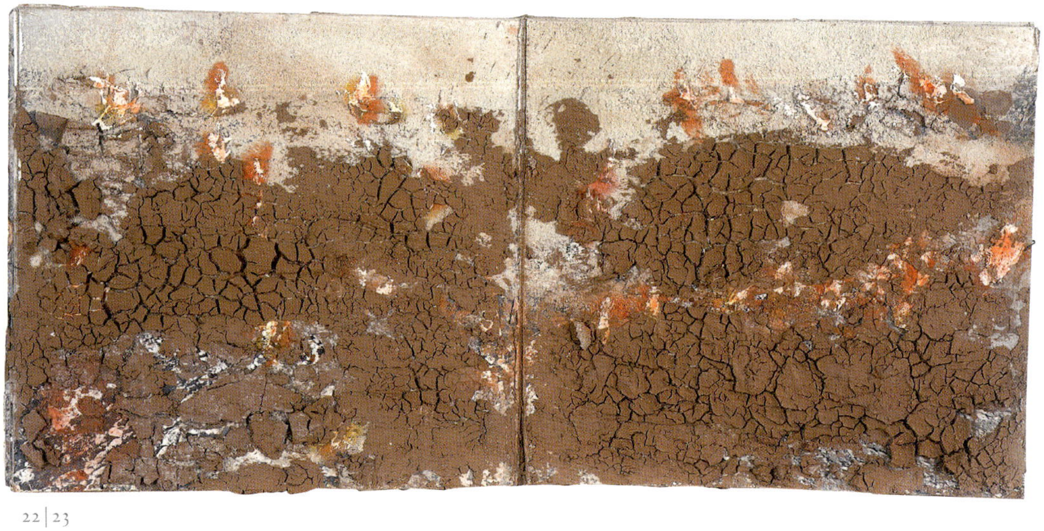

22 | 23

Elektra, 2005
Book, 29 double pages. Sand and clay on photographs on cardboard
23⅝ × 25⅛ × 6¼ inches (60 × 64 × 16 cm) (bound volume)

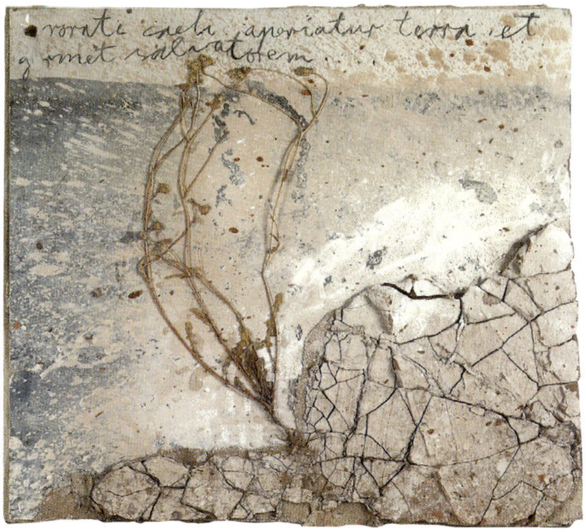

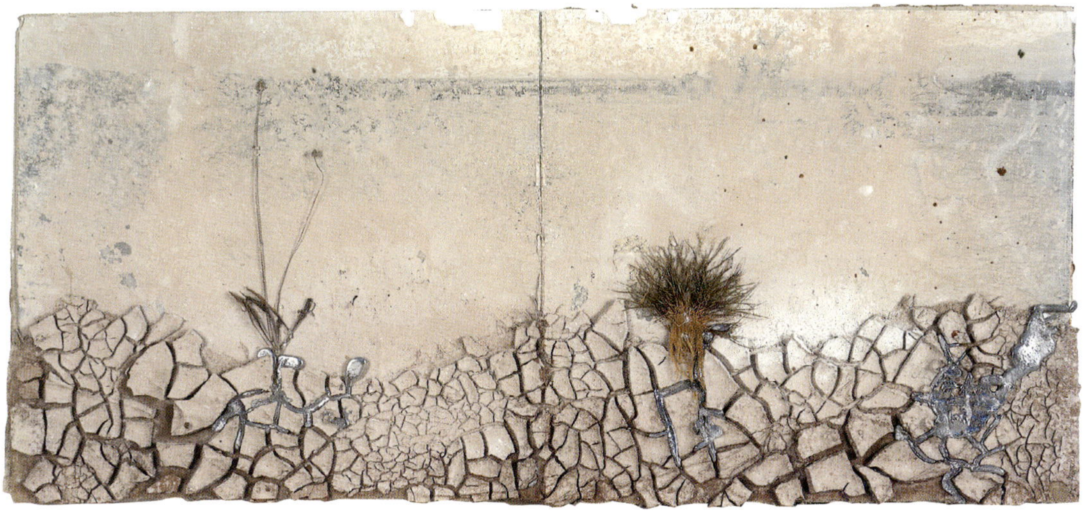

2 | 3

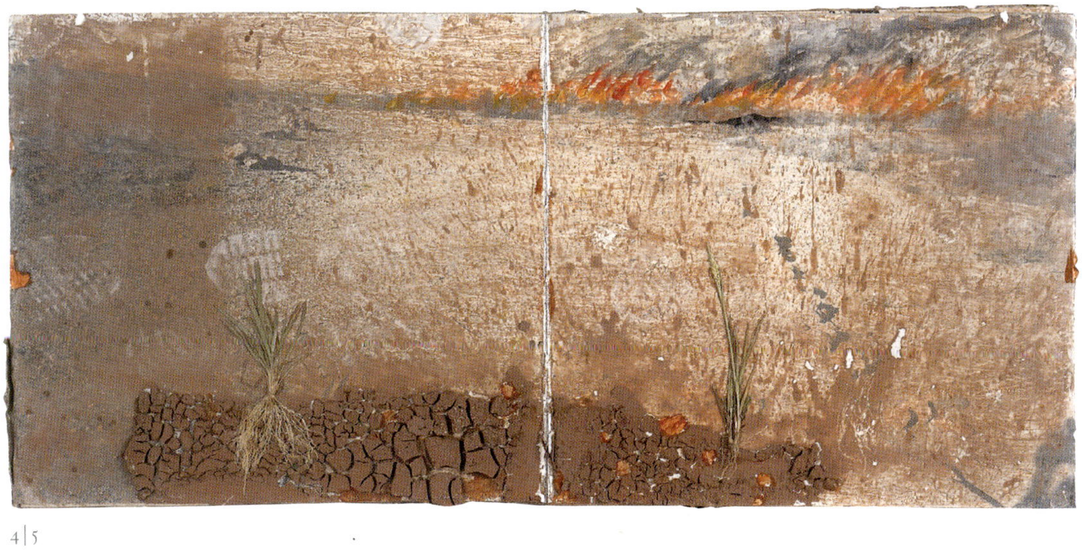

4 | 5

Rorate Caeli, 2005

Book, 17 double pages. Dried plants, clay, and sand on photographs on cardboard

$23\frac{5}{8} \times 25\frac{1}{2} \times 7\frac{1}{2}$ inches (60 × 65 × 19 cm) (bound volume)

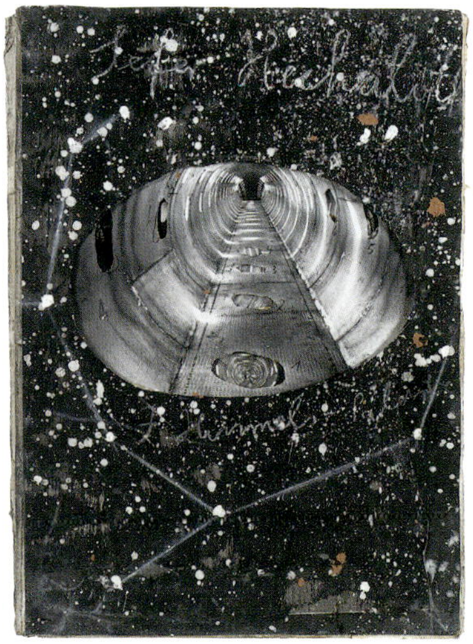

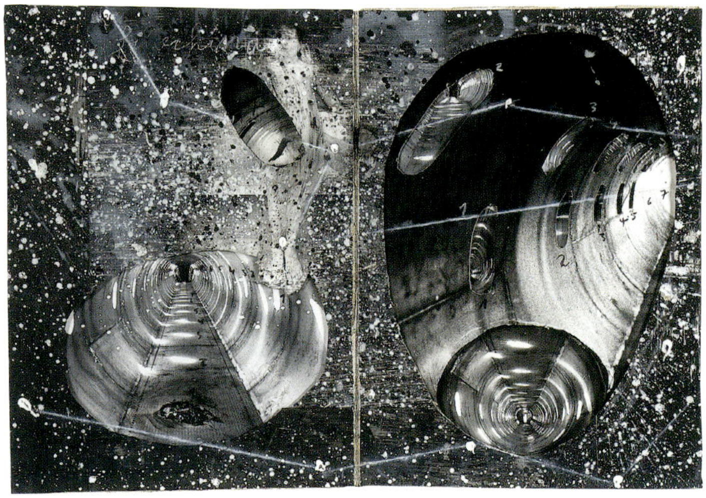

4|5

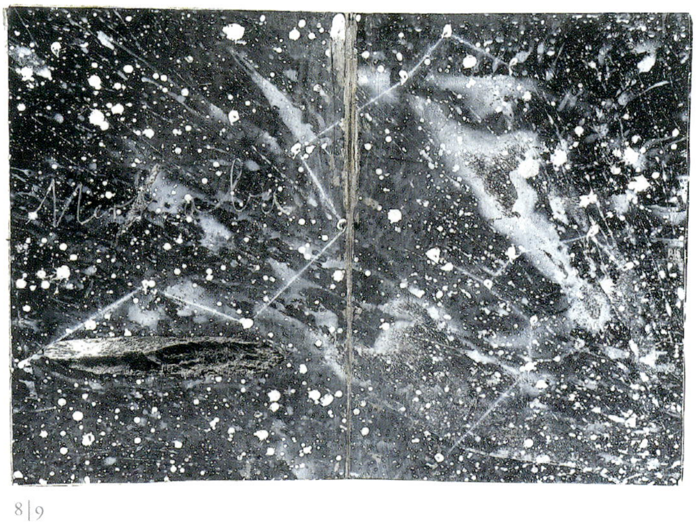

8|9

Sefer Hechaloth, 2005
Book, 11 double pages. Photographs and paper on cardboard
23⅝ × 16½ × 3 inches (60 × 42 × 7.5 cm) (bound volume)

Heaven Is an Idea

Photographs and Interview
Anselm Kiefer

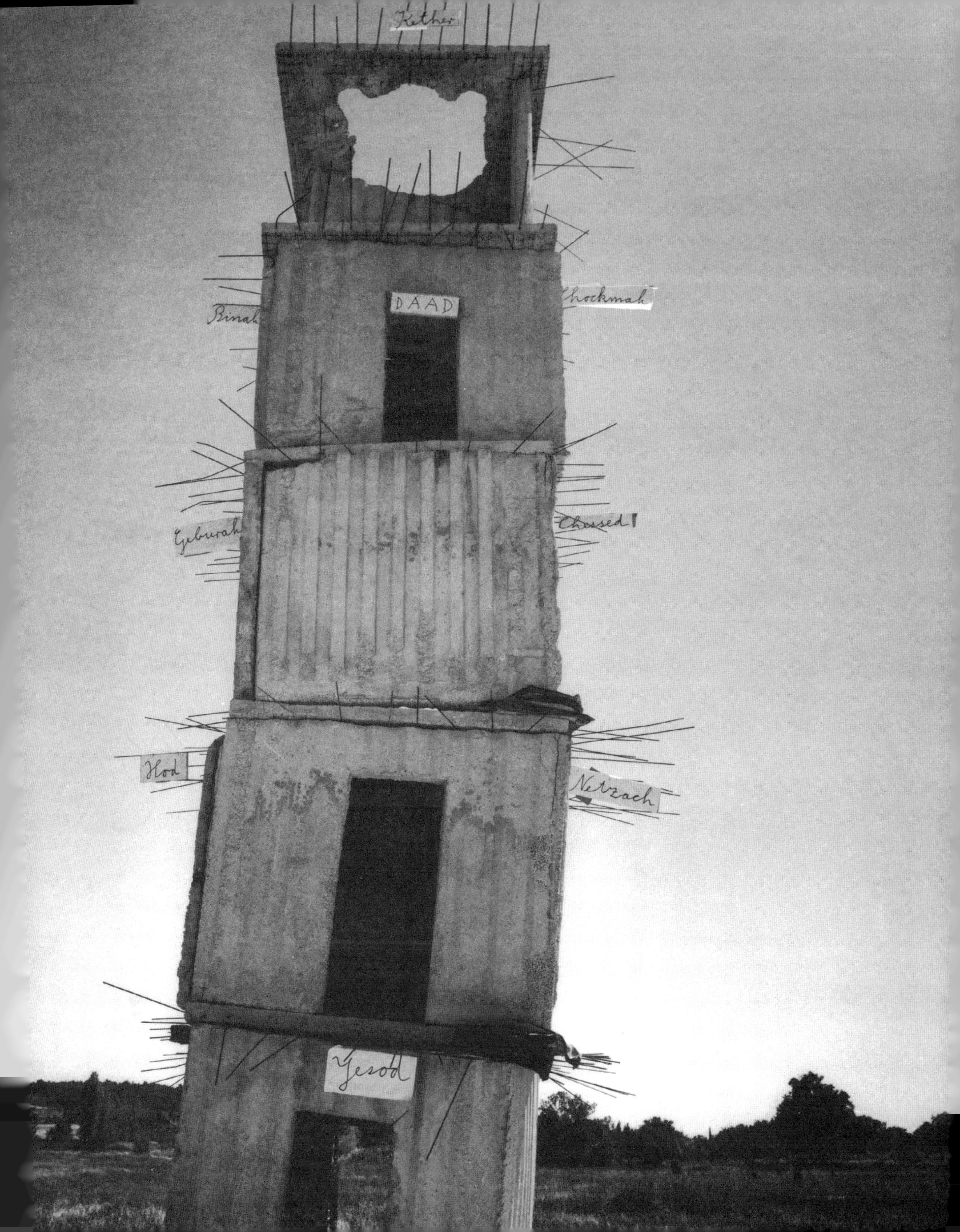
Kether
DAAD
Binah
Chockmah
Geburah
Chassed
Hod
Netzach
Yesod

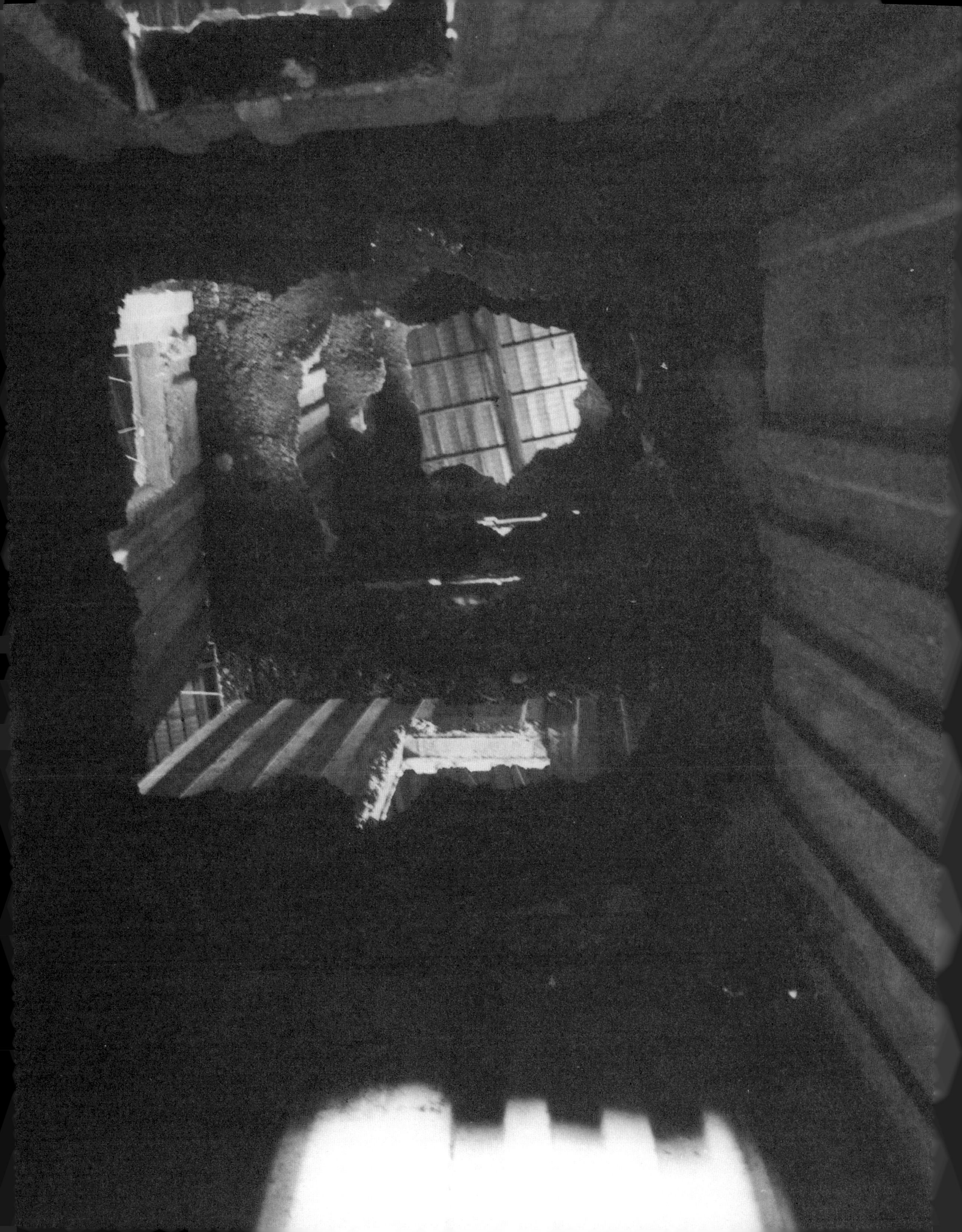

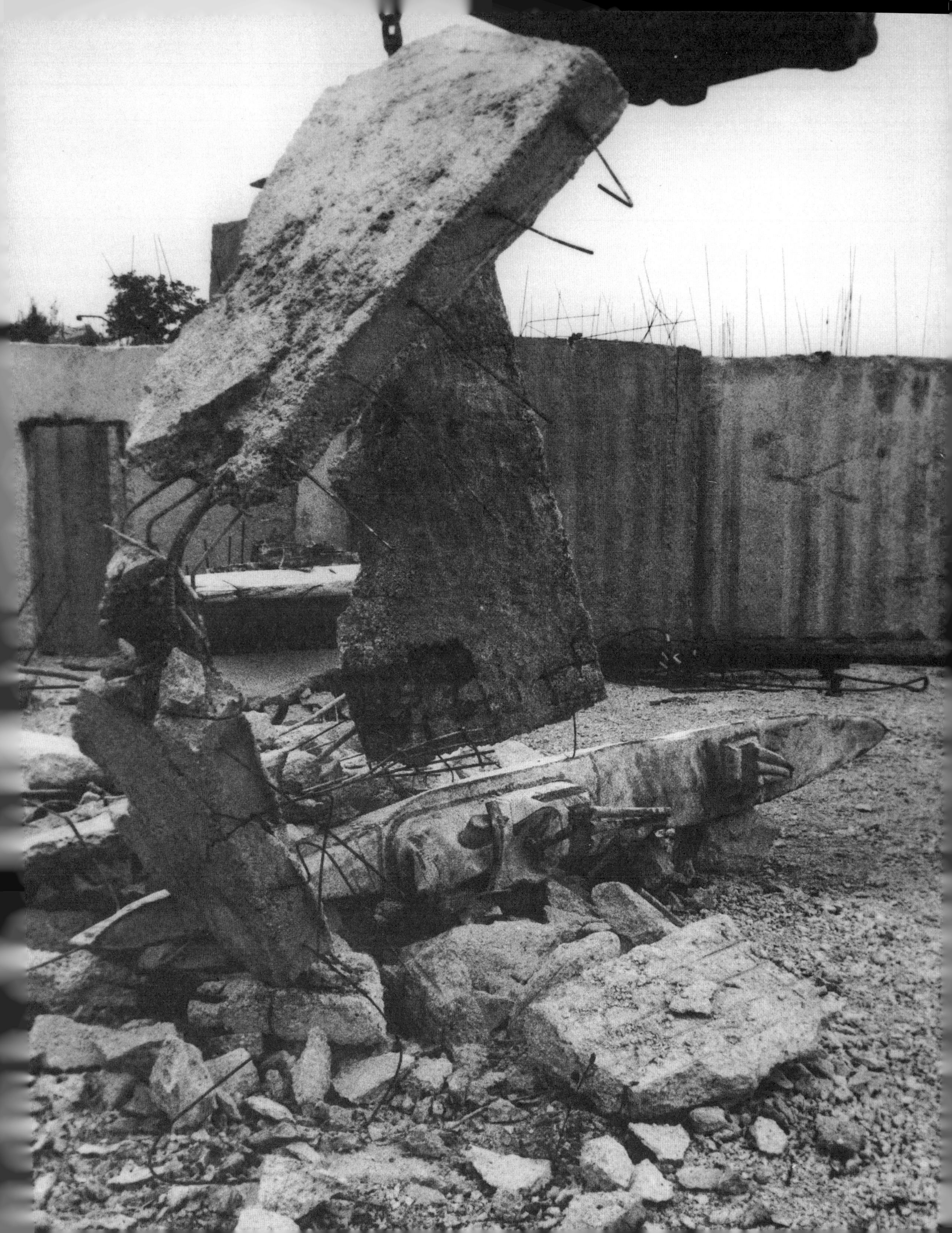

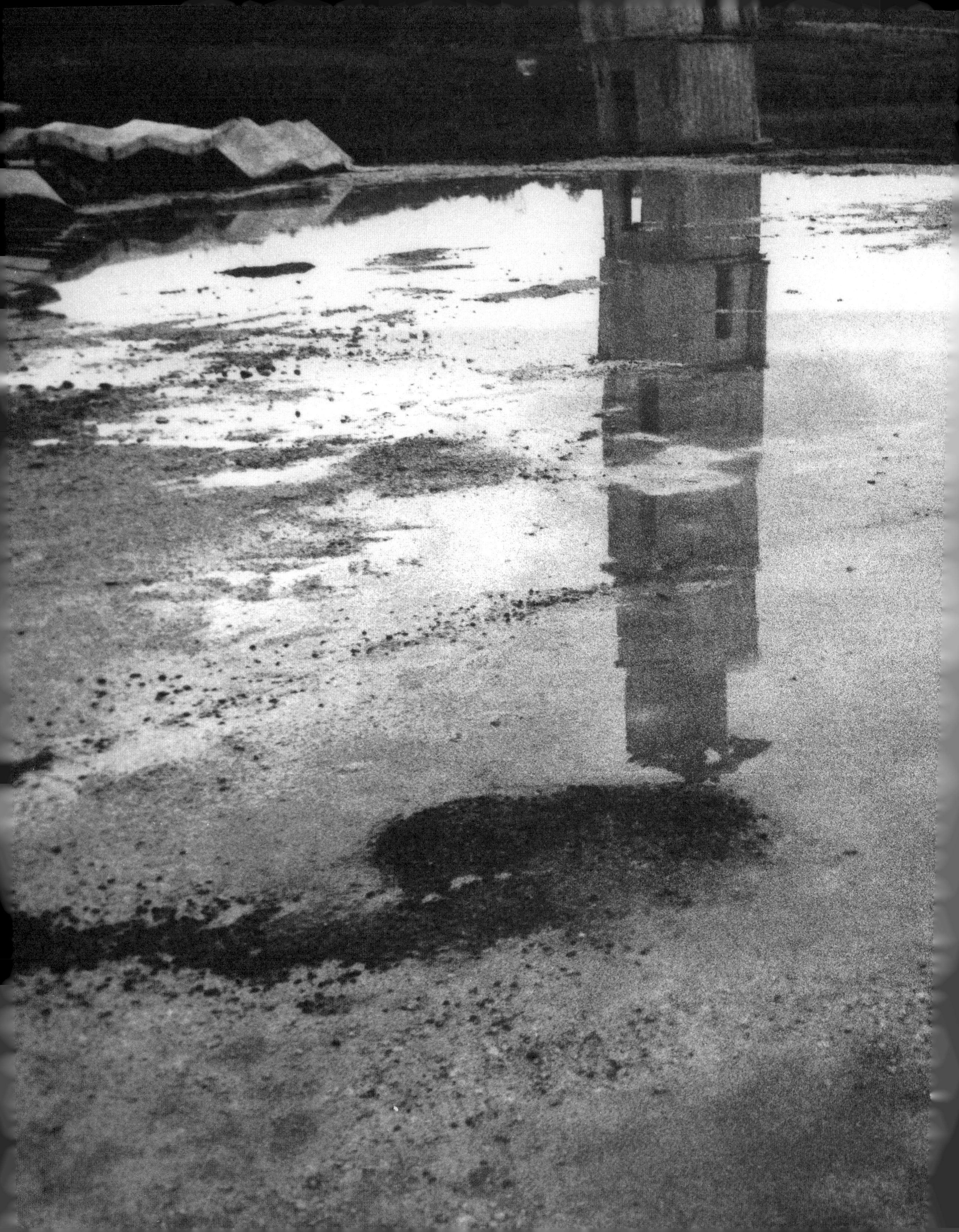

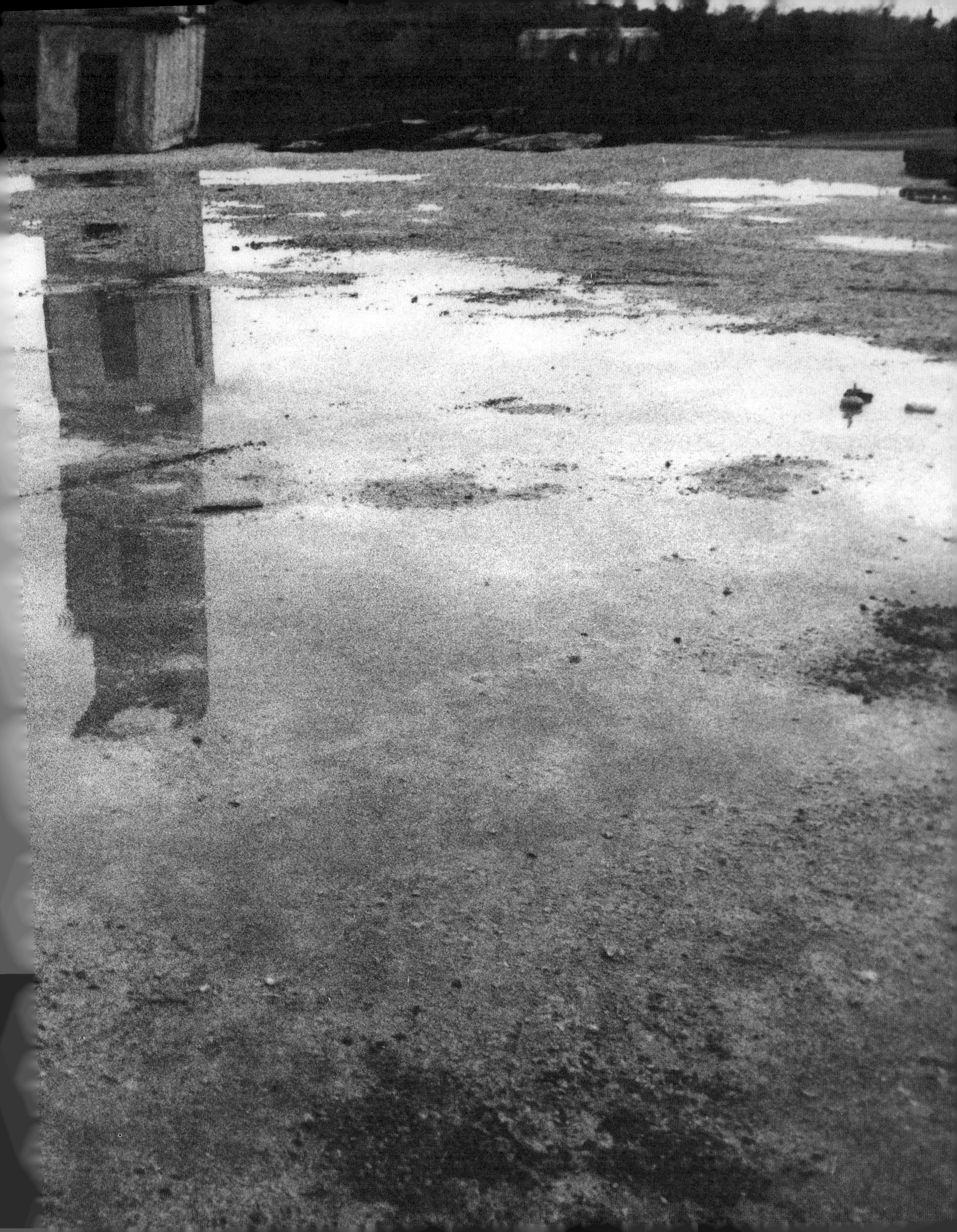

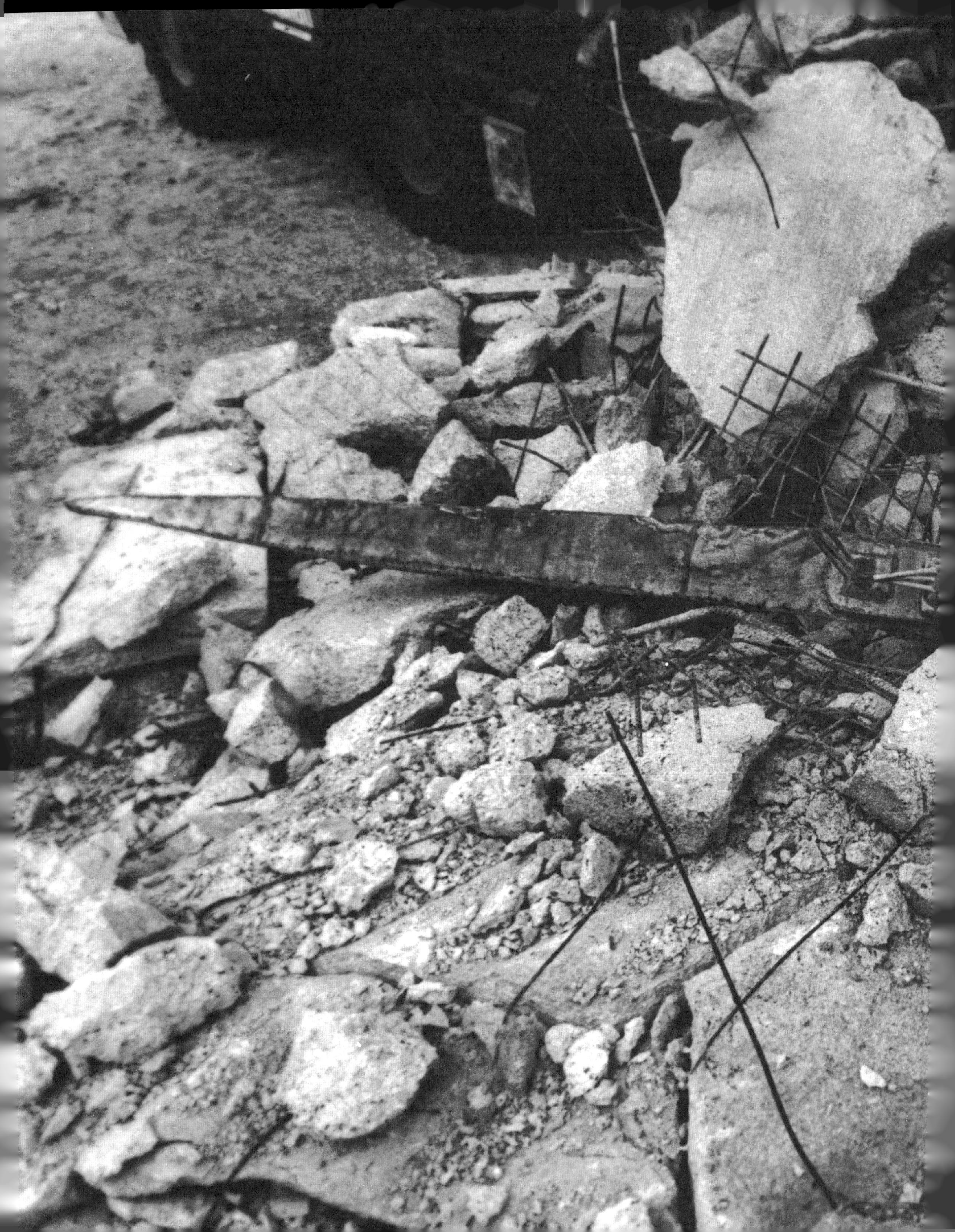

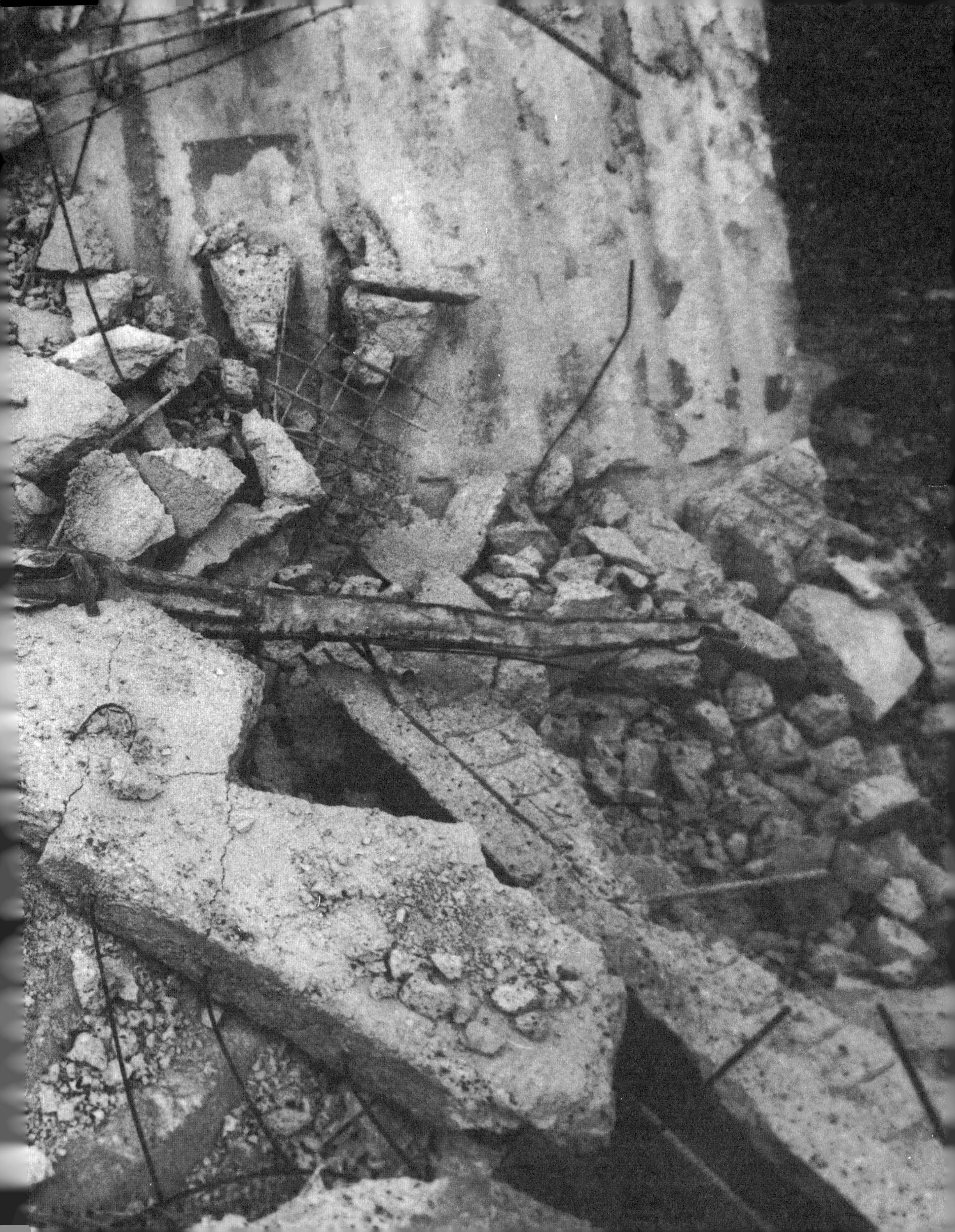

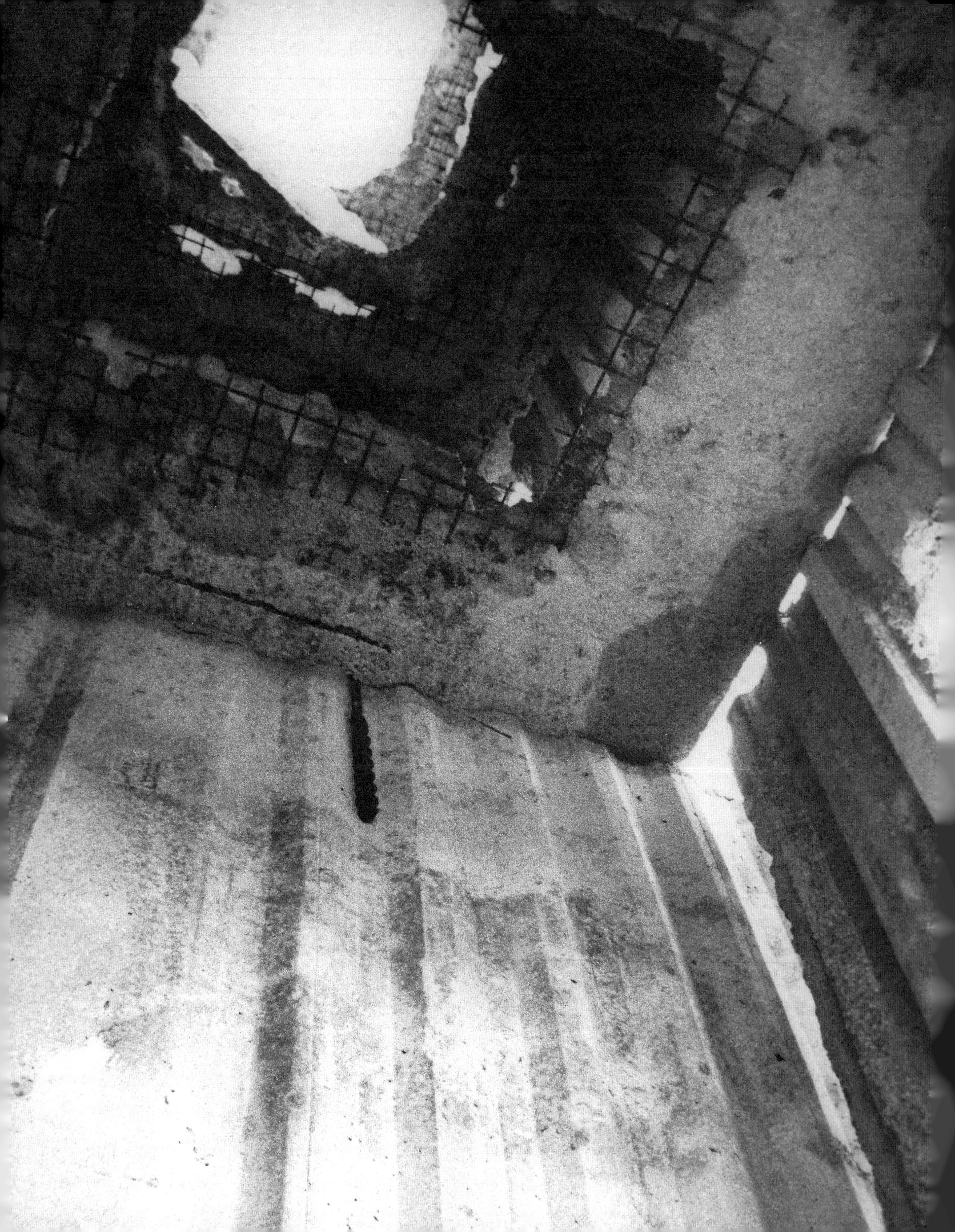

October 5, 2004 Barjac

MICHAEL AUPING: Titling an exhibition *Heaven and Earth*, as we have done here, requires a little explanation. Perhaps we should just begin with the very simple question, do you believe in heaven?

ANSELM KIEFER: The title *Heaven and Earth* is a paradox because heaven and earth don't exist anymore. The earth is round. The cosmos has no up and down. It is moving constantly. We can no longer fix the stars to create an ideal place. This is our dilemma.

MA: And yet we keep trying to find new ways to get to "the ideal place," the place we assume we came from—to find the right direction.

AK: It is natural to search for our beginnings, but not to assume it has one direction. We live in a scientific future that early philosophers and alchemists could not foresee, but they understood very fundamental relationships between heaven and earth that we have forgotten. In the Sefer Hechaloth, the ancient book that came before the kabbala, there is no worry of directions. It describes stages, metaphors, and symbols that float everywhere. Up and down were the same direction. The Hechaloth is the spiritual journey toward perfect cognition. North, south, east, and west, up and down are not issues. For me, this also relates to time. Past, present, and future are essentially the same direction. It is about finding symbols that move in all directions.

MA: Our religions all have heavens.

AK: We can't escape religion, but there is a difference between religion and heaven, and one doesn't necessarily lead to the other.

MA: You are not a "New Age" spiritualist. I know that for sure, but some people who see your images may wonder just what your position is in regard to religion.

AK: My spirituality is not New Age. It has been with me since I was a child. I know that in the last few decades religion has been made shiny and new. It's like a business creating a new product. They are selling salvation. I'm not interested in being saved.

I'm interested in reconstructing symbols. It's about connecting with an older knowledge and trying to discover continuities in why we search for heaven.

MA: I can see fragments of continuity in your works between symbols that are ancient and those that take a more modern form, and for me that suggests a kind of hope within your landscapes. But there are also some very dark shadows in your images, literally in terms of color, as well as in metaphor and content. It is as if in the same image we see a liberation of knowledge but the dark weight of history.

AK: There is always hope, but that must be combined with irony, and more important, skepticism. The context of knowledge is changing constantly. At one moment we pray from the top of a mountain and the next from a seat in a jet plane or a bomber cockpit. How can we not see that as ironic and skeptical?

MA: I understand what you are saying, but I'd like to backtrack a little. You were raised a Catholic.

AK: Yes.

MA: Did you attend church often?

AK: Sure. Religion was a part of my childhood and my youth. It was a very important thing. The rituals and rites were important. I can still do them in Latin. Of course, I knew the Latin before I knew what it meant. But I was involved, like many young people of my generation, in learning religion at an early age.

MA: Christian images are apparent in your work, but in many ways not as apparent as Jewish or even Gnostic references.

AK: Later, I discovered that Christian mythology was less complex and less sophisticated than Jewish mythology because the Christians limited their story to make it simple so that they could engage more people and defend their ideas. They had to fight with the Jewish traditions, with the Gnostics. It was a war of the use of knowledge. However, it wasn't just a defense against outside ideas. It was aggressive. Like politics, they wanted to win. You know, the first church in Rome was not defensive and not aggressive. It was quiet. It was spiritual in the sense of seeking a true discussion about God. It was exploring a new idea about humanity. But then there was "iglesias triumphant," the Triumph of the Church. And then the stones were stacked up and the buildings came, and the construction of the Scholastics, Augustine, and so on. They were very successful in limiting the meaning of the mythology. There were discussions about the Trinity and its meaning. Anyone who had ideas that complicated their specific picture was eliminated. This made Christianity very rigid and not very interesting. Whenever knowledge becomes rigid it stops living.

MA: In 1966, you visited the Monastery at La Tourette. Was this before you made the decision to be an artist?

AK: I began by studying law. I didn't study law to be a lawyer, but for the philosophical aspects of law, constitutional law. I was interested in how people live together without destroying each other.

I went to La Tourette while I was studying law. It may sound strange to go from the study of law to La Tourette, but it really wasn't. I had always been interested in law from a spiritual aspect. A constitution is not unlike the idea of church doctrine. People need a context or a content, something to bind them together. This could be stretched to mythologies. Law, mythology, religion—they are all structures for investigating human character. There was a well-known constitutional lawyer, Carl Schmitt. He was a very brilliant man who worked in the 1920s through the 1950s. Unfortunately, he got too involved with the Nazis. He was not really a fascist, but he got entangled with Nazi politics. They adopted him. He was very interesting in terms of bringing together legal theory and religious traditions—quite brilliant; but after the war, he was discriminated against. Nobody talked about him, even though he had made some very important contributions to constitutional law. I studied him because he was a very interesting man, as much a philosopher as a lawyer. When I was in Jerusalem, I found out that he was an adviser or consultant when they made their constitution. I think it was kept a secret for some time. He wrote a very interesting book about the Leviathan, the giant serpent that became an image of political power. I was interested in people like Schmitt because they got caught between the power of government and the power of God. We are all in that dilemma.

MA: Why did you go to La Tourette in the first place? I don't imagine that you went only to see a Le Corbusier building. You stayed there for three weeks.

AK: The Dominicans were there. I liked their teaching. They have an interesting history. I had read that they had many discussions with Le Corbusier about the shape of the building and the materials. It was a point in my life when I wanted to think quietly about the larger questions. Churches are the stages for transmitting knowledge, interpreting knowledge and ideas of transcendence. It's a history of conflicts and contradictions. A church is an important source of knowledge and power. Le Corbusier knew that. I stayed there for three weeks in a cell. I thought about things. In a place like that you are not simply encouraged to think about God but to think about yourself, *Erkenne dich selbst*. Of course, you think about your relationship to your god.

Also, for me it was an inspiring building in the sense that a very simple material, a modern material, could be used to create a spiritual space. Great religions and great buildings are part of the sediment of time; like pieces of sand. Le Corbusier used the sand to construct a spiritual space. I discovered the spirituality of concrete—using earth to mold a symbol, a symbol of the imaginative and the spiritual world. He tried to make heaven on earth—the ancient paradox.

MA: How do you mean that?

AK: Heaven is an idea, a piece of ancient internal knowledge. It is not a physical construction.

MA: Two years after visiting La Tourette, you made a small book titled *Die Himmel (The Heavens)*. I believe it was your first artwork.

AK: It was the first work that I didn't destroy.

MA: You did a lot of books at that time. Probably the most famous, or infamous, was the book of *Occupations* photographs. You photographed yourself doing a Nazi salute at different locations in Europe. That seems so radically different from a book titled *The Heavens*.

AK: Well, *Occupations* was done in stages over a longer period of time, but yes. One is a very specific topic and one is a very big topic. It's like the macrocosmic and the microcosmic. I wanted to deal with large issues in my art, but that didn't keep me from studying my own history as a German. Also, that first book, *The Heavens,* was not as romantic as it sounds.

MA: It's a collage book of shapes cut out of magazines—many of them little pieces of sky.

AK: I was very interested in media at that time. I realized that you could use any material to create imagery. What better than to use something so basic as popular magazines to create my own heaven? In a way I was testing to see if it worked.

MA: Did it?

AK: Of course, we can all create our own heaven using whatever materials we want. We always imagine heaven as something physical, as a place rather than as time. We have to have our illusions. I think heaven is about time, and is always changing. So there are many heavens in this book.

MA: Near the cover of the book is a black-and-white photograph of an Albert Speer building.

AK: Yes, but not a building. It was a very good artwork that he made. He collected all the light projectors (Klieg lights) that the army used to spot enemy aircraft. They had a lot of them and he put them together and pointed them up to the sky. It's like a cathedral, but much higher. It's a wonderful idea.

MA: Do you think Albert Speer was a spiritual man?

AK: You don't have to be spiritual to get in touch with spirituality. It's easier but it is not always necessary. It can happen that someone who does not think about spirituality, does not consider it in his life, can get in touch with the spiritual through circumstances he is not responsible for or aware of. Speer was a very focused man. He created spaces that in different circumstances could be considered spiritual, but were not used for spiritual purposes.

MA: You have made reference to Speer's buildings in a number of your works. Does Speer represent something specific for you?

AK: Speer's architecture is interesting, but because of his connection to the Nazis he was not being discussed at the time I was using his images. There are many artists who run into trouble on their way to paradise, philosophers also: Marx, Hegel, Mao, Wagner. They have all looked for ways to find their place, their salvation, through philosophy, art, or religion.

MA: It seems to me that Speer's buildings were meant to intimidate, not just inspire. They were powerfully political churches.

AK: The church has always been political. This is nothing new. And politics can pose as religion. Hitler abused religion. His speeches were full of prayers. We know all of this, which is why we have to have some skepticism in our spirituality. Anyway, this Light Dome we were discussing by Speer—I think he wanted to make something very special for the Reich Convention, a political convention. And he made this very beautiful Light Dome. Maybe he was doing it for beauty or for politics. The situation of the artist is not pure.

MA: Could we go back and talk a little bit more about your education as an artist? You went to the university in Freiburg.

AK: Yes. But first I had the nineteenth-century idea that the artist is a genius—that art comes out of him naturally and he doesn't need any education. I had always thought this, even as a child. You could say that I had too much admiration for artists. I thought they all came from heaven. Later I found out that an artwork is only partly done by the artist, that the artist is part of a larger state of things—the public, history, memory, personal history—and he must just work to find a way through it all, to remain free but connected at the same time. Peter Dreher, an artist and professor in Freiburg, was very important for me in this way. I had come from law school and was trying to figure out the rules of this new world of art. Peter Dreher opened me to the freedom of this new world, to the milieu of the artist, and how to operate within this freedom. If you are a genius, you don't need a milieu. So I figured out that maybe I wasn't a genius. He said to me, "Do what you want." And then we could talk about it later. He helped me to understand that first you have to work and then you can talk.

MA: And later on you went to see Joseph Beuys, although you didn't officially study with him.

AK: No. I was living in the forest in Hornbach and had made some canvases. I had heard of Beuys and so I took my canvases to Düsseldorf to show him. He was impressive. I liked him very much. His dialogue was broad and he could be very impressive. He had a world view, not just the view of an artist. I think I appreciated him more because I had studied law.

MA: How so?

AK: Art just cannot live on itself. It has to draw on a broader knowledge. I think both of us understood that at the time we knew each other.

MA: Although I never met him, you and Beuys seem very different to me. He was more extroverted and you are more introverted, or at least less public.

AK: We were different, and as a young artist I needed to question that difference. Nevertheless, I learned a lot from him, even though he was not my teacher. I could talk to him about larger issues.

MA: In his interviews and writings, Beuys often evoked the word "spiritual." How do you think he meant that?

AK: That is complicated. We were both in Germany at a certain time—a time when a dialogue about history and spirituality needed to begin. It was difficult to separate the two subjects. There was a sense of starting over. To evoke the spiritual not only looking at ourselves but into the history of our nation. It was not just a matter of a critique. It had to be deeper than that. So yes, Beuys was a spiritual man. The artist is naturally spiritual because he is always searching for new beginnings.

MA: Your use of the artist's palette image in many of your works seems to suggest various roles for the artist, not always spiritual in his effect.

AK: The palette represents the idea of the artist connecting heaven and earth. He works here but he looks up there. He is always moving between the two realms. The artists are like the shamans, who when they were meditating would sit in a tree in order to suspend themselves between heaven and earth. The palette can transform reality by suggesting new visions. Or you could say that the visionary experience finds its way to the material world through the palette.

MA: Sometimes your palettes are on the ground, a part of the earth, which is constantly referred to in your work, as a painted image or the material ground for a painting.

AK: All stories of heaven begin on earth.

MA: Often the earth appears to be plowed or burned or both. Many people see your landscapes as referring to battlefields.

AK: In some cases, that is true; but for me there is a larger metaphor. Plowing and burning, like slash-and-burn agriculture, is a process of regeneration, so that the earth can be reborn and create new growth toward the sun. Burning is a method to take out spirit. There is the alchemical reference to *nigredo*,[1] but it goes deeper than that. Burning is absolutely elemental. The beginning of the cosmos that we have conceived scientifically began with incredible heat. The light we see in the sky is the result of a distant burning. You might say heaven is on fire. But also our bodies are generators of heat. It is all related. Fire is the glue of the cosmos. It connects heaven and earth.

MA: Like fire, it seems to me that all of your images are symbolic mediators.

AK: Sure. Angels take many forms. Satan was an angel. We are not capable of imagining God in a pure state. We need symbols that are less pure, that include human elements.

MA: Like snakes.

AK: Yes. The snake can be an angel. It has played that role many times before in history.

MA: In a number of works you have referred to The Hierarchy of the Angels, and the concept of a celestial hierarchy. Is there a hierarchy to your symbols and the materials you use when you refer to this idea?

AK: No. There is no strict hierarchy to my images. They seem to be always evolving from one form or condition to another. This relates to the thinking of the Greek saint Dionysius the Areopagite. Do you know about the ideas attributed to him?

MA: The idea that heaven is organized in orders of different forms of angels?

AK: Yes—angels, archangels, seraphim, cherubim. More important was the concept that the spiritual realm is a spiral going up and down. So the spiritual realm is moving and twisting. This is important to the way I organize my pictures. I work with the concept that nothing is fixed in place and that symbols move in all directions. They change hierarchies depending on the context.

MA: An airplane propeller could be an angel or the spiral universe itself.

AK: Yes. And of course flying machines have played important roles in history, representing ambitions of transcendence or military power, from Icarus to moon rockets.

1 *Nigredo* is defined as "The initial, black stage of the opus alchymicum in which the body of the impure metal, the matter for the Stone, or the old outmoded state of being is killed, putrefied, and dissolved into the original substance of creation, the *prima materia*, in order that it may be renovated and reborn in a new form." Lyndy Abraham, *A Dictionary of Alchemical Imagery* (Cambridge: Cambridge University Press, 2003): 135.

MA: I was also thinking about the different levels of spheres and subspheres in the kabbala that deal with the evolution or hierarchies between matter and spirit, and how that might relate to your use of materials. Your studios are warehouses of everything from dead plants and human teeth to sprawling stacks of lead. Are you suggesting a kind of symbolic ladder through your materials?

AK: Not that directly. I collect all of these things as I read and they find their way into my reconstructed stories, but I usually become attached to materials that have more than one side to their meaning. So they can be used to go up and down the ladder. Lead is a very good example . . . The large sheets of lead that support the *20 Years of Solitude* books are from the roof of a cathedral . . . Lead can transform itself in all directions.

MA: I've also noticed that many of your paintings can be turned upside down and still carry their message, as if the heaven and the earth just switch identities. It seems to me the orientation is only fixed when you write on the canvas.

AK: I work on my paintings from all sides, so when I am working on them there is no up or down. The sky can be reflected in the water or material can come down from the sky. That is part of the content of the paintings. Heaven and earth are interchangeable. The writing is an attempt to fix a moment or a place, to suggest a fixed state, but the imagery denies. It is active.

MA: Like the stars, galaxies, and constellations you have been referring to—the Astral Serpent or the Milky Way.

AK: The title or language on my paintings is a starting point. The images should expand the meaning of the words. In *Die Milchstrasse*, I thought of the large cut in the land as a puddle of water. When the clouds are reflected on its surface, it looks like milk. A puddle is a very simple thing, but it has the ability to reflect into something much larger. It could be the Pacific Ocean.

MA: On this canvas it looks monumental, but it also looks like a wound in the belly of the earth.

AK: Yes. It could be. When you dig into the ground, you may find something—water, a buried meteorite, a piece of heaven. These kinds of pictures are always operating between the macrocosmic and the microcosmic. The lead strings reach to the sky and then converge down into the funnel, which dips into the puddle. The Milky Way, which has been observed for millenniums as a great and expansive constellation, is really a small thing in the cosmos. It is like a puddle in the cosmos. Establishing a heaven and earth is a way to try to orient ourselves, but cosmic space does not understand this. It is all relative. What is big can in fact be very small. What is up can be down.

MA: It's like size versus scale in your work. Your formats vary tremendously, where size and subject can sometimes seem contradictory—making a monumental canvas for what you call a "puddle," and then making a tiny book about heaven. The book *Die Himmel* is one of your smallest works.

AK: You cannot compete with heaven through size. The universe was once thought of as a large book. The human imagination creates its own heaven with things on earth.

MA: Books are clearly an important symbol for you—important mediators or containers.

AK: You know I did my first book when I was ten or eleven years old. I'll show it to you. [Reaches for a book high on a bookshelf.] You see here I gave it the number forty-two to indicate that it would be part of a large series. I must have been a bit pretentious. [Laughter.] As a young student, we were told to read a book and then write about the book, also making illustrations that would summarize the book from our memory. It was a very typical way of teaching in Germany.

The book, the idea of a book or the image of a book, is a symbol of learning, of transmitting knowledge. The story of our beginnings always begins in the oral tradition, but eventually finds its way into the form of a book. This has its double side. It preserves memory, but it also makes the story more rigid. Everyone tells a story differently, but when it is written down it can become frozen.

MA: It's always possible to interpret the written word differently.

AK: Yes, of course. But as civilization progresses there seems to be less interest in interpretation and more of simply an acceptance. This is why the Gnostics were important. They questioned, interpreted, and reinvented the story. We know very little about them except from later Christians who tried to dispel their questioning. But the questions continue to come. Science has not found our beginnings. The closest we can come to the beginnings are the old myths, the old stories. Questioning them keeps the story alive. I make my own books to find my own way through the old stories.

MA: When did you first become interested in the kabbala?

AK: I can't say for sure. Since childhood, I had studied the Old Testament, and sometime as a young man I began to read of Jewish mysticism. Then in the mid-1980s, I went to Jerusalem and began to read the books of Gershom Scholem. Beside the fact that kabbalistic stories and interpretations are very interesting, I think my attraction has something to do with the way that I work. People say that I read a lot, but in some ways I don't. I read enough to capture images. I read until the story becomes an image. Then I stop reading. I can't recite a passage, but I can recite it as an image. For an artist it is important to have a strong, complex subject. *Kabbala* means "knowledge that has been received," a secret knowledge; but I think of it as images that have been received. As I said before, the Christian church hardened in its knowledge and its symbolism at a certain point. The kabbalistic tradition is not one but many, forming a sophisticated spiritual discipline. It is a paradox of logic and mystical belief. It's part scholarship, part religion, part magic. For me, it is a spiritual journey anchored by images.

MA: Thinking of it as a journey, an image that has come to play a larger role in your art is that of the Merkaba—

AK: Of course, the chariot—the vehicle that rides to the throne of heaven.

MA: I think of the chariot as a kind of angel.

AK: It is more sophisticated than that. The image is that of a throne chariot of God, which could ascend and descend through the different heavenly palaces known as the Hechaloth—with the seventh or final palace revealing God. It comes from Ezekiel's vision of a mystical flight to heaven. But it is really a meditation tool. The kabbalistic mystics established a technique of using a chariot for a meditation tool. Using the chariot, the mystics would make an inward journey to the seven palaces in their correct order.

MA: Here on the grounds of your home in Barjac, France, you are creating a monumental installation of stacked concrete rooms or "palaces" that go up hundreds of feet into the air, as well as a sprawling series of connected underground tunnels and spaces containing palettes, books, and lead rooms. Are you working your way through the palaces of heaven?

AK: I follow the ancient tradition of going up and down. The palaces of heaven are still a mystery. The procedures and formulae surrounding this journey will always be debated. I am making my own investigation. You know this book the Sefer Hechaloth (Hechaloth Book)? Obviously, this is not just about traveling through palaces, but traveling through yourself in order to know yourself; the old saying *Erkenne dich selbst.*

MA: Recently you have made immense books the size of a human body that you can almost walk into, with the pages covered with stars. But you have given the stars numbers and connected them with lines. These star drawings have also appeared in huge paintings that include observatories and what look like navigation instruments.

AK: They are numbers given to stars by NASA scientists. Each number in the string of numbers indicates the distance, the color, the size, etc. This is the scientific heaven. But of course it is all illusion. All of the constellations are illusions or ghosts. They do not exist. The light we see today was emitted millions, billions of years ago and of course their source was constantly changing, moving, and dying. These lights we see, this heaven has nothing to do with our current reality. We are afraid, so we have to make sense of the world. We cannot stand not to have a heaven in our minds. If there really was a heaven, it would exist outside of science or religion. I am speaking of religions, with the plural; not just a religion.

MA: So the scientists are making up their own dome of heaven.

AK: Of course. They want to find heaven too, but their stars are always moving, always dying, and some breaking off, making new stars. Scientists are a little bit like artists. Their stars are like pieces of memory that find their way into a painting. You pull them out and stop them for a moment in the painting. It is stopped only for the instant you recognize it and then you change position and you see something else, another relationship in the image, but again, only for an instant. There are only glimpses.

Cette obscure clarté qui tombe des étoiles (This Dark Brightness which Falls from the Stars) (detail), 1996
Emulsion, acrylic, shellac, and sunflower seeds on canvas
204¾ × 220½ inches (520 × 560 cm)

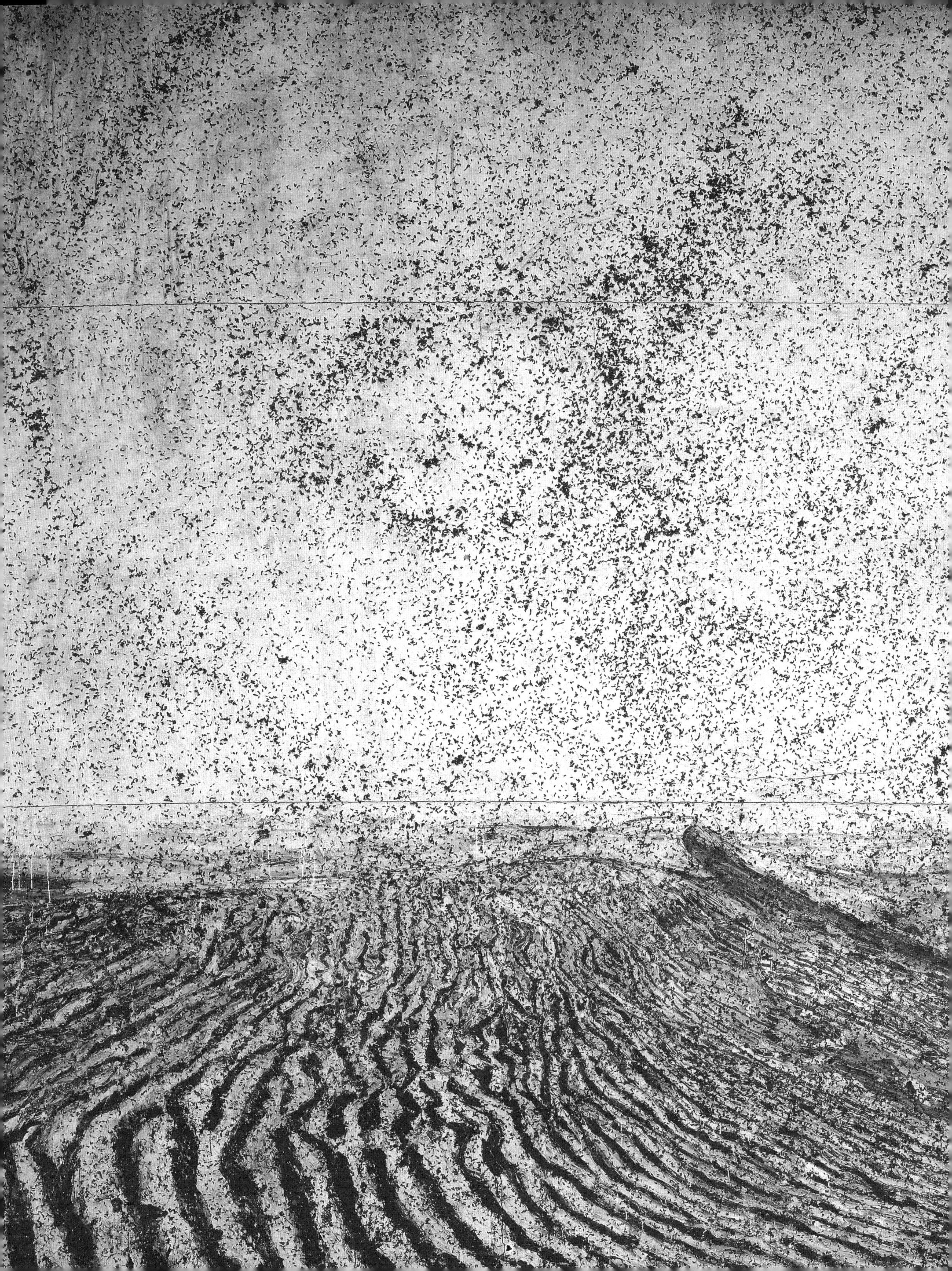

Checklist of the Exhibition

Die Himmel (The Heavens), 1969
Book, 79 pages. Oil and fragments of paper, photographs, and magazine pictures mounted on paper, thread-bound
9⅞ × 7½ × ⅜ inches (25 × 19 × 1 cm) (bound volume)
Private Collection
Pages 1–16

Die Himmel (The Heavens), 1969
Book, 220 pages. Oil and fragments of paper, photographs, and magazine pictures mounted on paper, thread-bound
9⅞ × 7½ × ⅜ inches (25 × 19 × 1 cm) (bound volume)
Buchhandlung Walther König, Köln

Jeder Mensch steht unter seiner Himmelskugel (Everyone Stands Under His Own Dome of Heaven), 1970
Watercolor, gouache, and graphite pencil on joined paper
15¾ × 18⅞ inches (40 × 47.9 cm)
The Metropolitan Museum of Art, Denise and Andrew Saul Fund, 1995 (1995.14.4)
(Fort Worth, Washington, and San Francisco presentations only)
Page 54

Winterlandschaft (Winter Landscape), 1970
Watercolor, gouache, and graphite pencil on paper
16⅞ × 14 inches (42.9 × 35.6 cm)
The Metropolitan Museum of Art, Denise and Andrew Saul Fund, 1995 (1995.14.5)
(Fort Worth, Washington, and San Francisco presentations only)
Page 53

Liegender Mann mit Zweig (Man Lying with Branch), 1971
Watercolor, gouache, and graphite pencil on paper
9⅝ × 10¾ inches (23.8 × 27.3 cm)
The Metropolitan Museum of Art, Gift of Cynthia Hazen Polsky, in memory of her father, Joseph H. Hazen, 2000 (2000.96.1)
(Fort Worth, Washington, and San Francisco presentations only)
Page 55

Mann im Wald (Man in the Forest), 1971
Oil on canvas
68½ × 74½ inches (174 × 189 cm)
Private Collection, San Francisco
Page 57

Landschaft mit Kopf (Landscape with Head), 1973
Oil, distemper, and charcoal on burlap, with charcoal on cardboard
82 11/16 × 94½ inches (210 × 240 cm)
Private Collection, Berlin
Page 59

Quaternität (Quaternity), 1973
Oil and charcoal on burlap
117½ × 170¼ inches (298.4 × 432.4 cm)
Collection of the Modern Art Museum of Fort Worth, Museum purchase, The Friends of Art Endowment Fund
Pages 62/63

Resurrexit, 1973
Oil, acrylic, and charcoal on burlap
114 3/16 × 70⅞ inches (290 × 180 cm)
Private Collection Sanders, Amsterdam
Page 61

Himmel – Erde (Heaven – Earth), 1974
Oil on canvas
27½ × 37⅜ inches (70 × 95 cm)
Private Collection
Page 65

Malerei der verbrannten Erde (Painting of the Scorched Earth), 1974
Oil on burlap
37⅛ × 49¼ inches (95 × 125 cm)
Céline Bastian, Berlin
Page 71

Sende Deinen Geist aus (Send Forth Your Spirit), 1974
Watercolor, gouache, pen and ink, ballpoint pen, and colored pencil on paper
13⅜ × 9½ inches (34 × 24.1 cm)
The Metropolitan Museum of Art, Purchase, Lila Acheson Wallace Gift, 1995 (1995.14.6)
(Fort Worth, Washington, and San Francisco presentations only)
Page 66

Ausbrennen des Landkreises Buchen (Cauterization of the Rural District of Buchen), 1975
Seven bound volumes, each oil, charcoal, and glue on twenty strips of burlap
23⅝ × 16½ × 3⅛ inches (60 × 42 × 8 cm) each
Private Collection
Pages 72/73

Deutsche Heilslinie (German Lineages of Salvation), 1975
Watercolor, gouache, and ballpoint pen on paper
9½ × 13⅜ inches (24.1 × 34 cm)
The Metropolitan Museum of Art, Denise and Andrew Saul Fund, 1995 (1995.14.19)
(Fort Worth, Washington, and San Francisco presentations only)
Page 67

Essenz/Ek-sistenz (Essence/Ex-sistence), 1975
Watercolor and gouache on paper
11¾ × 15⅝ inches (29.8 × 39.7 cm)
The Metropolitan Museum of Art, Purchase, The Barnett Newman Foundation Gift, 1995 (1995.14.17)
(Fort Worth, Washington, and San Francisco presentations only)
Page 68

Himmel auf Erden (Heaven on Earth), 1974–75
Watercolor, gouache, and ballpoint pen on paper
9½ × 12⅝ inches (24.1 × 32.1 cm)
The Metropolitan Museum of Art, Purchase, Lila Acheson Wallace Gift, 1995 (1995.14.13)
(Fort Worth, Washington, and San Francisco presentations only)
Page 69

Aaron, c. 1979
Oil on canvas
28 × 35⅞ inches (71 × 91 cm)
Private Collection, Berlin
Page 75

Der gestirnte Himmel (The Starred Heaven), 1980
Photograph (1969), with acrylic and emulsion
32⅞ × 23 inches (83.5 × 58.5 cm)
Collection of Eric Fischl and April Gornik
Page 77

Palette, 1981
Oil and mixed media on canvas
114 × 157½ inches (290 × 400 cm)
Anthony d'Offay, London
Pages 78/79

Dem unbekannten Maler (To the Unknown Painter), 1982
Watercolor and pencil on paper
34⅝ × 21⅝ inches (88 × 55 cm)
Private Collection, San Francisco
Page 81

Das Buch (The Book), 1979–85
Oil, lead, photographic paper, straw, and fabric on canvas
130 × 217⅝ inches (330.2 × 552.8 cm)
Hirshhorn Museum and Sculpture Garden, Smithsonian Institution, Thomas M. Evans, Jerome L. Greene, Joseph H. Hirshhorn, and Sydney and Francis Lewis Purchase Fund, 1985
(Washington presentation only)

Emanation, 1984–85
Shellac on photograph, mounted on cardboard, with lead
22½ × 32 inches (57 × 81 cm)
Jerry and Emily Spiegel
Page 83

Das Schlangenwunder (The Miracle of the Serpents), 1984–85
Collage and shellac on photographic paper
22 13/16 × 32 11/16 inches (58 × 83 cm)
Collection of Dr. and Mrs. Konrad M. Weis, Pittsburgh; and the Carnegie Museum of Art
Page 85

Die Milchstrasse (The Milky Way), 1985–87
Emulsion paint, oil, acrylic, and shellac on canvas with applied wires and lead
overall 150 × 221⅝ inches (381 × 563 cm)
Albright-Knox Art Gallery, Buffalo, New York, In Celebration of the 125th Anniversary of The Buffalo Fine Arts Academy, General and Restricted Purchase Funds, 1988
(Fort Worth, Montreal, and Washington presentations only)
Pages 86/87

Die Ordnung der Engel (The Hierarchy of Angels), 1985–87
Oil, emulsion, shellac, acrylic, chalk, lead propeller, curdled lead, steel cables, band-iron, and cardboard on canvas
133½ × 220⅞ × 22¾ inches (339.1 × 561 × 57.8 cm)
Collection Walker Art Center, Minneapolis
Gift of Penny and Mike Winton, 1987
Pages 88/89

Karfunkel Fee, 1990
Oil, emulsion, shellac, charcoal, and ashes on canvas, with lead airplane, poppy, lead strips, copper wire, and dress
150 × 110½ × 15 inches (381 × 280.5 × 38 cm)
Ludmer Collection, Montreal
On loan, Musée d'art contemporain de Montréal
(Montreal presentation only)
Page 182

Himmel – Erde (Heaven – Earth), 1991
Photograph on cardboard and lilies of the valley on lead in a glazed steel frame
67 × 51⅛ inches (170 × 130 cm)
Private Collection

Johannisnacht (Midsummer Night), 1987–91
Acrylic, soil, lead on cardboard, separators, singed spots, and fern on lead in a glazed steel frame
94½ × 51⅛ inches (240 × 130 cm)
Private Collection
Page 91

20 Jahre Einsamkeit (20 Years of Solitude), 1971–91
Five books, semen, five pallets of lead
Dimensions variable
Private Collection
Pages 92/93

Buch mit Flügeln (Book with Wings), 1992–94
Lead, steel, and tin
74¾ × 208⅝ × 43⅜ inches (189.9 × 529.9 × 110.2 cm)
Collection of the Modern Art Museum of Fort Worth, Museum purchase, Sid W. Richardson Foundation Endowment Fund
Page 95

Sternenfall (Falling Stars), 1995
Oil on canvas
90½ × 67 inches (230 × 170 cm)
Private Collection, London
Page 97

Cette obscure clarté qui tombe des étoiles (This Dark Brightness which Falls from the Stars), 1996
Emulsion, acrylic, shellac, and sunflower seeds on canvas
204¾ × 220½ inches (520 × 560 cm)
Dallas Museum of Art, Frances Moss Ryburn Memorial Fund
(Fort Worth presentation only)
Page 177

Dein und Mein Alter und das Alter der Welt (Your Age and Mine and the Age of the World), 1996
Emulsion, acrylic, shellac, and sunflower seeds on canvas
109⅜ × 218¾ inches (280 × 560 cm)
Maxine and Stuart Frankel Foundation for Art
Pages 98/99

Ich halte alle Indien in meiner Hand (I Hold All Indias in My Hand), 1996
Oil, emulsion, and acrylic on canvas with wire cages
74¾ × 110¼ inches (190 × 280 cm)
Private Collection
Page 109

Merkawa, 1996
Book, 32 pages. Mixed media
41⅛ × 32¼ × 3⅞ inches (104.5 × 81.9 × 9.8 cm) (bound volume)
Maxine and Stuart Frankel Foundation for Art
Pages 101–8

Papst Alexander VI: Die goldene Bulle (Pope Alexander VI: The Golden Bull), 1996
Emulsion, acrylic, and gold leaf on canvas
130 × 218¾ inches (330.2 × 555.6 cm)
Collection of the Modern Art Museum of Fort Worth, Museum purchase, The Friends of Art Endowment Fund
Pages 110/111

Die Aschenblume (Ash Flower), 1983–97
Oil, emulsion, acrylic paint, clay, ash, earth, and dried sunflower on canvas
149⅝ × 299¼ inches (380 × 760 cm)
Collection of the Modern Art Museum of Fort Worth, Gift of The Burnett Foundation in honor of Michael Auping
Pages 112/113

The Secret Life of Plants, 2001
Paint and mixed media on lead
122 inches (309.9 cm) diameter;
79 × 58 inches (200.7 × 147.3 cm) each page
Private Collection
Page 117

Die Himmelspaläste (The Heavenly Palaces), 2002
Oil, emulsion, acrylic, and lead objects on lead and canvas
248 × 212½ inches (630 × 540 cm)
Collection the artist, Courtesy of Gagosian Gallery
(Fort Worth presentation only)
Page 119

Sefer Hechaloth, 2002
Oil, emulsion, acrylic, metal shelves, and burned books on canvas
147½ × 130 inches (375 × 330 cm)
Private Collection
Page 121

Am Anfang (In the Beginning), 2003
Oil, acrylic, and emulsion on canvas with polyhedron
74¾ × 110¼ inches (190 × 280 cm)
Private Collection
Page 135

Asijah, 2003
Gouache on photo paper
46⅜ × 50 inches (117.7 × 126.8 cm)
Private Collection
Page 125

Asijah, 2003
Gouache on photo paper
46¼ × 46⅝ inches (117.5 × 118.5 cm)
Private Collection
Page 126

Benija, 2003
Gouache on photo paper
43½ × 43⅜ inches (110.5 × 110 cm)
Private Collection
Page 127

Für Robert Fludd (For Robert Fludd), 2003
Book, 28 pages. Lead and paint
41 × 32¼ × 3½ inches (104 × 82 × 9 cm) (bound volume)
From the Collection of Lester Marks
Pages 138–43

Hexen, 2003
Gouache on photo paper
30⅛ × 49¾ inches (76.5 × 126.3 cm)
Private Collection
Page 130

Die Himmelspaläste (The Heavenly Palaces), 2003
Gouache on photo paper
44¼ × 31¼ inches (112.5 × 79.3 cm)
Private Collection
Page 128

Die Lorelei, 2003
Gouache on photo paper
46⅛ × 40⅝ inches (117.3 × 103.3 cm)
Private Collection
Page 129

Nagpur, 2003
Gouache on photo paper
41¾ × 30¾ inches (106 × 78 cm)
Private Collection
Page 131

Sefer Hechaloth, 2003
Gouache on photo paper
44⅞ × 29 inches (114 × 73.5 cm)
Private Collection
Page 132

Sefer Hechaloth, 2003
Gouache on photo paper
32½ × 22⅞ inches (82.5 × 58 cm)
Private Collection
Page 133

Aschenblume (Ash Flower), 2004
Oil, acrylic, and emulsion on canvas
95⅝ × 110⅞ inches (243 × 281.5 cm)
Private Collection
Page 145

Himmel auf Erden (Heaven on Earth), 1998–2004
Oil, emulsion, and acrylic on canvas
with barbed wire
110¼ × 220½ inches (280 × 560 cm)
Private Collection
Pages 146/147

Die Himmelspaläste (The Heavenly Palaces), 2004
Oil, emulsion, and acrylic on canvas with wire cages
110¼ × 130 inches (280 × 330 cm)
The Jewish Museum, New York, Purchase,
Melva Bucksbaum Contemporary Art Fund, 2005-3
Page 123

Melancholia, 2004
Oil, acrylic, and emulsion on canvas
with glass polyhedron
110⅝ × 150⅜ inches (281 × 382 cm)
Private Collection
Page 137

Voyage au bout de la nuit, 2004
Oil, acrylic, and emulsion on canvas
with metal strips
75 × 111⅜ inches (190.5 × 283 cm)
Private Collection
Page 149

Burda Moden 90, 2005
Book, Mixed media
31⅞ × 20½ × 2½ inches (81 × 52 × 6.5 cm)
(bound volume)
Private Collection

Burda Moden 92, 2005
Book, 21 double pages. Photographs
and paper on cardboard
31⅞ × 20½ × 2¾ inches (81 × 52 × 7 cm)
(bound volume)
Private Collection
Pages 150/151

La Conversion de Saint Paul, 2005
Mixed media
74⅞ × 130 inches (190 × 330 cm)
Private Collection

Elektra, 2005
Book, 29 double pages. Sand and clay on
photographs on cardboard
23⅝ × 25⅛ × 6¼ inches (60 × 64 × 16 cm)
(bound volume)
Private Collection
Page 152

Hafis, 2005
Dried plants, acrylic, and oil on canvas in a glazed
steel frame
34¼ × 45⅞ inches (87 × 116.5 cm)
Private Collection

Hafis, 2005
Dried plants, acrylic, and oil on canvas in a glazed
steel frame
34¼ × 45⅞ inches (87 × 116.5 cm)
Private Collection

Des Herbstest Runengespinst – für Paul Celan, 2005
Oil, acrylic, and emulsion on canvas
with burned wood
110¼ × 150⅝ inches (280 × 380 cm)
Private Collection

Meteoriten (Meteorites), 1998/2005
Steel bookcase with lead books and lead objects
135½ × 59 × 65 inches (344.2 × 149.9 × 165.1 cm)
Private Collection, Courtesy of Gagosian Gallery

Rorate Caeli, 2005
Book, 17 double pages. Dried plants, clay,
and sand on photographs on cardboard
23⅝ × 25½ × 7½ inches (60 × 65 × 19 cm)
(bound volume)
Private Collection
Page 153

Sefer Hechaloth, 2005
Book, 11 double pages. Photographs and paper on
cardboard
23⅝ × 16½ × 3 inches (60 × 42 × 7.5 cm)
(bound volume)
Private Collection
Page 154

Solo Exhibitions

1969
Galerie am Kaiserplatz, Karlsruhe. *Anselm Kiefer*

1973
Galerie im Goethe-Institut/Provisorium,
Amsterdam. *Der Nibelungen Leid*
Galerie Michael Werner, Cologne. *Nothung*

1974
Galerie Felix Handschin, Basel. *Alarichs Grab*
Galerie Michael Werner, Cologne. *Malerei der verbrannten Erde*
Galerie t'Venster/Rotterdam Arts Foundation,
Rotterdam. *Heliogabal*

1975
Galerie Michael Werner, Cologne. *Bücher*

1976
Galerie Michael Werner, Cologne. *Siegfried vergisst Brünhilde*

1977
Galerie Helen van der Meij, Amsterdam. *Heroische Sinnbilder*
Galerie Michael Werner, Cologne. *Ritt an die Weichsel*
Kunstverein, Bonn. *Anselm Kiefer*

1978
Galerie Maier-Hahn, Düsseldorf. *Anselm Kiefer: Wege der Weltweisheit—Hermannsschlacht*
Kunsthalle, Bern. *Anselm Kiefer: Bilder und Bücher*

1979
Galerie Helen van der Meij, Amsterdam.
Anselm Kiefer: Bücher
Stedelijk Van Abbemuseum, Eindhoven.
Anselm Kiefer

1980
Galerie Helen van der Meij, Amsterdam.
Anselm Kiefer
Galerie Sigrid Friedrich/Sabine Knust, Munich.
Bilder und Zeichnungen
Groninger Museum, Groningen, The Netherlands.
Anselm Kiefer: Holzschnitte und Bücher
Kunstverein, Mannheim. *Anselm Kiefer*
West German Pavilion, Thirty-ninth Biennale,
Venice. *Verbrennen, verholzen, versenken, versanden*
Württembergischer Kunstverein, Stuttgart.
Anselm Kiefer

1981
Ehinger-Schwarz Galerie, Ulm. *Anselm Kiefer*
Galerie Paul Maenz, Cologne. *Anselm Kiefer: Urd, Werdandi, Skuld*
Galleria Salvatore Ala, Milan. *Anselm Kiefer*
Galerie Sigrid Friedrich/Sabine Knust, Munich.
Anselm Kiefer: Bücher
Kunstverein, Freiburg. *Anselm Kiefer: Aquarelle 1970–1980*

Marian Goodman Gallery, New York. *Anselm Kiefer*
Museum Folkwang, Essen. *Anselm Kiefer: Bilder und Bücher.* Exhibition also shown at Whitechapel Art Gallery, London

1982
Galerie Helen van der Meij, Amsterdam. *Anselm Kiefer*
Galerie Paul Maenz, Cologne. *Anselm Kiefer*
Marian Goodman Gallery, New York. *Anselm Kiefer*
Mary Boone Gallery, New York. *Anselm Kiefer*

1983
Anthony d'Offay Gallery, London. *Anselm Kiefer: Paintings and Watercolours*
Hans-Thoma-Museum, Bernau. *Anselm Kiefer: Bücher und Gouachen*
Maximilian Verlag Sabine Knust, Munich. *Der Rhein*
Sonja Henie/Niels Onstad Foundations, Oslo. *Anselm Kiefer*

1984
Galerie Paul Maenz, Cologne. *Anselm Kiefer*
Musée d'Art Contemporain, Bordeaux. *Anselm Kiefer: Peintures 1983–1984*
Städtische Kunsthalle, Düsseldorf. *Anselm Kiefer.* Exhibition also shown at ARC/Musée d'Art Moderne de la Ville de Paris and The Israel Museum, Jerusalem

1985
Marian Goodman Gallery, New York. *Anselm Kiefer: Auszug aus Ägypten (Departure from Egypt)*

1986
Galerie Paul Maenz, Cologne. *Anselm Kiefer*
Stedelijk Museum, Amsterdam. *Anselm Kiefer: Bilder 1986–1980*

1987
The Art Institute of Chicago and the Philadelphia Museum of Art. *Anselm Kiefer.* Exhibition also shown at the Museum of Contemporary Art, Los Angeles and The Museum of Modern Art, New York
Galerie Foksal, Warsaw. *Anselm Kiefer*
Marian Goodman Gallery, New York. *Anselm Kiefer: Bruch und Einung*

1989
Anthony d'Offay Gallery, London. *Anselm Kiefer: Zweistromland—The High Priestess*
Galerie Foksal, Warsaw. *Anselm Kiefer: Mohn und Gedächtnis*
Galerie Paul Maenz, Cologne. *Anselm Kiefer: Der Engel der Geschichte*

1990
The Douglas Hyde Gallery, Dublin. *Jason*
Israel Museum, Jerusalem. *Mohn und Gedächtnis*
Kunsthalle Tübingen. *Anselm Kiefer: Bücher 1969–1990.* Exhibition also shown at Kunsthaus Zürich and Kunstverein, Munich
Marian Goodman Gallery, New York. *Anselm Kiefer: Lilith*
Mönchehaus Museum, Goslar. *Kaiserring Goslar 1990: Anselm Kiefer*
Städelsches Kunstinstitut, Frankfurt. *Anselm Kiefer: Über Räume und Völker*

1991
Galerie Yvon Lambert, Paris. *Anselm Kiefer: Nachtschattengewächse*
Neue Nationalgalerie, Berlin. *Anselm Kiefer.* Exhibition also shown at Staatliche Museen zu Berlin—Preußischer Kulturbesitz

1992
Anthony d'Offay Gallery, London. *Anselm Kiefer: The Women of the Revolution*
Fuji Television Gallery, Tokyo. *Anselm Kiefer*
Lia Rumma Gallery, Naples. *Anselm Kiefer*

1993
Marian Goodman Gallery, New York. *Anselm Kiefer: Twenty Years of Solitude*
Sezon Museum of Art, Tokyo. *Anselm Kiefer—Melancholia.* Exhibition also shown at Kyoto National Museum of Art and Hiroshima Museum of Contemporary Art

1995
Kukje Gallery, Seoul. *Anselm Kiefer*

1996
Astrup Fearnley Museum of Modern Art, Oslo. *Anselm Kiefer*
Centro Cultural Arte Contemporáneo, Mexico City. *Del Paisaje a la Metaphora: Anselm Kiefer en Mexico: Pinturas y Libros Del Artista Aleman*
Galerie Yvon Lambert, Paris. *Anselm Kiefer: Cette obscure clarté qui tombes des étoiles*
South London Gallery, Anthony d'Offay Gallery, London. *Anselm Kiefer: I Hold All Indias in My Hand*

1997
Museo Correr, Venice. *Himmel – Erde*
Museo e Gallerie Nazionale di Capodimonte, Naples. *Anselm Kiefer: Holzschnitte*

1998
Fundación Proa, Buenos Aires. *Anselm Kiefer*
Gagosian Gallery, New York. *Your Age and Mine and the Age of the World*
Galerie Camargo Vilaca, São Paulo. *Anselm Kiefer*
The Metropolitan Museum of Art, New York. *Anselm Kiefer: Works on Paper in The Metropolitan Museum of Art*
The Museum of Modern Art, São Paulo. *Anselm Kiefer*
Museo Nacional Centro de Arte Reina Sofía (Palacio de Velázquez), Madrid. *El viento, el tiempo, el silencio*
Shoshana Wayne Gallery, Los Angeles. *Woodcuts*

1999
Galleria d'Arte Moderna, Bologna. *Stelle cadenti*
Galerie Yvon Lambert, Paris. *Die Frauen der Antike*
Lia Rumma Gallery, Milan. *Die Frauen der Antike*

2000
Anthony d'Offay Gallery, London. *Let a Thousand Flowers Bloom*
Chapelle de la Salpêtrière, Paris. *Anselm Kiefer: Chevirat Ha-Kelim*
Gagosian Gallery, New York. *Anselm Kiefer*
Stedelijk Museum voor Actuele Kunst, Ghent. *Anselm Kiefer: Recent Works 1996–1999*

2001
Fondation Beyeler, Basel. *Die sieben Himmelspaläste*
Louisiana Museum of Modern Art, Humlebæk. *Anselm Kiefer: Paintings 1998–2000*
Le Rectangle, Lyon. *Anselm Kiefer: Les Reines de France*

2002
Gagosian Gallery, New York. *Anselm Kiefer: Merkaba*
Galerie Yvon Lambert, Paris. *Anselm Kiefer: La vie secrète des plantes*

2003
Galerie Thaddaeus Ropac, Salzburg. *Anselm Kiefer: Am Anfang*

2005
White Cube, London. *Anselm Kiefer: Anselm Kiefer für Chlebnikov, Schicksale der Völker*

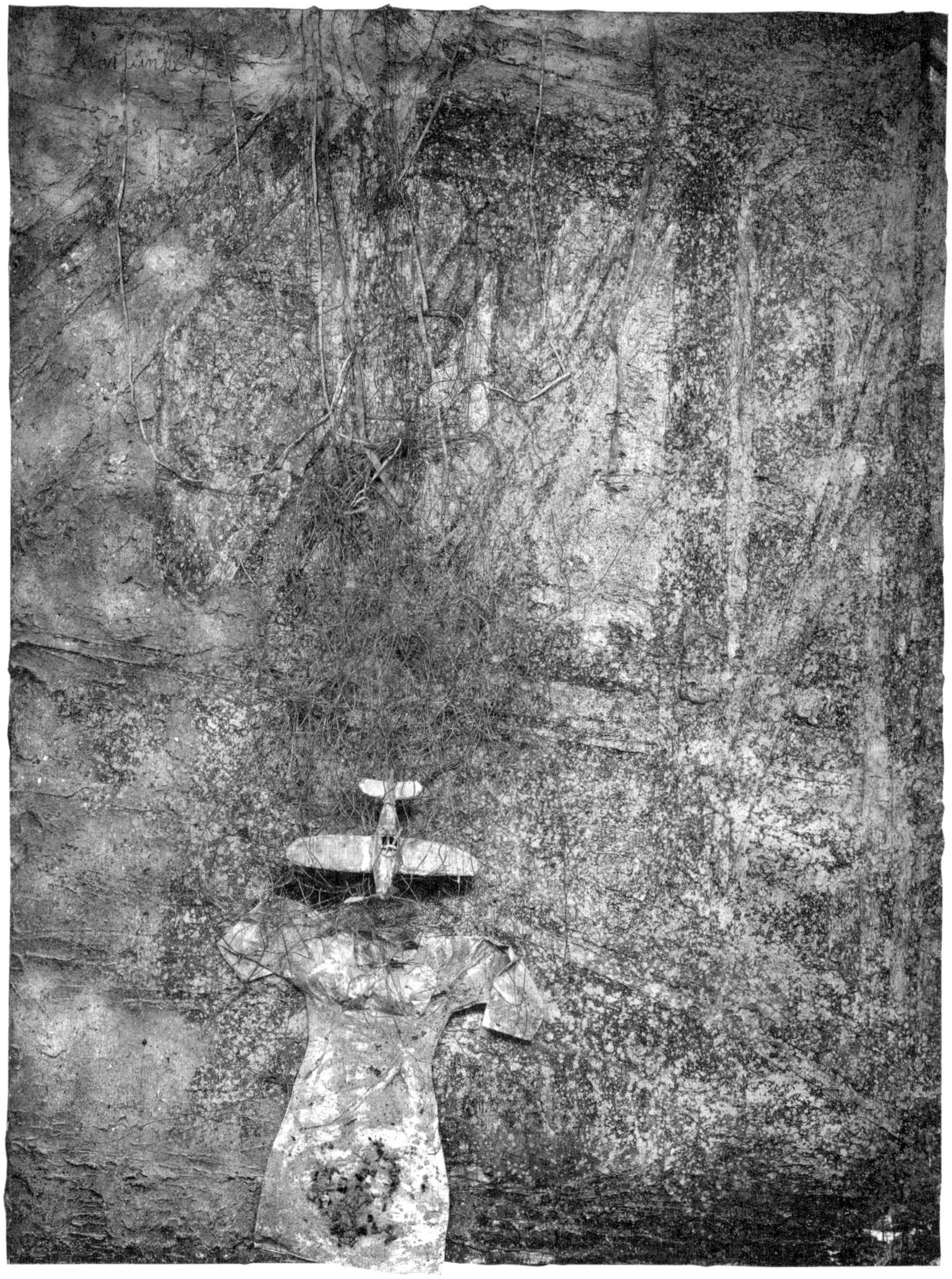

Karfunkel Fee, 1990
Oil, emulsion, shellac, charcoal, and ashes on canvas, with lead airplane, poppy, lead strips, copper wire, and dress
150 × 110½ × 15 inches (381 × 280.5 × 38 cm)

Selected Bibliography

ARTIST'S STATEMENTS, INTERVIEWS, AND PUBLICATIONS

"Besetzungen 1969." *Interfunktionen* 12 (Cologne, 1975): 133–44.

"Selbstbiographie." In *Anselm Kiefer*. Bonn: Kunstverein, 1977.

Die Donauquelle. Cologne, 1978.

Hoffmann von Fallersleben auf Helgoland. Groningen, The Netherlands, 1980.

"Gilgamesch und Enkidu im Zedernwald." *Artforum* 19 (Summer 1981): 67–74.

Nothung. Baden-Baden, 1983.

Grasskamp, Walter. "Conversaciones con los artistas: Anselm Kiefer." In *Origen y visión: Nueva pintura alemana*. Madrid: Palacio Velázquez, 1984: 40–43.

Interview with Donald Kuspit, in *Art Talk: The Early Eighties*. Ed. Jeanne Siegel. Ann Arbor, Mich.: UMI Research Press, 1988; repr., Cambridge, Mass.: Da Capo Press, 1990: 85–90.

"Zweistromland." In *Anselm Kiefer: The High Priestess*. London: Anthony d'Offay Gallery, Thames & Hudson, 1989.

"Die Argonauten." In *Jason*. Dublin and Stuttgart: Douglas Hyde Gallery, Edition Cantz, 1990.

"Das grenzenlose Licht des Ain Soph" Speech at the Knesset, Jerusalem, October 3, 1990, in *Das Plateau*. Stuttgart: Radius Verlag.

Über Räume und Völker. Frankfurt: Suhrkamp Verlag, 1990.

Interview with Christian Kämmerlin and Peter Pursche, "'Nachts fahre ich mit dem Fahrrad von Bild zu Bild.' Ein Werkstattgespräch mit Anselm Kiefer." *Süddeutsche Zeitung Magazin* 46 (November 16, 1990): 24–30.

"Boundaries, Tracks, Traces, Songs." *Art Australia* 30 (Summer 1992).

Interview with Bernard Comment, "Cette obscure clarté qui tombe des étoiles." *Art Press* 216 (September 1996): 19–27.

Twenty Years of Solitude. Pampelune: I. G. Castuera, 1998.

Ich halte alle Indien in meiner Hand, ed. Heiner Bastian. Munich: Schirmer/Mosel, 1999.

Über euren Städten wird Gras wachsen, ed. Heiner Bastian. Munich: Schirmer/Mosel, 2000.

Les Reines de France. Lyon: Le Rectangle, 2001.

Interview with Jill Lloyd, "Lad tusind blomster blomstre." *Louisiana Magasin* 2 (2001): 2–6.

Interview with Thomas H. Macho, in *Am Anfang*. Salzburg: Galerie Thaddaeus Ropac, 2003.

EXHIBITION CATALOGUES AND BOOKS

Von Stetten, Dorothea, and Evelyn Weiss, *Anselm Kiefer*. Exh. cat. Bonn: Kunstverein, 1977.

Gachnang, Johannes, and Theo Kneubühler. *Anselm Kiefer: Bilder und Bücher*. Exh. cat. Bern: Kunsthalle Bern, 1978.

Fuchs, Rudi H. *Anselm Kiefer*. Exh. cat. Eindhoven: Stedelijk Van Abbemuseum, 1979.

Blotkamp, Carel, and Günther Gercken. *Anselm Kiefer: Holzschnitte und Bücher*. Exh. cat. Groningen, The Netherlands: Groninger Museum, 1980.

Fuchs, Rudi H. *Anselm Kiefer*. Exh. cat. Mannheim: Kunstverein, 1980.

Gallwitz, Klaus, and R. H. Fuchs. *Anselm Kiefer: Verbrennen, verholzen, versenken, versanden*. Exh. cat. Venice: West German Pavilion, Thirty-ninth Biennale, 1980.

Osterwold, Tilman. *Anselm Kiefer*. Exh. cat. Stuttgart: Württembergischer Kunstverein, 1980.

Felix, Zdenek, and Nicholas Serota. *Anselm Kiefer*. Exh. cat. Essen: Museum Folkwang; London: Whitechapel Art Gallery, 1981.

Schmidt, Katharina. *Anselm Kiefer: Bücher und Gouachen*. Exh. cat. Bernau/Schwarzwald: Hans-Thoma-Museum, 1983.

Seymour, Anne. *Anselm Kiefer: Paintings and Watercolours, 1970–1982*. Exh. cat. London: Anthony d'Offay Gallery, 1983.

Denizot, René. *Anselm Kiefer: Peintures 1983–1984*. Exh. cat. Bordeaux: Musée d'Art Contemporain, 1984.

Fuchs, Rudi H., Suzanne Pagé, and Jürgen Harten. *Anselm Kiefer*. Exh. cat. Düsseldorf: Städtische Kunsthalle; Paris: ARC/Musée d'Art Moderne de la Ville de Paris, 1984.

Schjeldahl, Peter. "Anselm Kiefer." In *Art of Our Time: The Saatchi Collection*, vol. 3. London: Lund Humphries; New York: Rizzoli, 1984.

Anselm Kiefer: Auszug aus Ägypten (Departure from Egypt), 1984–1985. Exh. cat. New York: Marian Goodman Gallery, 1985.

Burckhardt, Jacqueline, ed. *Ein Gespräch/ Una Discussione: Joseph Beuys, Jannis Kounellis, Anselm Kiefer, Enzo Cucchi*. Zürich, 1986.

Inboden, Gudrun. *Anselm Kiefer*. Exh. cat. Edited by Paul Maenz and Gerd de Vries. Cologne: Galerie Paul Maenz, 1986.

Beeren, Wim. *Anselm Kiefer: Bilder 1986–1980*. Exh. cat. Amsterdam: Stedelijk Museum, 1987.

Neff, John Hallmark. *Anselm Kiefer: Bruch und Einung*. Exh. cat. New York: Marian Goodman Gallery, 1987.

Rosenthal, Mark. *Anselm Kiefer*. Exh. cat. Chicago: The Art Institute of Chicago; Philadelphia: Philadelphia Museum of Art, 1987.

Stebbins, Theodore E., and Susan Cragg Ricci. *A Book by Anselm Kiefer*. Boston: The Museum of Fine Arts; New York: George Braziller, 1988.

Zweite, Armin. *Anselm Kiefer: The High Priestess*. Exh. cat. London: Anthony d'Offay Gallery, Thames & Hudson, 1989.

Adriani, Götz, Peter Schjeldahl, Toni Stooss, and Zdenek Felix. *Anselm Kiefer: Bücher 1969–1990*. Exh. cat. Tübingen: Kunsthalle Tübingen; London: Thames & Hudson, 1990.

Gilmour, John C. *Fire on Earth: Anselm Kiefer and the Postmodern World*. Philadelphia: Temple University Press, 1990.

LeVitté-Harten, Doreet. *Anselm Kiefer: Lilith*. Exh. cat. New York: Marian Goodman Gallery, 1990.

Mohn und Gedächtnis. Comments by Heiner Bastian. Jerusalem: Friends of the Israel Museum Society, 1990.

Schneckenburger, M. *Anselm Kiefer: "Osiris + Isis,"* Arbeitsbuch Kunstunterricht Sekundarstufe II, Spätmoderne und Postmoderne, Düsseldorf: Cornelsen Verlag Schwann-Girardet, 1991.

Schuster, Peter-Klaus. *Anselm Kiefer*. Exh. cat. Berlin: Nationalgalerie Berlin, 1991.

Vuarnet, Jean-Noël. *Anselm Kiefer: Nachtschattengewächse*. Exh. cat. Paris: Galerie Yvon Lambert, 1991.

Esser, Werner. *Anselm Kiefer: Glaube, Hoffnung, Liebe*. Stuttgart: Edition Cantz, 1992.

Rosenthal, Mark. Takashi Hiraide, et al. *Anselm Kiefer: Melancholia*. Exh. cat. Tokyo: Sezon Museum of Art, 1993.

Shinoda, Tatsumi. *Anselm Kiefer: The Winged Zeitgeist*. Exh. cat. Tokyo: Fuji Television Gallery, 1992.

Arasse, Daniel. *Anselm Kiefer: Cette obscure clarté qui tombe des étoiles*. Exh. cat. Paris: Galerie Yvon Lambert, 1996.

Francis, Richard. *Negotiating Rapture*. Chicago: Museum of Contemporary Art, 1996.

López-Pedraza, Rafael. *Anselm Kiefer: The Psychology of "After the Catastrophe."* New York: George Braziller; London: Thames & Hudson, 1996.

McEvilley, Thomas. *I Hold All Indias in My Hand*. Exh. cat. London: South London Gallery, Anthony d'Offay Gallery, 1996.

Nestegard, Jutta. *Anselm Kiefer at the Astrup Fearnley Museum of Modern Art*. Oslo: Astrup Fearnley Museum of Modern Art, 1996.

Cacciari, Massimo, and Germano Celant. *Anselm Kiefer*. Exh. cat. Venice: Museo Correr; Milan: Edizioni Charta, 1997.

Bastian, Heiner. *Anselm Kiefer: Your Age and Mine and the Age of the World*. Exh. cat. New York: Gagosian Gallery; Munich: Schirmer/Mosel, 1998.

Biro, Matthew. *Anselm Kiefer and the Philosophy of Martin Heidegger*. Cambridge: Cambridge University Press, 1998.

Chillida, Alicia, et al. *Anselm Kiefer: El Viento, El Tiempo, El Silencio*. Exh. cat. Madrid: Palacio de Velázquez, 1998.

Littman, Robert, et al. *Anselm Kiefer*. Exh. cat. Buenos Aires: Fundación Proa, 1998.

Littman, Robert, and Alberto Tassinari. *Anselm Kiefer at the Museu de Arte Moderna de São Paulo*. Exh cat. São Paulo: Museu de Arte Moderna de São Paulo, 1998.

Rosenthal, Nan. *Anselm Kiefer: Works on Paper in The Metropolitan Museum of Art*. Exh. cat. New York: Metropolitan Museum of Art, Harry N. Abrams, 1998.

Clair, Jean, ed. *Cosmos: From Romanticism to the Avant-garde*. Munich: Prestel, 1999.

Comment, Bernard. *Anselm Kiefer: Die Frauen der Antike*. Exh. cat. Paris: Galerie Yvon Lambert, 1999.

Eccher, Danilo. *Anselm Kiefer: Shooting Stars*. Exh. cat. Bologna: Galleria d'Arte Moderna di Bologna, 1999.

Saltzman, Lisa R. *Anselm Kiefer: Art After Auschwitz*. Cambridge: Cambridge University Press, 1999.

McEvilley, Thomas. *Anselm Kiefer: Let a Thousand Flowers Bloom*. London: Anthony d'Offay Gallery, 2000.

Strasser, Catherine. *Anselm Kiefer: Chevirat Ha-Kelim*. Exh. cat. Paris: Chapelle de la Salpêtrière, Editions du Regard, 2000.

Arasse, Daniel. *Anselm Kiefer*. New York: Harry N. Abrams, 2001.

Ransmayr, Christoph. *Die Sieben Himmelspaläste*. Riehen/Basel: Fondation Beyeler, 2001.

Steingrim, Larsen, and Thomas McEvilley. *Anselm Kiefer: Paintings 1998–2000*. Humlebæk: Louisiana Museum of Modern Art, 2001.

ARTICLES, ESSAYS, REVIEWS

Brock, Bazon. "Avantgarde und Mythos." *Kunstforum International* 40 (1980): 86–103.

———. "The End of the Avant-Garde? And So the End of Tradition; Notes on the Present 'Kulturkampf' in West Germany." *Artforum* (Summer 1981): 62–74.

Johnen, Jörg. "Anselm Kiefer: Galerie Paul Maenz, Köln." *Kunstforum International* 43 (1981): 148–49.

Liebmann, Lisa. "Anselm Kiefer at Marian Goodman: New York." *Art in America* (Summer 1981): 125–26.

Januszczak, Waldemar. "Beuys/Kiefer: Whitechapel/d'Offay." *The Guardian* (April 3, 1982): 10.

Kuspit, Donald. "The Night Mind." *Artforum* (September 1982): 64–67.

Liebmann, Lisa. "Anselm Kiefer." *Artforum* (Summer 1982): 90–91.

Bos, Saskia. "Anselm Kiefer: Helen van der Meij Gallery." *Artforum* (January 1983): 85.

Cowart, Jack. "Expressions." *Expressions: New Art from Germany*, St. Louis Art Museum (June–August 1983): 9–25.

Kuspit, Donald. "Acts of Aggression: German Painting Today, Part II." *Art in America* (January 1983): 90–101, 131.

———. "Flak from the 'Radicals': The American Case against Current German Painting," *Expressions: New Art from Germany*, St. Louis Art Museum (June–August 1983): 43–55.

Marano, Lizbeth. "Anselm Kiefer: Culture as Hero." *Portfolio* (May–June 1983): 102–5.

Martin, Rupert. "Anselm Kiefer's Ironic Vision." *Artscribe* (October 1983): 26–30.

Schjeldahl, Peter. "Up against the Wall: A Berlin Story." *Vanity Fair* (April 1983): 93–96, 162.

Schwartz, Sanford. "Anselm Kiefer, Joseph Beuys, and the Ghosts of the Fatherland." *New Criterion* (March 1983): 1–9.

Bell, Jane. "What is German about the New German Art?" *ARTnews* (March 1984): 96–101.

Blistène, Bernard. "Anselm Kiefer—Waterloo, Waterloo." *Terrae Motus* (Herculaneum: Villa Campolieto, 1984): 81–82.

Caldwell, John. "Anselm Kiefer's 'Dem unbekannten Maler.'" *Carnegie Magazine* (January–February 1984): 6–8.

Dietrich, Dorothea. Anselm Kiefer's 'Johannisnacht II': A Textbook." *The Print Collector's Newsletter* (May–June 1984): 41–45.

Godfrey, Tony. "Jerusalem: Anselm Kiefer at the Israel Museum." *Burlington Magazine* (September 1984): 590–93.

Hall, Douglas and Keith Hartley. "Anselm Kiefer: 'Johannis Nacht,' 1979." *Creation: Modern Art and Nature* (Scottish National Gallery of Modern Art, August–October 1984): 38.

Kuspit, Donald. "Transmuting Externalization in Anselm Kiefer." *Arts Magazine* (October 1984): 84–86.

Ronnen, Meir. "Kiefer's Twilight of the Gods." *The Jerusalem Post Magazine*, July 27, 1984.

Schneider, Michael. "Fathers and Sons, Retrospectively: The Damaged Relationship Between Two Generations." *New German Critique* (Milwaukee, Winter 1984): 3–51.

Fisher, Jean. "A Tale of the German and the Jew." *Artforum* (September 1985): 106–10.

Landau, Suzanne. "Landscape as Metaphor: Anselm Kiefer's 'Aaron'." *Israel Museum Journal* 4 (1985): 63–66.

Schjeldahl, Peter. "Anselm Kiefer and the Exodus of the Jews." *Art and Text* (South Yarra, Australia, October–December 1985): 5–11.

Schmidt, Katharina. "'To the Supreme Being': Ein Gemälde von Anselm Kiefer." *Artefactum* (April–May 1985): 8–15.

Harrison, Charles. "Importance: Kiefer and Serra at the Saatchi Collection." *Artscribe* (November–December 1986): 50–55.

Schneckenburger, Manfred. "Anselm Kiefer." *Positionen: Malerei aus der Bundesrepublik Deutschland* (Berlin, 1986): 94–97.

Draxler, Helmut. "Verbrennen und verholzen: Feldwege einer deutschen Mythologie." *Kunstforum International* 87 (1987).

Flam, Jack. "Assessing an Enigmatic Painter." *The Wall Street Journal* (December 16, 1987): 31–36.

Groot, Paul. "Anselm Kiefer." *Artforum* 8 (1987).

Madoff, Steven Henry. "Anselm Kiefer—A Call to Memory." *Artnews* 9 (1987).

Ratcliff, Carter. "Kiefer's Heart of Darkness." *Harper's Bazaar* (December 1987).

Russell, John. "A Painter Who Lends Fire to the Gods." *The New York Times* (May 24, 1987): 19, 24.

———. "Art: A Kiefer Retrospective." *The New York Times* (December 5, 1987).

Storr, Rob. "Anselm Kiefer." *Galeries Magazine* 22 (1987).

Watson, Scott. "Anselm Kiefer: Bilder 1980–1986." *Wolkenkratzer Art Journal* 2 (1987).

Dietrich, Dorothea. "Decoding Kiefer." *Print Collector's Newsletter* (September–October 1988): 156–58.

Gilmour, John C. "Original Representation and Anselm Kiefer's Postmodernism." *The Journal of Aesthetics and Art Criticism* (1988).

Gopnik, Adam. "Alchemist." *The New Yorker* (November 21, 1988).

Kuspit, Donald. "Anselm Kiefer's Will to Power." *Contemporanea* (November–December 1988).

Meister, Hanns. "Prophet im fremden Land." *Stern* (October 20, 1988).

Schjeldahl, Peter. "Kieferville," *7 Days* (November 2, 1988).

———. "Our Kiefer." *Art in America* (March 1988): 116–27.

Stevens, Mark. "A Poet of the Apocalypse." *The New York Republic* (February 8, 1988).

West, Thomas. "Interview at Diesel Strasse" and "The Energy of Broken Images." *Art International* (Spring 1988): 62–65, 75–83. Parts 1, 4 of the 4-part article "Evaluating Kiefer."

Barron, Eric J. "Earth's Shrouded Future." *The Sciences* (September–October 1989).

Danto, Arthur. "Anselm Kiefer." *The Nation* (January 2, 1989).

Fisher, Jean. "London—Anselm Kiefer—Anthony d'Offay Gallery." *Artforum* (November 1989).

Graham-Dixon, Andrew. "Anselm Kiefer." *Vogue* (June 1989).

Haxthausen, Charles Werner. "Kiefer in America." *Kunstchronik* (January 1989).

Huyssen, Andreas. "Anselm Kiefer: The Terror of History, the Temptation of Myth." *October* (Spring 1989): 25–45.

LeVitté-Harten, Doreet. "Anselm Kiefer." *Nike* (July–September 1989).

———. "Anselm Kiefer." *Kunst und Kirche* (September 1989).

———. "Szlaki Anselm Kiefer." *Odra* 12 (1989).

Trommler, Frank. "Germany's Past as an Artifact." *Journal of Modern History* (December 1989).

Barber, Fiona. "The Postmodern Sublime: Kiefer in Dublin." *Circa Art Magazine* (September–October 1990).

Bühler, Dietrich. "Anselm Kiefer: Die Bücher—Requisiten der Mythologie." *Zyma Art Today* (September–October 1990).

Fallon, Brian. "The Flight of the Argonauts." *The Irish Times* (June 13, 1990).

———. "The World Messengers of Anselm Kiefer." *The Irish Times* (June 15, 1990).

Kimmelman, Michael. "Anselm Kiefer Explores and Confronts the Past." *The New York Times* (May 11, 1990).

Lewis, James. "Anselm Kiefer: Marian Goodman Gallery." *Artforum* (September 1990).

Meinhardt, Johannes. "Tübingen—Anselm Kiefer—Kunsthalle." *Artforum* (December 1990).

Panicelli, Ida. "Theory of Flight." *Artforum* (January 1990).

Ronnen, Meir. "Decoding Kiefer." *Weekend, The Jerusalem Post Magazine* (May 20, 1990).

Benjamin, Andrew. "Kiefer's Approaches." In *Thinking Art: Beyond Traditional Aesthetics* (London: Institute of Contemporary Arts, 1991).

Brock, Bazon. "Ist Anselm Kiefer ein Neofaschist?" *Pan* (October 25, 1991).

Haxthausen, Charles W. "The World, the Book, and Anselm Kiefer." *The Burlington Magazine* (1991).

Müller, Hans-Joachim. "Der Alchemist, der Erlöser." *Die Zeit* (March 22, 1991).

Rein, Ingrid. "Anselm Kiefer—Neue Nationalgalerie Berlin." *Artforum International* (September 1991).

Richter, Manfred. "Saturn im Horizont der Kabbala." *Blickpunkt Prag, Kunst und Kirche* 2 (1991).

Schmied, Wieland. "Ein Alchemist in Bleigewittern." *Kunstpresse* (June 1991).

Stooss, Toni. "Anselm Kiefer: Bücher 1969–1990." *Kunsthaus Zürich* 1 (1991).

Esser, Werner. "Anselm Kiefer—Glaube, Hoffnung, Liebe." In *Werkstudien 3, Staatsgalerie Stuttgart* (Stuttgart: Edition Cantz, 1992).

Flam, Jack. "The Alchemist." *New York Review of Books* (February 13, 1992): 31–36.

Huyssen, Andreas. "Kiefer in Berlin." *October* (Fall 1992): 84–101.

Kozloff, Max. "Anselm Kiefer's Books." *Print Collector's Newsletter* (March–April 1992): 1–5.

Kuspit, Donald. "Anselm Kiefer's Will to Power." In *Signs of Psyche in Modern and Postmodern Art* (Cambridge: Cambridge University Press, 1993): 228–36.

Koerner, Lisbet. "Nazi Medievalist Architecture and the Politics of Memory." In *Medievalism in Europe* (Cambridge: D. S. Brewer, 1994): 48–75.

Hyman, James. "Journey to the Centre of the Earth," *Tate Magazine* (Spring 1997): 47–51.

Neff, John Hallmark. "A 'Gnostic' Triptych by Anselm Kiefer," *North Carolina Museum of Art Bulletin* 17 (1997): 70–89.

Alvarez, José. "Anselm Kiefer: An Art of Completion," *Connaissance des Arts* 551 (June 1998): 79–85.

Schjeldahl, Peter, "Lost in the Terrain: Anselm Kiefer." *Village Voice* (December 12, 1998).

Alvarez, José. "Anselm Kiefer. Un peuple de statues dont le silence épouvante les maîtres." *Connaissance des Arts* (November 1999): 90–93.

Arasse, Daniel. "La mémoire sans souvenirs d'Anselm Kiefer." In *Mémoire et Archive: Définition de la culture visuelle IV, Actes du colloque tenu au Musée d'art contemporain de Montréal les 23, 24, 25 mars 2000*, Montreal (2000): 21–32.

This catalogue is published on the occasion of the exhibition *Anselm Kiefer: Heaven and Earth*, organized by Michael Auping for the Modern Art Museum of Fort Worth.

First published in 2005 by the Modern Art Museum of Fort Worth in association with Prestel

Modern Art Museum of Fort Worth
3200 Darnell Street
Fort Worth, Texas 76107
www.themodern.org

Prestel Verlag
Königinstrasse 9, 80539 Munich
Tel. +49 (89) 38 1709-0; Fax +49 (89) 38 1709-35

Prestel Publishing Ltd.
4 Bloomsbury Place, London WC1A 2QA
Tel. +44 (020) 7323-5004; Fax +44 (020) 7636-8004

Prestel Publishing
900 Broadway, Suite 603, New York, NY 10003
Tel. +1 (212) 995-2720; Fax +1 (212) 995-2733

www.prestel.com

All measurements are in inches and centimeters.

Edited by Pam Hatley, Modern Art Museum of Fort Worth
Design and layout by Peter B. Willberg
Origination: Reproline mediateam GmbH
Printing and binding: Aumüller Druck KG
Produced by Prestel Verlag
Printed and bound in Germany on acid-free paper

Library of Congress Cataloging-in-Publication Data

Kiefer, Anselm, 1945-
Anselm Kiefer : heaven and earth / organized by Michael Auping.— 1st ed.
p. cm.
Catalog of an exhibition organized by Michael Auping, as chief curator of the Modern Art Museum of Fort Worth, 2005.
Includes bibliographical references.
ISBN-13: 978-0-929865-24-9 (pbk. : alk. paper)
ISBN-10: 0-929865-24-3 (pbk. : alk. paper)
ISBN-13: 978-3-7913-3387-8 (hardcover : alk. paper)
ISBN-10: 3-7913-3387-9 (hardcover : alk. paper)
1. Kiefer, Anselm, 1945—Exhibitions. 2. Cosmology in art—Exhibitions. I. Auping, Michael. II. Modern Art Museum of Fort Worth. III. Title.
N6888.K43A4 2005
709'.2—dc22

2005013717

British Library Cataloguing-in-Publication Data: a catalogue record for this book is available from the British Library. Deutsche Bibliothek holds a record of this publication in the Deutsche Nationalbibliografie; detailed bibliographical data can be found under: http://dnb.ddb.de

Paperback ISBN 0-929865-24-3
Cloth ISBN 0-929865-25-1
Prestel Cloth ISBN 3-7913-3387-9.

Photographic Credits
Pages 26, 38, 41, 44, 47, 48, 157–64: Anselm Kiefer; pages 29/30: Le Corbusier, Couvent Sainte Marie de La Tourette, © 2005 Artists Rights Society (ARS), New York / ADAGP, Paris, / FLC; pages 43, 45: Michael Auping; pages 53, 54, 55, 66, 67, 68, 69: Photograph © 1997 The Metropolitan Museum of Art; pages 59, 109, 135, 125–33, 145, 137, 149: J. Littkemann; pages 62/63: Tom Jenkins; pages 72/73, 101–8; pages 110/111: Uwe Seyl; page 77: Ellen Page Wilson; page 83: Zindman/Fremont; page 182: Richard-Max Tremblay; pages 92/93: Margrit Olsen; page 97: Mike Bruce, Gate Studios, London, UK; page 119: Robert McKeever; pages 138–43: Thomas R. DuBrock; page 117: Christopher Burke Studio; page 123: The Jewish Museum / Art Resource, NY. Photograph by Richard Goodbody, Inc.; pages 146/147: Jean-Michel Tardy.

On pages 1–16: *Die Himmel* (detail), 1969